Beyond Live/Work

CW00797222

Beyond Live/Work: the architecture of home-based work explores the old but neglected building type that combines dwelling and workplace, the 'workhome'. It traces a previously untold architectural history illustrated by images of largely forgotten buildings. Despite having existed for hundreds, if not thousands, of years in every country across the globe this dual-use building type has long gone unnoticed.

This book analyses the lives and premises of 86 contemporary UK and US home-based workers from across the social spectrum and in diverse occupations. It generates a series of typologies and design considerations for the workhome that will be useful for design professionals, students, policy-makers and home-based workers themselves.

In the context of a globalising economy, more women in work than ever before and enabling new technologies, the home-based workforce is growing rapidly. Demonstrating how this can be a socially, economically and environmentally sustainable working practice, this book presents the workhome as the house of the future.

Frances Holliss is an architect and Emeritus Reader in Architecture at London Metropolitan University, UK. Her research concerns the emerging field of design for home-based work.

'In *Beyond Live/Work*, Frances Holliss has combined documentary, historical research with ethnographic/architectural investigations of people who occupy workhome spaces. The book reveals not only a phenomenon of the past and present, but also a probable future in which people will increasingly want to reintegrate their working and domestic lives. This timely and beautifully illustrated book has important lessons for clients, architects and policy-makers, and powerful implications for the nature of the emerging city.'

Howard Davis, Professor of Architecture, University of Oregon, USA, and co-director of the Collaborative for Inclusive Urbanism

'*Beyond Live/Work* is a highly accessible and copiously illustrated book. It is a testament to the individual's, and sometimes the collective's, ingenuity in shaping personal space to suit their specific life and work needs, and the multi-layered, complex cities that result. She argues compellingly that the workhome is transforming our cities, offering not only a vital economic driver, but a truly sustainable model for the future.'

Sarah Wigglesworth RDI MBE, Director, Sarah Wigglesworth Architects and Professor of Architecture, University of Sheffield, UK

Beyond Live/Work

The architecture of home-based work

Frances Holliss

Routledge
Taylor & Francis Group

LONDON AND NEW YORK

First published 2015
by Routledge
2 Park Square, Milton Park, Abingdon, Oxon OX14 4RN

and by Routledge
711 Third Avenue, New York, NY 10017

Routledge is an imprint of the Taylor & Francis Group, an informa business

British Library Cataloguing-in-Publication Data
A catalogue record for this book is available from the British Library

Library of Congress Cataloging-in-Publication Data
Holliss, Frances.
Beyond live/work : the architecture of home-based work / Frances Holliss.
pages cm
Includes bibliographical references and index.
1. Multipurpose buildings. 2. Architecture--Human factors. 3. Work environment. 4. Domestic space. I. Title.
NA4177.H65 2015
728--dc23
2014024435

ISBN: (hbk) 978-0-415-58548-4
ISBN: (pbk) 978-0-415-58549-1
ISBN: (ebk) 978-1-315-73804-8

Typeset in Avenir LT Pro
by Fakenham Prepress Solutions, Fakenham, Norfolk NR21 8NN

Printed and bound in India by Replika Press Pvt. Ltd.

For A.H.

To see what is in front of one's nose needs a constant struggle.
George Orwell, 'In Front of Your Nose', *Tribune* (22 March 1946)

Contents

Introduction

1. For example: R. Banham 'Ateliers D'Artistes: Paris Studio Houses and the Modern Movement'. Architectural Review (August 1956) pp. 75–84; G. Walkley, Artists' Houses in London 1764-1914, (1994); Chesterton Planning and Developments, Live/Work Developments: An analysis of their role in economic regeneration (2003).

This book is about the building type that combines dwelling and workplace. It exists in every country and culture across the world in both vernacular and elite architectural traditions. Old but neglected, it is distinct according to culture and often hidden, disguised as house, shop, workshop or studio. These buildings range from the White House to the Mumbai 'hutment' where President and slum-dwelling handbag-maker respectively live and work with their families. In the UK, such buildings commonly include the vicarage, the pub, shop or funeral parlour with proprietor living above, the house with an office in a spare bedroom or shed at the bottom of the garden, the artist's studio-house and the live/work unit. This building type is important today because people all over the world increasingly work from home or live at their workplace.

These dual-use buildings are currently nameless as a type, which may explain why they have gone unnoticed for so long. While the word 'dwelling' applies to all the buildings people live in, there is no equivalent in the English language, or in any other language that I have found, that refers to all the buildings in which people both live and work. The terms that exist, such as 'studio-house' or 'live/work unit', describe subsets, and previous research and writing have focused on these.[1]

Until the Industrial Revolution, these buildings were called 'house', with subsets of 'longhouse', 'manor house', 'ale-house', 'bath-house', 'bakehouse', 'fire-house', etc. In the twentieth century, however, the term 'house' came to mean a building in which unpaid domestic, rather than paid productive, work took place and which provided a base from which people could 'go out to work' to earn their living. And so the buildings that combine dwelling and workplace became nameless.

Perhaps there is no general term because the overall field has not been analysed. But this is a chicken and egg situation, because without a name it is difficult to conceptualize. In 1751, the Swedish botanist Carl Linnaeus (whose classification system for the biological sciences is still in use today) said: 'If you do not know the name of things, the knowledge of them is lost too.'[2] This seems to be what has happened here. For us to be able to identify, think about, analyse, and develop a conceptual framework for it, this little-written-about building type needs a name.

So, in the same way that 'dwelling' refers to all the buildings from igloo to bungalow that we live in, and 'workplace' refers to all the buildings from factory to theatre that we work in, I have coined the term 'workhome' to describe all the buildings from longhouse to live/work unit that combine dwelling and workplace.[3]

Although as common as the house or shop, the workhome has not previously been identified or systematically analysed. Plenty of books have been published that celebrate the recent spate of imaginative live/work schemes.[4] Some open with a nod towards historical examples of buildings that combine dwelling and workplace, such as weavers' houses or shops with living accommodation above. But none interprets 'live/work' as just the most recent version of a building type that, existing all around us in our cities, towns and villages, has been built and continuously inhabited, worldwide, for centuries. In the context of the information revolution and a global environmental crisis, this building type is ripe for rediscovery.

For globalized, on-line economies, the geographical location of a great deal of work is unimportant. While industrial capitalism depended on a spatial separation between workplace and dwelling, informational capitalism tends to bring these spheres back together. People in developed countries across the world are increasingly choosing to work at home or live at their workplace, supported by new information technologies and telecommunications. Individual lives, buildings and whole neighbourhoods are, as a consequence, being transformed.

The number of home-based workers globally is currently estimated at 100 million and growing rapidly.[5] In the USA, the numbers of those working at home more than tripled between 1980 and 1997, and have continued to rise since; regular 'telecommuting'[6] grew by 79.7 per cent between 2005 and 2012.[7] In the UK, around a quarter of the working population is currently estimated either to live at their workplace, or work at or from home for at least eight hours a week, the point at which it is considered to be spatially significant: 12.8 per cent worked mainly from home in 2009, a rise of 21 per cent since 2001.[8] A social and spatial reordering is taking place as a consequence. Although no mills are being built and no massive rural migration to the city is causing overcrowded and insanitary slums, it is a new industrial revolution.

Thinkers such as Manuel Castells have been theorizing this transformation for decades.[9] But practice lags behind and we do not

2. C.V. Linné and S. Freer, Linnaeus' Philosophia Botanica (2002).

3. I used the alternative generic term 'live/workplace' throughout my doctoral research.

4. This architectural movement will be discussed in detail in Chapter Two

5. S. Sinha, Rights of Home-based Workers (2006), p. 10.

6. 'Telecommuting' is one of the many terms that have been coined to describe flexible working practices and that are used loosely. In the context of these US statistics it is defined to mean zero commute or work-at-home.

7. See more at http://www. globalworkplaceanalytics. com/telecommuting-statistics#sthash.sUrsoNBr. dpuf. Accessed 02.10.13.

8. F. Holliss, The workhome... a new building type?, PhD, London Metropolitan University (2007); <http:// www.flexibility.co.uk/ flexwork/location/ homeworking-statistics-2009. htm>.

9. Castells, M., The Rise of the Network Society The Information Age: Economy, Society and Culture. Vol. 1, (2000).

currently design our buildings or our cities, or organize our society, around it. Dwellings continue to be designed as places where people cook, eat, bathe, sleep, watch TV and bring up their children, nothing more. Workplaces rarely incorporate residential space for those who work there. To make up for this, many people appropriate buildings designed for a single function, residential or industrial, as places where they can both live and work, generally covertly for reasons that will be discussed later.

One of the most interesting and important aspects of home-based work is its inherent social, economic and environmental sustainability. This will be discussed in Chapter Six. This working practice also has some major disadvantages, however, that are often the result of home-based workers living and working in inappropriate buildings. There is substantial scope for innovation here.

The recent growth of live/work might have been expected to kick-start this process but it has in fact run into difficulty in both the UK and the USA. A lack of knowledge and understanding of home-based workers and of the spaces and buildings that they need, and of the inhibiting role of national governance systems, is central to this and will be discussed in Chapters Three and Five. There is also a deep-seated problem of awareness and fixed thinking. Home-based work continues in the shadows despite much evidence that it is an increasingly mainstream practice involving 'proper' work.

This book should help change this. It sets out the benefits of this working practice and identifies home-based work as an idea that can contribute to a more sustainable future. It establishes some momentous implications that this shift in lifestyle has for the future shape of our neighbourhoods and cities. And finally it recognizes that many of the disadvantages of home-based work result from people inhabiting buildings and cities that have not been designed for this working practice.

Considering these buildings as a specific type makes it possible to identify spatial principles that apply to all buildings that combine dwelling and workplace, no matter how big or small, opulent or humble. It also draws attention to the effect on such buildings of government regulations that, though they may vary from country to country, are based on mono-functional building classification systems. This gives us an insight into the ways we could design and regulate the built environment better to accommodate home-based work, at both the building and the urban scale.

A tradition

A Tradition

1. For example, G. Meirion Jones, 'The Long House', Medieval Archaeology 17 (1973); J.M. Prest, The Industrial Revolution in Coventry (1960); T. Ando and F. Dal Co, Tadao Ando : Complete Works (1995); P. Barnwell, M. Palmer, and M. Airs (eds), The Vernacular Workshop: From Craft to Industry, 1400–1900 (2004); T. Benton, The Villas of Le Corbusier, 1920–1930 (1987); D. Vellay, La Maison de Verre: Pierre Chareau's Modernist Masterwork (2007).

2. This is necessarily and unashamedly a condensed history and is included as a means to establish the existence of this previously unidentified building type. It is no substitute for further exploration by the reader.

The workhome has existed for hundreds, even thousands, of years. Examples can be found worldwide, from the Japanese *machiya* to the Malaysian shop-house, the Iranian courtyard house to the Vietnamese tube house, the Lyons silk-weaver's atelier to the Dutch merchant's house. Taking different forms according to culture and climate, workhomes are often so familiar that they are no longer noticed.

Their history has not previously been pieced together, but it can be found, fragmented and often disguised, in publications about houses or workplaces, about individual buildings or architects' œuvres, or about particular geographical locations or periods of time.[1] While an encyclopaedic approach to assembling this history would be valuable, this is not the place for it. The aim of this book is to establish the existence of this building type and to consider its contemporary relevance and potential. So a more limited approach will be adopted here. A small number of examples, all vernacular buildings, will be used to trace some aspects of the history of this overlooked building type from the Middle Ages to the present day, as a way of establishing its existence.

England

There was little differentiation between domestic and productive work in medieval England. Most people inhabited workhomes.[2] Lifestyles varied radically according to social status, however, and the buildings of the time reflected this. A snapshot of mid fourteenth-century life in England includes three typical workhomes: the longhouse, the merchant's house and the manor house. These buildings were sometimes transformed according to activity, time of day or night, or season, and sometimes accommodated the separate functions of dwelling and workplace in distinct spaces.

The longhouse was both home and workplace to peasant families in areas of rural England where animals had to be kept indoors at night and in the winter. Single-storied and built from local materials, it consisted of a single open-plan space with animals living at one end and people at the other, separated only by a cross-passage. By sharing the peasants' space, the animals were protected from predators and extremes of cold; the warmth of their bodies contributed to the peasants' comfort. All the activities of daily life, including cultivating the ground, tending animals, spinning wool, weaving and making clothing from the wool of their sheep, making leather from the hides of their cattle, preserving food for the winter months, cooking, cleaning and looking after their children, were woven seamlessly together in and around this single space. **Figure 1.1** is based on the excavation of a cluster of longhouses in a medieval village, Wharram Percy in North Yorkshire, which was deserted shortly after 1500. It shows a reconstructed interior combining kitchen and spinning/weaving/dressmaking workshop, bedroom and dairy, dining room, butchery, tannery and byre. Peasants' lives were structured by

FIG. 1.1 Reconstruction of daily life in a medieval longhouse in the deserted medieval village of Wharram Percy, North Yorkshire

the seasons, the weather, and the rhythms of day and night, as well as by the need to work for the local lord to pay the rent and to attend the Manor Court. Despite an obligation to their landlord, the villagers lived and worked in a state of relative autonomy, cultivating the fields surrounding their workhomes collectively and exercising control over many aspects of their lives.[3]

The tall, tightly packed townhouses of medieval England also integrated workspace with living accommodation. Ralph Treswell, an early seventeenth-century map-maker, drew surveys of a series of London buildings, medieval in layout and crammed together in tenements, that show that even the smallest tended to have a ground-floor shop, workshop, warehouse, inn or bake-house, and living spaces above [**Fig. 1.2**]. Individual craft workers inhabited workhomes like this, clustered together on the streets of market towns, in which they made, stored and sold their goods. The form and inhabitation of these buildings continued virtually unchanged for centuries. Samuel Pepys was born in 1633 in one, his father's tailor's shop. The household, his biographer Claire Tomalin tells us, centred on the ground-floor shop and cutting room, a rear kitchen opening onto a yard: '… older children, maids and apprentices slept on the third floor … or in the garret, or in trundle beds, kept in most of the rooms, including the shop and the parlour; sometimes they bedded down in the kitchen for warmth'.[4] Domestic life was also inextricably entwined with the business of trade in the medieval merchant's

3. F. Gies and J. Gies, Life in a Medieval Village (1990).

4. C. Tomalin, Samuel Pepys: The Unequalled Self (2002).

FIG. 1.2 Ralph Treswell survey plan, Cowe Lane, London, 1612

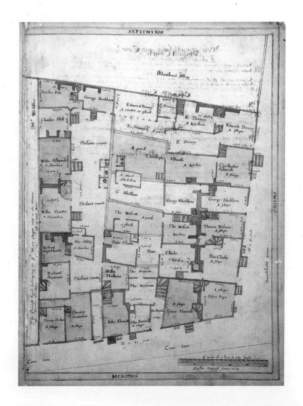

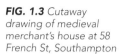

FIG. 1.3 *Cutaway drawing of medieval merchant's house at 58 French St, Southampton*

5. C.M. Woolgar, *The Great Household in Late Medieval England* (1999), p. 9.

house. The much-restored example at 58 French St, Southampton, was built for a wealthy thirteenth-century wine merchant [**Fig. 1.3**]. It was entered through a narrow entrance passage that led past a shop where goods were displayed. Passers-by were served over a fold-down counter that acted as a shutter when not in use, protecting the building from theft and bad weather and indicating when the establishment was closed for business. The front shop and rear counting house, where the merchant made his most important transactions, opened off a large central, semi-public double-height space (the 'hall'), where customers were offered hospitality and meals were eaten. Family and guests slept in small front and rear first-floor rooms. Trading and family life, public and private, were integrated in this workhome in a way that is generally unfamiliar in twenty-first-century England. The unglazed shop was part of the street, but also part of the home; the business of selling involved the whole family. The main living room was a workspace where business was carried out and customers entertained, but also the space where children played and meals were prepared. The rear room where deals were struck was a comparatively informal domestic-scale space, to a contemporary eye a far cry from the corporate office.

Work and life were similarly undifferentiated in the manor houses of the English medieval gentry. Fourteenth-century Penshurst Place in Kent, inhabited over generations by a lord of the manor, his family, guests and household of employees, was built to the standard 'H' plan of the time. Its immense central double-height hall is sandwiched between two two-storey wings that contain a series of smaller spaces, little altered despite centuries of extensions. All members of the household, from the most menial to the most powerful, lived and worked in and around this building, the two activities generally being indistinguishable. The work of the lord of the manor revolved around the maintenance of his 'honour, status, profit and wellbeing',[5] and involved keeping a huge household and offering extensive hospitality. Some 519 people, including 319 guests, sat down to

lunch at Epiphany at Thornbury Castle (an equivalent establishment to Penshurst) in 1508, and 400 to supper.[6] The list of foods consumed at this event indicates the scale and splendour of the feast:

… from the lord's store: 36 rounds of beef, 12 carcasses of mutton, two calves, four pigs, one dry ling, two salt cods, two hard fish, one salt sturgeon. In achats [i.e. purchased]: three swans, six geese, six suckling pigs, ten capons, one lamb, two peacocks, two herons, 22 rabbits, 18 chickens, nine mallards, 23 widgeons, 18 teals, 16 woodcocks, 20 snipes, nine dozen great birds, six dozen little birds, three dozen larks, nine quails, half a fresh salmon, one fresh cod, four dog fish, two tench, seven little breams, half a fresh conger, 21 little roaches, six large fresh eels, ten little whitings, 17 flounders, 100 lampreys, 400 eggs, 24 dishes of butter, 15 flagons of milk, three flagons of cream, and 200 oysters. Together with 678 loaves of bread, 33 bottles and 13 and a half pitchers of wine and 259 flagons of ale (20 of which were drunk by the gentry for breakfast…).[7]

6. A. Gage, Archaeologia, Vol. XXV (1834).

7. Woolgar, op. cit.

8. Falstof Paper 43, Magdalen College Oxford, cited in T. Hosking, (1994), p. 63.

Armies of peasants worked in the fields to provide the basic ingredients, and swarms of servants in the kitchens to prepare such a feast. Brewing and baking on a huge scale were continuous processes. The noble family and their most important guests sat for meals on a raised platform at the end of the hall, looking down on rows of tables where the other members of the household ate. The lavish food and drink were served from small rooms near the kitchen, separated from the main building to minimize hazard from cooking on an open fire. Served with great pomp and ceremony, these feasts were followed by entertainment from minstrels, strolling players, jugglers or jesters. At night the servants cleared away the trestle tables and the household slept on the rush-covered floor around the fire in the Hall. The gentry withdrew to a first-floor space, private for reasons of status rather than modesty, where the lord, his family and closest servants relaxed, prayed and then slept, in some cases all together in a huge bed. This withdrawing room, reached via a narrow stair off the raised dais, had a small window that allowed the antics in the hall to be watched from a distance.

Many people, including grooms and stable boys, cooks and kitchen boys, slept in the spaces they worked in, as a 1431 inventory at a similar institution, Caister Castle, shows:

… some servants were accommodated in their offices; in the bakehouse there was a mattress, blanket, sheet and coverlet; grooms slept in the stable; sumpterman's stable was endowed with bedding; gardener's chamber had two mattresses, two bolsters, one pair of sheets, two blankets, one old carpet, three coverings or coverlets and a celure (worn) of blue.[8]

But the Hall was not just a space to eat, sleep and make merry in. It transformed every few weeks into a courtroom. This Manor Court provided a forum to determine rents, resolve inheritance issues, decide where cattle should be grazed and bracken cut, and check the condition of dwellings and waterways. It also mediated disputes and punished offenders, controlled the quality of bread and ale, and even determined what occupation a son should follow or who a daughter should marry.[9] The lord directed it from the dais and all male tenants over the age of 12 had to attend. Our contemporary understanding of the nature of a courtroom makes it unimaginable that its space could be transformed at the end of the day into, first, a riotous dining room and then a collective sleeping space. Similarly, the idea of bedding down in our workplace, whether kitchen or office, garage or bakery, is unfamiliar today. Or is it? We will return to this later.

While medieval workhomes generally consisted of a few, simple, multi-purpose transformable spaces, over time these were replaced by workhomes with smaller, functionally differentiated spaces in which waged work was separated from the other aspects of daily life. In the 1940s, Francis Steer, an archivist working in the Essex Records Office, transcribed a recently discovered chest-load of seventeenth- and eighteenth-century inventories of the belongings of several hundred inhabitants of the villages of Writtle and Roxwell, near Chelmsford in Essex, at the time of their deaths.[10] These list the occupation of the deceased and the contents of their house room by room, casting light on the social and spatial organization of the time. Although there are no photographs, plans of buildings or even addresses to accompany the inventories, the naming of rooms helps us to understand the relationships between spaces and their uses.

Most of the subjects were small farmers; the occupations of the rest covered the necessities of life: mason, bricklayer, labourer, sawyer, carpenter, blacksmith, weaver, tanner, glover, tailor, barber surgeon, miller, baker, victualler, grocer, grocer and draper, butcher, inn-holder and gardener. Almost all inhabited workhomes. These generally had four to eight rooms, at least one of which can, from its contents, be seen to be a workspace. The inventories show that while work was, for most people, still carried out in and around the home, in these workhomes it was increasingly allocated a separate space. Thomas Raynebeard, the weaver, had five rooms:

In the Hall – One Table & a frame, 2 formes, two little ioyne stooles, the bench & bench board, one little playne table, one fyr shovil, a payer of tongs, two Cobyrons, 2 potthookes, one payer of Bellowes, the painted Clothes with the ymplements prised at £1 13s 4d. –In the Parlour – One halfe headded bed stead, one old Feather bed with script feathers, one boulster, one pillow, 2 blanketts, one Coverlett at £2; one presse cupboard, 13s 4d; 20lb weight of pewter, 6s 8d; 3 earthen Dishes & 3 glasses at 1s; one ioyne Chest & 2 plaine chests, one Chayer with other ymplements in ye parlour 13s 4d. – In the Chamber ouer ye Hall – One plaine bedstead, one Flockbed, one boulster, one pillow, 2 blanketts, with other ymplements at £1. – In the Butterey – Two little barrels, one Kneading troffe, two little Tubs, one little troffe, the shelves with all other ymplements at £1. – In the

9. P.B. Park, *My Ancestors Were Manorial Tenants* (2002).

10. F.W. Steer (ed.), *Farm and Cottage Inventories of Mid-Essex, 1635–1749*, Essex Record Office publication no. 8 (1950), p. 305.

Brasse – Three Kettles, one little brasse pot, one little postnett, one frying pan, one gridiorn at £1 10s. – In the Shop – Three old loomes with all other ymplements belonging to them at £5 10s. [my emphasis]

While his inventory indicates a spatial separation between his weaving shop and the rooms used for cooking, brewing, eating and sleeping, the physical relationship between them is not clear. His shop may have been a workshop in the basement or behind the building, rather than a retail space facing the street as we might expect today. It seems likely that three people lived and worked there (probably Thomas, his wife and an adult child) because there were three looms in the weaving shop and just two beds, a double in the 'chamber ouer the hall' and a single in the parlour. The absence of any stocks of cloth or thread in the loom-shop suggests that Raynebeard worked for a master who delivered raw materials and collected the finished product. The integration of three large wooden looms into a dwelling seems spatially and environmentally problematic. Handloom weaving is a dirty business, producing large quantities of dust. It is also very noisy and these looms would have clattered away when working. Work must have dominated the space and the weavers' lives. So this was not a home as conceived by the Victorians, a feminine space of domesticity, a haven from the world of work. It was a workhome, where all members of the family could, in some way, be involved in production and where work was embraced and interwoven with the other aspects of life. Remarkably similar set-ups exist today, pushed into the shadows by the influence that the Victorian ideal of home continues to exert. These will be discussed later.

The home of Richard Porter, the baker, included a bake-house. That of Thomas Poultar, the glover, included a shop containing hides, tools and twelve pairs of gloves. Isaac Adames, the inn-holder, had a number of rooms with tables and chairs and a 'bruehouse'. The home of John Putto, the miller, consisted of a hall, parlour, best chamber, chamber over the hall, mill chamber (containing a bed, covers 'and other small things'), dairy, brew-house, stable, windmill and watermill, giving an indication of both the way the various rooms were used and their spatial relationship. That of William Poole, the blacksmith, included a workshop

with twenty-five barrs of new ireon weighing 8cwt and a half at 14s per hundredweight, £5 19s; twelve streaks of old ireon, one pair of bellows, one slick-trough, three old gloomes al's anvils, hamers, tongs and other tooles with several peeces of old ireon, eleaven pare of hanges, one pair of eyes for gates, three pair of fork tines, tenn dozen of new horse-shooes, two box moulds, one beame, scales & weights, with other implements.[11]

Ann George ran a small shop, her home consisting of a hall, hall chamber, little chamber, shop chamber, buttery, brewhouse and a shop which contained a motley collection of goods including '1 parsell of sope, 1 parsell of gingerbread and candells, thread, tape, laces & spindles & balls.'[12] Joseph Clarke was a more prosperous

11. *Ibid.*, p. 172.
12. *Ibid.*, p. 188.

grocer and glover. The goods in his shop included a large number of bolts of cloth and haberdashery items as well as a wide range of groceries.[13]

These inventories are tantalizing. Because we cannot link them to actual buildings, our understanding of the workhomes they refer to is limited. Self-servicing communities, continuously inhabiting the space through day and night, are intimated, similar in many ways to the medieval village. But a shift has taken place from a feudal economy based on aristocratic control of land to a capitalist economy in which proto-industrialists controlled the production of goods through the 'putting out' system: masters delivered raw materials to craftworkers, who were paid by the piece for their work, and then collected and sold the finished items. Paid productive work began to be distinguished from, and valued above, unpaid domestic work. A spatial differentiation followed and workspaces, distinct from domestic spaces, started to appear in workhomes. Technological innovations contributed to this: the invention of the fireplace and hearth with a chimney meant different activities could take place simultaneously in separate, individually heated spaces in the workhome. And developments in glassmaking technology reduced the price of glass so that even modest workhomes could have large glazed openings to their purpose-built workrooms.

13. The inventories of these people are No. 37, 49, 71, 103, 129, 146, 149, 169 in ibid.

14. D. Defoe, A Tour through the Whole Island of Great Britain ([1727] 1974), p. 195.

In his *Tour though Britain*, Daniel Defoe paints a picture of daily life that suggests a large proportion of the early eighteenth-century rural population worked from home in the textile industry in isolated cottages and villages:

Among the manufacturers' houses are likewise scattered an infinite number of cottages or small dwellings, in which dwell the workmen which are employed, the women and children of whom are always busy in work such as carding or spinning so that no hands being unemployed, all can gain their bread, even from the youngest to the ancient, hardly anything above four years old but its hands are sufficient to itself. This is the reason why we saw so few people without doors; but if we knocked at the door of the master manufacturer, we presently saw a house full of lusty fellows, some at the dye-fat, some dressing the cloths, some at the loom, some one thing, some another, all hard at work and full employed upon the manufacture and all seeming to have sufficient business.[14]

Each class of worker had a distinct lifestyle, and workhomes were built to accommodate these differences. Three broad categories emerged: the larger, often grand, residences of the masters; the 'middling' sort in which family businesses were run; and the more humble buildings inhabited by craftspeople to whom work was put out.

All three types of workhome could be found in the Spitalfields area of London, a major centre for the textile industry after the influx of highly skilled, silk-weaving Huguenot refugees in the late

FIG. 1.4 *Eighteenth-century master silk-weavers' workhomes with weaving attics, Spitalfields, London*
FIG. 1.5 *Weaver's workhome, No. 16 Elder Street, Spitalfields, London, 1724*

15. F. Sheppard, 'Spitalfields and Mile End New Town', Survey of London, vol. XXVII, (1957), p. 199.

seventeenth century. Many of these buildings still exist. Large and elaborate workhomes were built for prosperous master-weavers in Fournier St [**Fig. 1.4**]. After a recession hit the industry, an additional loom-shop was added to the top of many masters' houses initially planned and constructed as dwellings. This was fully glazed to front and rear to maximize the natural light because silk thread is fine and therefore difficult to see. We know little about how the two functions co-existed in the single building. Apprentices and employee weavers probably ate with the household servants and slept among the looms. However, the racket caused by their long working days in the attic weaving-lofts must have carried through the whole building and disturbed the elegant lifestyle of the silk-master and his family below. Putting the looms in the attic separated dwelling and workplace to some extent. But silk waste found packed between the attic floor joists in some of these workhomes in an attempt to soundproof the loom-shop suggests that this was not altogether successful.[15]

A family weaving business occupied the 1724 workhome at 16 Elder St, London [**Fig. 1.5**]. Wide arched windows lit large loom-shops at the second and third floor level, the two floors of living accommodation below having smaller more domestic-scale windows. Family members, employees and apprentices would all have worked

FIG. 1.6 *Early nineteenth-century weavers' workhomes, Crossland Square, Bethnal Green, London*

the looms, lived, worked and eaten together as a large extended family, with employees and apprentices sleeping in the workshop.

Smaller, simpler workhomes, such as those illustrated in **Figure 1.6**, were occupied by less skilled piece-working silk-weavers. They often had a small upper-floor loom-shop lit by an oversized window that dominated the building's elevation. A contemporaneous interior view gives an idea of how the cramped space may have been inhabited [**Fig. 1.7**]. A man weaves at a well-lit loom while a woman sits beside him at a table with an unfinished meal on it. Again, frustratingly, it is difficult to tell how the building functioned, but the noise and dirt generated by the loom working day in, day out must have had a major impact on the household.

Workhomes such as these, built all over England, were in common use for centuries. They took different forms according to local building traditions and particular occupations. We can get a glimpse of some home-based workers' daily life at the turn of the nineteenth century from the picture George Eliot draws of Silas Marner, a Warwickshire linen-weaver. Pallid and stooped from working indoors sixteen hours a day over his loom, his life was reduced 'to the unquestioning activity of a spinning insect' as it revolved around his loom and essential trips out to collect materials and deliver completed goods.[16] Marner inhabited a single-roomed stone workhome. It contained nothing more than a bed, a table, three chairs and a loom, with a brick hearth for heating and cooking. This was primarily a working environment, and as such it presented a potential hazard to young children. Eliot describes Eppie, Marner's adopted daughter, being tied to the loom to keep her safe while Silas worked:

16. G. Eliot, *Silas Marner* (1861).

FIG. 1.8 *Nineteenth-century Coventry top-shops*

17. *Ibid., p. 110.*
18. *Prest, op. cit., p. 75.*

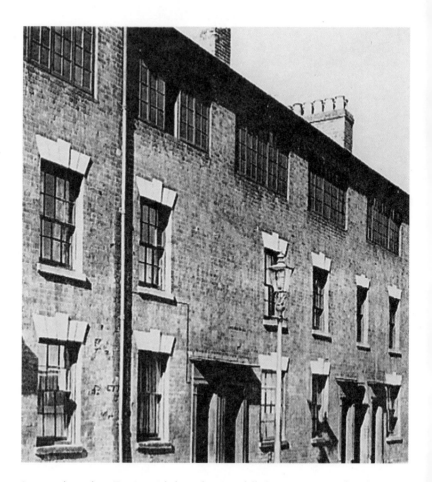

It was clear that Eppie with her short toddling steps, must lead father Silas a pretty dance on any fine morning when circumstances favoured mischief. For example, he had wisely chosen a broad strip of linen as a means of fastening her to the loom when he was busy. It made a broad belt around her waist, and was long enough to allow of her reaching the truckle-bed and sitting down on it, but not long enough for her to attempt any dangerous climbing.[17]

Coventry's craftworkers' workhomes were called 'top-shops' because they had top-floor workshops [**Fig. 1.8**]. Number 11 Vernon St, Hillfields, was typical of those built for nineteenth-century silk-weavers working in the putting-out system, with living accommodation on the ground and first floor and an extensively glazed, second-floor loom-shop. There was no door between this and the first floor, and once again rags were found stuffed between the floor-joists of the workshop in an attempt to insulate the home below from the noise of the top-floor weaving.[18] Number 32 Queen St, Hillfields was built for a small ribbon-weaving master. It was a classic street-facing top-shop with a large rear workshop [**Fig. 1.9**]. The whole building was organized around the business of making silk cloth, from taking orders to production. It included an office, separate workshops for

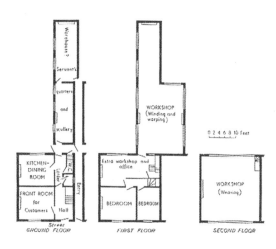

FIGS. 1.9, 1.10. *32 Queen St, Hillfields, Coventry. Street elevation and plan*

winding and warping, a warehouse and a front room where customers were received, as well as a kitchen and bedrooms. A separate entrance and staircase for the master, his family and customers reinforced the underlying class structure [**Fig. 1.10**].

Watchmakers, probably for reasons of security or status, preferred their workhomes to look like houses from the street, so these workshops tended to be placed at the rear. They had big windows, as the fiddly work of watchmaking involved the manufacture and assembly of tiny components and required high levels of natural light. But unlike those of the weavers, these workshops were single-aspect; the watchmaker's workshop was designed around a single narrow well-lit bench at which a number of craftsmen worked. At 27 Gloucester St, Spon End, five indentations can be seen worn into the workshop floor, a trace of the watchmakers who stood and worked there.

Once again these workhomes came in a variety of shapes and sizes, depending on the status of the watchmakers and their relationship to the means of production. The master-watchmaker's workhome at 61 Allesley Old Road, Chapelfields, housed a substantial business

[**Fig. 1.11, 1.12**]. Family and customers used the formal front entrance and sitting room, while a separate back door used by employees led to workshops, warehouse space and offices on two floors. Apprentices and some employees slept in the workshops. Watchmakers who worked on their own account had smaller, simpler workhomes that reflected both their status and the less complex business being carried out. In 34 Craven Street, Spon End, the workshop was on the first floor, a type sometimes called a 'middle-shop'. Once again, this workhome looks like a house from the street; the work function is visible only from the back.

There was a struggle in the mid-nineteenth-century Coventry silk industry between highly skilled weavers who wanted to continue to work from home and the less skilled workers who were prepared to work in factories:

… detesting the factory system as an infringement of their time-honoured liberty to work when they chose, and despising the lower class of improvident weavers with no looms of their own, who had already taken work in the factories, they were determined to preserve their way of life, and their respectable, propertied virtues. If steam was inevitable – and competition made it that – then they would not be driven out of their homes to work in factories. Why should they journey to the steam-engine when the steam engine could be brought to them?[19]

The 'cottage factory', apparently peculiar to Coventry, was a compromise between home-based and factory-based work. A single shaft from a common steam engine ran between individual weavers' attic workshops in a terrace of top-shops, driving all the looms. This brought the advantages of the power loom to the home-based weavers, allowing them to compete with factory-based weavers while maintaining their autonomy and enabling all members of the family to be involved in the weaving processes, thus combining childcare

19. Ibid., p. 95.

20. The invention of the factory generated a crisis in childcare; in many cases children locked in their houses 'for safe keeping' while their parents went out to work were accidentally burned to death. Women often, as a result, found piece-work they could carry out at home.

21. Prest, op. cit., p. 95.

22. Ibid., p.101.

FIGS. 1.11, 1.12. *Street elevation and plans, master-watchmaker's workhome at No. 61 Allesley Old Rd, Coventry*

and domestic work with their paid work.[20] By 1859, the silk-weaving industry in Coventry was divided more or less equally between 15 factories with 1,250 power looms and 300 cottage factories with between two and six looms each.[21]

Wealthy silk-master Eli Green built 67 cottage factories in the Hillfields area of Coventry in 1858, each with its own front door, living accommodation and attic loom-shop. The development took the form of a triangular block around the engine.

From his window at the top of his house the first-hand journeyman could see over the little gardens of the community, and watch the other weavers at work. Down in the middle the communal steam engine revolved – common not in the sense that the weavers had clubbed together to buy it, but common in the sense that they all paid rent to 'the proprietors of steam property' to hire it, at a rate of two or three shillings per week per loom. The noise of the revolving shafting, and of the looms, must have reverberated all the way around the enclosure. In prosperous times it was a sizeable organization.[22]

A sense of community would have been strengthened through neighbourly meetings on the small central allotments where each household grew food to supplement its income, and in the corner shop, and also through the weavers' common cause in relationship to their masters. Similar street elevations of cottage factories at Little South Street, a couple of blocks south of Eli Green's, are a fusion of industrial and domestic elements, expressing their dual functions [**Fig. 1.13**]. The 16-pane traditional sliding sash windows, with their flat stone arches and raised keystones, pronounce 'home' while the wrought iron glazing above shouts 'factory'. The rear view in **Figure 1.14** shows Eli Green's top-shops were fully glazed at the back, and that the upper industrial storey was taller than its lower domestic counterparts.

Another development of cottage factories, 'Cash's One Hundred', was built a year earlier. A hundred workhomes were planned, as terraces of traditional two-up/two-down houses with weaving-shops above, but only 48 were built. More than half as tall again as the domestic

storeys and designed around the newly invented Jacquard loom, the top-shops were accessed by ladders from the living quarters below and had vast windows front and back to light the looms. The drive shaft from a steam engine at the end of the block ran up the side of the building and along the attics [**Fig. 1.15**]. Again these workhomes were built around allotments, and paths linking the fronts and backs of the cottage factories allowed easy movement between them.

S.L. Sidwell, son and grandson of Coventry silk-weavers, describes such a community among the weaving families in the Hillfields cottage factory, where he grew up some generations later when the engine was gas-powered, and conveys a general sense of collective contentment:

My grandfather had five sons and three daughters, all married. It was these large families that provided the labour force so necessary to the silk trade. All families went up to the Top Shop, about 4am with their food for the day, gas being laid on for cooking, lighting and for the motive power for the looms. Crossley gas engines were in use for this purpose, the shaftings being run from house to house, there being no electricity in those days. I can remember about 1899 going up to the looms and observing my grandfather in his frock coat and top hat, who after seeing the looms were operating OK left to journey to the Drapers Hall to sell his wares, drink a bevy and return much later in the day to his beloved looms … When working, the looms did not stop, only for breakdown, meals being taken al Fresco. The weaving families, although not well off for money, were very happy together, and when trade was bad, pawnbrokers supplied the necessary cash to live.[23]

Harnessing their looms to a common engine altered home-based weavers' awareness of time. Previously working at will, they were used to building plenty of leisure time into the working day despite starting in the small hours of the morning and finishing late at night. However, once their looms were powered in this way, they could work only while the engine was running, and as a consequence had to begin work when it started up and to finish when it stopped. The machine, or rather the owner of the machine, began to regulate their working day. However, because the work was taking place in the home and family members took turns on the looms, leisure activities and domestic duties continued to be combined with productive work. Self-determination was highly valued, many preferring to be home-based rather than to go out to work in a mill or factory.[24] The prominence of the chimney and clock tower in a contemporaneous painting of Cash's cottage factory indicates the importance of both the steam engine and the regulation of time.

By the end of the eighteenth century there also were more than 20,000 home-based knitters in England, generally working on stocking-frames in their living rooms. Over time, separate frame-shops were created, usually on the upper floor of the house and with large windows to maximize natural light.[25] By the nineteenth century, detached workshops for between five and 20 stocking-frames were built next door to the knitters' cottages. The complex shown in

23. S. Sidwell, 'The Weavers and Watchmakers of Hillfields', (1972).

24. Prest, op. cit., p. 94.

25. Royal Commission Enquiring into the Condition of Framework-Knitters (1845), p. 117. William Felkin was the son of a framework knitter, apprenticed at the age of 12 years to his grandfather. Felkin reported his findings on the accommodation of French framework knitters to the Royal Commission Enquiring into the Condition of Framework-Knitters in 1845. Outlining the industry, which remained a 'domestic employment', he described each house as having up to five stocking-frames in their living room, which also contained, in one case, 'a square horizontal piano-forte and five other musical instruments and 20 or 30 larger or smaller volumes of books upon the shelves' and was 'as clean and decent [a room] as the one we are sitting in …'

26. D.M. Shrimpton, The Parkers of Rantergate: Framework Knitters (1989).

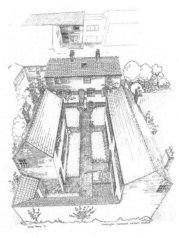

FIG. 1.15 Cash's One
Hundred cottage factory,
Kingfield, Coventry, 1857
FIG. 1.16 Nineteenth-
century stocking-knitters'
complex, Ruddington

Figure 1.16 included five stocking-knitters' cottages, two frame-shops, and communal facilities including a chapel, a laundry, a pump, a wash-house, a bake-oven, a privy and a pig-sty, giving an idea of the lifestyle of the inhabitants.[26] All members of this small community, men, women and children, contributed to the process of knitting, and domestic work was carried out in this context. Dwelling and workplace sat side-by-side, giving a bit of spatial separation between the two functions. This remains a popular model for contemporary home-based work that will be examined in more depth later.

The classic characterization of nineteenth-century England is of a nation divided by class: the poor living in atrocious conditions and working in factories while the middle classes retreated to the suburbs, emerging only to go to work in the City. This, however, represents only a partial truth, and it is the other part of the story that is of interest in this book. Industrialization and the development of public transport systems did lead to a large proportion of the population going out to work, but a substantial number, rich and poor, urban, suburban and rural, continued in home-based work throughout the Industrial Revolution, often in buildings specifically designed for the purpose. This ongoing tradition has, however, become invisible, as work and home have frozen in their separateness. For some people, working at home meant they could maintain their autonomy, often organizing their paid work around looking after children, the sick or the elderly. For others, such as the publicans, caretakers, proprietors of hotels or lodging houses, undertakers, shopkeepers, nurses, nannies, domestic servants or prostitutes, it was the result of intrinsically long or anti-social hours. It was also often the way small 'manufactories' were set up.

Many of the workhomes these people inhabited are familiar and some continue in dual use. They often incorporated a ground-floor workshop or a sales space with a display window and had living accommodation for a craftworker or shopkeeper above. **Figure 1.17** shows a terrace in East London, inhabited by a grocer, a furniture-maker and a draper. The single entrance onto the street served the ground-floor shop (or workshop) and home above. Some had their main living space on the ground floor behind the shop:

FIG. 1.17 *Nineteenth-century speculative 'shop-houses' in Brick Lane, Spitalfields, first occupied by a grocer, a draper, a cabinet-maker and their families*

27. Booth notebook, A20, 'Dressmakers and Milliners', (1886–1903), p. 99.

28. C. Dickens, Hard Times (1854).

29. Booth notebook, A19, 'Tailors and Bootmakers', (1886–1903), p. 103.

In small shops worked by a draper and his family, while the hours are often longer, the conditions are not so irksome. The family lives in the room at the back of the shop and during the slack hours the shop is watched from that vantage point.[27]

Steven Blackpool, Dickens' hero in *Hard Times*, lived in a room *above a little shop. How it came to pass that any people found it worth their while to sell or buy the wretched little toys, mixed up in its window with cheap newspapers and pork (there was a leg to be raffled for tomorrow night), matters not here. He took his end of candle from the shelf, lighted it at another end of candle on the counter, without disturbing the mistress of the shop who was asleep in her little room, and went upstairs to his lodging.*[28]

The shopkeeper slept in a small ground-floor room behind her shop, probably using the shop itself as a living room and boosted the shop's takings by renting out a room. Contemporary shopkeepers across England continue to live above and behind their shops. Renting out a room to boost the household income is also still common.

Evidence of ordinary nineteenth-century workhomes can be found in the raw material collected by the philanthropic industrialist Charles Booth, in his survey of life and labour in London between 1886 and 1903 (see Appendix). Booth's team of researchers walked every street of London twice, noting what they saw in pencil in a series of more than 350 small notebooks. These are now held in the London School of Economics' archive and provide a wealth of information on working practices of the time. One anonymous researcher, identifiable only by the handwriting, made detailed descriptions of the workshops of eleven master-clothiers, each of whom employed between seven and 25 people in their homes [**Fig. 1.18**]. Six of these workshops were in the backyard of the clothiers' houses, four occupied the top storey and in one case a waistcoat-maker used his parlour as a workshop where he 'employed four machinists' and 'some girls'.[29]

It is possible to start to build up a picture of the life of these clothing

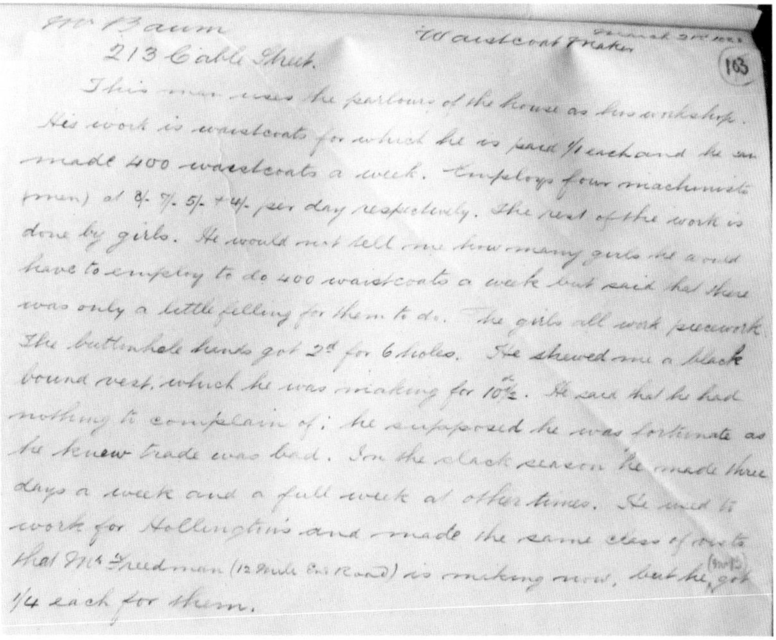

FIG. 1.18 Booth notebook, Page 103, A19, Tailors and Bootmakers

workers and the buildings they inhabited from these descriptions. But many aspects remain unclear, such as whether the apprentices or any of the employees also lived on the premises, what breaks they took and whether they went home for lunch or were given their meals in part payment. There is no mention of the overlap between domestic and employment functions at the start and finish of the working day, a particularly intriguing question to ask about those working in workshops at the top of the house. Did the employees arrive punctually, all at the same time, to be ushered swiftly through the house and up to the workshop, without making contact with the family of the employer on the lower floors? Or did they drift in and wander up to the top floor having greeted the other members of their employer's household? Was the house primarily a family home, with an isolated workplace incorporated in the attic or yard? Or was the whole building devoted to the business, the domestic arrangements being secondary? Or was there was a switch, inside or outside working hours? Or perhaps arrangements took a different form from one establishment to another, depending on the character of the employer and their relationship with their employees. The workhome, as a building type, always combines two functions, and these often come into conflict in terms of public/private, dirty/clean, noisy/ quiet, etc. Architectural history is, frustratingly, usually written as a commentary on buildings, their form, materiality and quality of light, for example, and tends to ignore the people that inhabit them, unless they are remarkable in some way. In the case of the dual-use workhome, we are therefore left guessing which buildings were successful in use, and which caused major problems for their inhabitants. This is a theme that will be touched on repeatedly through this book.

The tradition of home-based work and its associated dual-use buildings continued throughout the nineteenth century but adapted

30. It was not until more than a hundred years later that most houses had private bathrooms. See L. Wright, Clean and Decent: The Fascinating History of the Bathroom and Water Closet (1960).

31. Following the 1846 Act to Encourage the Establishment of Public Baths and Wash-houses.

32. A.W.S. Cross, Public Baths and Wash Houses (1906), p. 200.

33. Ibid.

34. Ibid.

35. Builder, 13 March 1897, p. 256, cited in Dictionary of Scottish Architects.

to the new industrial context. The explosion of new institutions that accompanied industrialization included many workhomes.

A developing understanding of the importance of cleanliness to public health, at a time when most houses did not have private bathrooms,[30] led to the widespread construction of public baths and wash-houses, especially in densely occupied urban areas.[31] These generally combined a swimming pool, 'slipper baths' (where people could pay to have a hot bath) and a laundry. Often conceived by architects as imposing houses or palaces, their grandeur was in some ways at odds with their function: providing facilities for some of the poorest members of society to clean their bodies and clothes.

In the UK, a live-in married couple ran each establishment and provided security when the building was closed. The superintendent was expected to be

a man [sic] who has received a fairly sound education, as it will often fall to his lot to be entrusted with the control of the books connected with the working expenses and receipts of the establishment. He must also be a good organizer and a strict disciplinarian, who is capable of dealing with his subordinates in a manner that tends to secure the regular and prompt performance of their various duties … The matron, his wife, should render him assistance in his general duties and take complete charge of the female departments of the establishment.[32]

This was a responsible and respectable appointment. And as a result the living accommodation that went with it, generally placed on the top floor, was generous. In Wills and Anderson's public baths for Chelsea, separate offices for the superintendent and matron sit on either side of the grand entrance. Their second-floor home, accessed via a private stair from one of the offices, overlooks both street and courtyard and forms the (lesser) attic storey to the classical façade [**Fig. 1.19**]. This allowed the staff to overlook the premises even when they were at home. In Henry Cross's 1904 Haggerston Baths in East London, a Board Room sits above the main entrance, on axis with the main swimming pool and flanked by slipper baths, with the superintendent's apartment above. Its central living room has a balconied window, while kitchen and bedrooms are tucked into the roof-space.[33] In R. Stephen Ayling's 1898–1900 Bethnal Green Baths, where the superintendent's apartment shares a side entrance with the Board Room, the two functions of the building are given distinct architectural treatments inside and out. A Portland stone and red brick base unifies the different elements of the building. This morphs into alternating bands of brick and stone for the first-floor apartment, which has a less generous storey-height and smaller windows, and picks out the oriel window that shelters the side entrance to dwelling and Board Room.[34] A generous stair, leading to the upper ground-floor Board Room, narrows to a domestic scale as it continues up to the first-floor flat.

While only the most senior members of staff lived at the bathhouse, the fire service was a living, working community with many employees living at the fire station. Edinburgh's authorities formed the UK's first properly organized municipal brigade in 1824. Robert Moreham's 1898 Edinburgh central fire station

comprises an engine house for four fire engines, stabling for six horses, a duty room, private and clerks' offices for the fire-master, gymnasium, recreation room and baths for the firemen, workshops for the engineer, joiners and painters, quarters for nine single men and dwelling houses for 21 married men, residence for the fire-master, hose tower, and stores and boiler houses.[35]

The complex, with workspaces on the ground floor and living spaces above, fills an entire block [**Fig. 1.20**]. Its main façade onto Lauriston Place has a rusticated granite base and grand arched openings for the fire engines, which were horse-drawn from 1900, when the

FIG. 1.19 *Public Baths, Chelsea, London. Wills and Anderson, 1907*

FIG. 1.20 *Central Fire Station, Lauriston Place, Edinburgh. Robert Moreham, 1898*

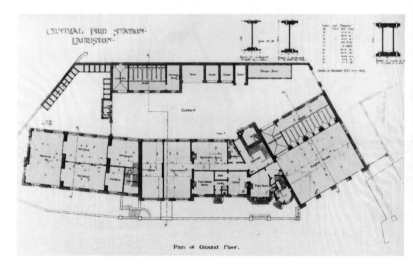

FIG. 1.21 Ground floor plan, Central Fire Station, Lauriston Place, Edinburgh. Robert Moreham, 1898

Plan of Ground Floor.

36. This means that the front door of each flat opened onto a continuous balcony at each level.

station opened, until 1910. The Fire Master had a spacious first-floor apartment, with bay windows above the fire hall, where he lived with his wife and two daughters. It had its own grand front door and staircase in a circular turret to one side, and its own pole down into the fire hall. It also included servants' rooms and had its own flat roof area and greenhouse. The Assistant Fire Master and his family lived above, in a smaller second-floor apartment, while the Divisional Officers' houses were in the roof-space. Less important (and therefore less prominently positioned) spaces that opened off the side street included ground-floor offices, workshops and stores, with firemen's living accommodation above. This had two staircases, one for home and one for work; the pole stair meant firefighters could be ready for action in under a minute [**Fig. 1.21**]. On the first floor there was a dormitory for unmarried firefighters, who had a cook and ate together in a canteen. Married firefighters lived in modest deck-accessed houses on the first and second floors [**Fig. 1.22**].[36] A ground-floor games room had a billiards table, a card room and a gymnasium, all open 24 hours a day for the use of the firefighters on duty. A communal laundry on

FIG. 1.22 Rear deck access, Central Fire Station, Lauriston Place, Edinburgh. Robert Moreham, 1898

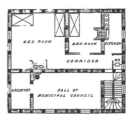
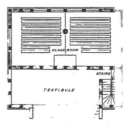

FIG. 1.23 *Nineteenth-century rural French school at St Pardoux les Cars*
FIG. 1.24 *Plan, nineteenth-century rural French school at St Pardoux les Cars*

37. *This section is based on a series of conversations with Ian McMurtrie, MBE, fireman since 1950 and former Assistant Fire Master at Lauriston when the fire officers, firemen and their families still lived there.*

the top floor had an external drying 'green' and 'drying horses' inside. These consisted of large steam-heated cupboards with pull-out racks for drying laundry when the weather was bad. Curtains emphasize the domestic aspect of this workhome. Staff had to apply for the residential accommodation, which was popular as it was central, spacious and well serviced, and those with families took priority. There was a bell in every house, which woke the children whenever there was a fire at night and meant that families were aware of it, and wives often lay awake when their men were attending a fire. People stopped living at the fire station in the 1980s, when the shift system changed. Before that, firefighters were on duty 24 hours a day: on station duties from 9 a.m. till 5 p.m., and in their houses after that. They were allowed to be off duty from 4 until 11 p.m. once a week, had a day off once a fortnight and a weekend off once a month. But when the Scottish Fire Service was reorganized, shifts changed to a five-days-on two-days-off pattern, so there was no need for staff to live in. And when the Lauriston building became the organization's Lothian and Borders Headquarters, its living accommodation was converted into offices.[37]

Many other fire stations in the UK were built to a similar pattern. The Arts and Crafts Euston Road example was one of a number built by the London County Council between 1896 and 1914. While its similar spatial hierarchy is imprinted on its form, the municipal approach has been discarded in favour of a more domestic architecture, resembling that of a large country house.

The introduction of universal elementary education (in 1870 in the UK) led to a boom in the construction of schools across the developing world. In 1874, Edward Robert Robson, architect for hundreds of London Board schools, many of which are still in use more than a century later, wrote a treatise, *School Architecture. Being Practical Remarks on the Planning, Designing, Building and Furnishing of School-Houses*, that includes a survey of schools in the US and Europe. Some of the French schools he included, for example, S. Pardoux les Cars, placed the teacher's living accommodation above the schoolroom [**Fig. 1.23, 1.24**]. In others, school and dwelling were

FIG. 1.25 *Erinside school and teacherage, Manitoba, Canada, 1914*

in separate buildings, between the street and covered playground. And in Austria and Germany, schools included living space for both caretaker and Director. In the USA, historic responsibility for housing teachers stretches back to the eighteenth century. In rural areas, a teacher's house, or 'teacherage' (a less common word, but taking the same approach as 'vicarage' or 'parsonage'), was often built next to the one-room schoolhouse [**Fig. 1.25**]. An equivalent connection was expected between school and rural community to that between church and community, which was forged by the priest in his parsonage.[38]

In England and Wales only rural or very large schools included a Master's House, for reasons that have a contemporary echo:

The practice of placing the headmaster's house within the bounds of the school precincts is not in vogue except in our large towns and there only in establishments of the largest size. It is considered better for the master of an elementary school to reside at some distance, sufficient to compel him every day to take a walk and to breathe fresh air. Attached to the new Board Schools of London, no masters' residences have been erected. Country schools, on the contrary, are incomplete without these adjuncts. They are generally built detached from the school-building. When close to it, particularly if a door of communication be added, the teacher is apt to forget the difference between work and leisure. There must be no internal communication between the house and the school.[39]

A school-keeper's dwelling was often embedded in the Board Schools, however, the domestic-scale home abutting the much taller classrooms [**Fig. 1.26**]. Others were built as detached cottages on the street, overlooking both school entrance and playground. In a small school, the caretaker simply provided security, and as a result had only a pair of rooms. In larger schools, however, the role involved carrying out minor repairs to the buildings and keeping the heating systems running too, so the accommodation was more generous. Limited funds often 'forbade the employment of a caretaker permanently, or for the whole of his time. He was expected for a small sum to take charge of the building, and to earn his main living during the day in other ways.'[40] This approach to the security and maintenance of schools deserves closer scrutiny. Although many London Board Schools still have a resident school-keeper, most modern school buildings have no residential element, making them vulnerable when the school is not in use. The cost of fire damage to schools in the UK rose to a record amount of £96.6 million in 2002, an estimated 90 per cent of this caused by arson attacks.[41] While there is growing concern about this, the resulting recommendations focus on improvements to physical factors such as boundary security, alarm systems, sprinklers, fire breaks in wall, ceiling and roof voids and the storage of flammable material. Reinstating the residential caretaker could be a cheaper, more effective strategy that would also build social capital. More on this in Chapter Six.

Cultural memory is short, however, and such buildings tend to be ignored in contemporary architectural discussions about live/work, despite the fact that many are still in dual use. While few firefighters still live above fire stations, many institutional buildings, including schools, prisons, hospitals and university colleges continue to combine dwelling and workplace for people working in a wide variety of occupations. These buildings challenge commonly held notions about the nature and meaning of home and of home-based work. This will be discussed further in Chapter Three.

This brief fragment of history shows workhomes evolving over a few hundred years, largely in England. It is, however, inevitably a limited picture. This building type takes radically different forms in

38. S.J. Maxcy, 'The Teacherage in American Rural Education', (1979), p. 273.

39. E.R. Robson, School Architecture. Being Practical Remarks on the Planning, Designing, Building, and Furnishing of School-Houses (1874), pp. 221–2.

40 Ibid., p. 273.

41. Zurich News, 'Fire Damage to Schools', 27 March 2003.

FIG. 1.26 School caretaker's workhome, William Patten School, Stoke Newington, London, 1892

different contexts. Japan emerges as of particular interest in this field. Familiar images of Tokyo do not appear to have anything to do with home-based work or its architecture [**Fig. 1.27**], but the high-rise neon streetscapes conceal an inner world where home-based work has been accommodated for centuries with little interruption [**Fig. 1.28**]. This has resulted in the development of a sophisticated contemporary architecture of home-based work. The history of the Japanese workhome therefore provides a useful counterpoint to that of its English cousin.

Japan

From 1185 to 1868, Japan was a feudal society ruled by warlords. As in medieval England, home-based work was the norm and the workhome was in almost universal use. Three building types, mirroring the power relations in society, dominated the Japanese city during these years: the 'buke-yashiki' or 'spread-out houses' of the ruling classes and warriors, the 'machiya' where shopkeepers and merchants lived and worked, and the 'nagaya' workhomes of artisans and craftsmen.

FIG. 1.27 *Neon Tokyo streetscape, 2008*

FIG. 1.28 *Contemporary Tokyo* machiya *streetscape, 2008*

The *buke-yashiki* of the most powerful were defensive castles, enclosed by massive, concentric stone walls and wide moats. The shogun's was built in the centre of Tokyo (known at the time as Edo) over generations and completed in 1636. A whole town of smaller workhomes, inhabited by warriors, merchants and artisans, developed inside its enclosures. Although having power and responsibility in outlying areas of Japan, provincial warlords were forced to keep their primary residence (which took the form of a smaller spread-out house) where their wife and children lived in Edo and to spend alternate years living there. This was a deliberate and effective strategy to prevent uprisings against the shogun: the families were in effect held hostage, the gates in and out of Edo being guarded to prevent them leaving. These workhomes were unlike the grand houses of the European nobility, in that they did not have imposing façades onto street or square. Instead they consisted of a sprawling collection of buildings set in acres of landscaped garden, with dozens of rooms, often connected by walkways, all contained and enclosed by a tall wall. A large, sometimes fortified gate in the wall would be the only evidence of its existence to the passer-by, not very urban at all to the

FIG. 1.29 *Kyoto machiya street elevation*

European eye. Inside the gates, these workhomes, like the English manor houses, were home and workplace to vast households that included family, guests and employees. The huge gardens containing *buke-yashiki*, inhabited by less than a tenth of the city's population, occupied 70 per cent of the area of Edo. Scattered across the city, these walled spread-out houses formed a series of nuclei around which the commoners' workhomes were crammed.

Merchants and their multigenerational families lived and worked in *machiya* (or town-houses), buildings so long and thin that they were nicknamed 'eel's bedrooms', their narrowness a result of a policy that taxed buildings according to the width of their street façade. Built side by side along the main streets, a shop or workshop faced directly onto the street. The façade consisted of a latticed timber screen, the slats arranged in such a way that it made it difficult to see in but easy to see out [**Fig. 1.29**]. When the shop was open, the façade screens had three possible positions. In cold weather they might remain closed and the entrance to the shop would be through a door to one side of the lattices. Then the only indication that the shop was open would be a '*noren*' (a sign-curtain) at the door, bearing the name of the shop and the type of goods being sold or service provided [**Fig. 1.30**]. This would be taken down when the shop shut. In better weather the latticed screens would be slid to a partially open position or removed altogether during the day, making the shop part of the street and the street part of the shop. Bruno Taut described the

FIG. 1.30 *Kyoto machiya with 'noren' or sign curtain*

42. B. Taut, *Houses and People of Japan* (1937), pp. 43–4, 45, cited in B. Shelton, (1999).

impact of the *machiya* on the street in his account of a trip to Japan in the 1930s:

Looking at the bustle of the town, we also got used to its way of life and the many stores and workshops that lined its streets in an unbroken chain ... The displays of every kind of merchandise, as well as the entire interior life of the store and workshop were open to the eyes of the passers-by ... A little way back the matted living-part adjoined the shop ... When the paper sliding doors were pulled apart one could often see the family at their meal or the children at their studies. Sometimes you could see right through these rooms into the garden beyond. One night we drove home very late and all the houses that at daytime were so free and open had been shut up like wooden boxes. Without exception all the wooden shutters had been drawn close ...[42]

The spaces of the *machiya* open progressively off each other, separated by sliding timber and paper screens. This sequence is interspersed with a number of pocket gardens with open verandas running around them, allowing natural light and ventilation into all the spaces of a very deep site. Larger *machiya* include a minimum of two pocket gardens, one small and shady and the other larger and sunny. This generates a passive ventilation system, drawing cool air through the *machiya* in hot weather. A narrow, solid-floored circulation and service space ('*niwa*'), containing cooking and bathing areas, runs alongside the tatami-rooms. Double-height and open to the roof structure, it is lit and ventilated from above [**Fig. 1.31**]. A change in level and floor surface from street to tatami-mat marks the entrance; customers remove their shoes and step up into the shop. Mainly constructed from timber and paper, *machiyas* are structurally independent from their neighbours. This is so that they can be rebuilt

FIG. 1.31 Kyoto machiya 'niwa' or service passage

on a piecemeal basis, essential in a city that was, for centuries, regularly devastated by fire.

Artisans and labourers inhabited *nagaya* (row-houses). These were tiny, terraced and often back-to-back single-roomed buildings, crammed together in blocks behind the comparatively spacious *machiya*, and accessed through alleyways. They were often inhabited as workhomes, with adjacent dwelling and workshop elements. An exhibit at the Edo-Tokyo Museum shows the layout of a typical block of *nagaya*, surrounded by streets of *machiya* [**Fig. 1.32**]. The reconstruction of an individual *nagaya* gives us an idea of how these diminutive spaces were inhabited [**Fig. 1.33**].

It is not difficult to find buildings five hundred years old or more in most European cities, as they are largely built from durable materials such as brick and stone. The rigidity imposed on the Western city through its construction in long-lasting materials leads to the re-inhabitation of buildings and also to the wholesale demolition and redevelopment of areas of the city as society develops. In contrast, it is difficult to find a building that is 50 years old in Tokyo. Extraordinarily, from a European perspective, the overall footprint of Tokyo, its communication networks and even the actual plot sizes were constant from the early seventeenth century to the mid-nineteenth century and remain largely unchanged to the present day. In 1995, Professor Hidenobo Jinnai superimposed a

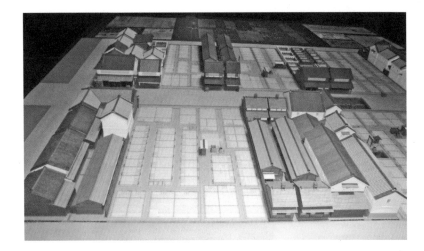

FIG. 1.32 *Nagaya and machiya reconstruction, Edo-Tokyo Museum, 2008*

43. H. Jinnai, *Tokyo: A Spatial Anthropology* (1995), p. 9.

44. *Although not in Kyoto or provincial towns such as Kanezawa, where streets are still lined with historic examples, often in a considerable state of disrepair, but also having been freshly renovated. Japan appears only recently to have woken up to the fact that these buildings constitute an important part of the country's architectural heritage.*

contemporary map of Tokyo at 1:2500 on an Edo map, as part of his investigation into the spatial anthropology of the city:

To my surprise, I found that not only the old Edo streets, but also the pattern of district divisions and even the lot boundaries corresponded, in almost every instance, to the contemporary map. The old city of Edo lay almost entirely within the loop of the Yamanote train line.[43]

The traces of the old feudal structure remain engraved on the urban landscape of the modern Japanese city. The short-lived nature of much of its construction has led to a constant renewal, individual buildings often only having a life of thirty years or so. The majority of Tokyo's buildings are detached, for the historic fire reasons mentioned earlier, so the turnover has ensured a large proportion of the city lots have remained the same over centuries. And, as a consequence, traditional forms have gradually been adapted to accommodate the changing needs of society. Although originating as early as the twelfth century, the *machiya* is still an essential component of the contemporary Japanese city. While many of the old timber *machiya* have vanished,[44] this type of workhome is still to be found in many contemporary commercial streets in Japan. Constructed today from

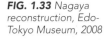

FIG. 1.33 *Nagaya reconstruction, Edo-Tokyo Museum, 2008*

concrete and steel and the latticed screens replaced by metal roller-shutters, this building type is still both common and relevant to modern life in Japan [**Fig. 1.34**].

The transition from feudal society to a more democratic form of governance in Japan happened fairly abruptly in the second half of the nineteenth century. Once divested of their power, provincial warlords returned to the regions, their empty properties appropriated by the government for public use. The vast garden settings of the former rulers' workhomes, unimaginable in a Western city, provided pools of underdeveloped land within the city. These made ideal sites for a range of urban buildings necessary to Tokyo as the capital of a modern state, such as hospitals and universities. In contrast to the periods of massive reconstruction that many European cities went through in the nineteenth century, there was no need to demolish areas of the Japanese city to accommodate industrialization. The large, previously walled sites of the former *buke-yashiki*, now occupied by university campuses, foreign embassies, government buildings, schools or sports complexes, are clearly visible on contemporary maps, with densely populated areas in the interstices between them.[45] It is in these areas that home-based work and its architecture continue to flourish. For reasons that will be explored in Chapter Five, there is no reason to hide home-based work in Japan, so workhomes are both visible on the street and regularly published in architectural journals.

45. Jinnai, op. cit.

FIG. 1.34 *Contemporary upholsterer's machiya, Tokyo, 2008*

Architecture

Architecture

1. Vernacular buildings discussed in Chapter One can be defined as 'the local, indigenous, ordinary, everyday, popular, nostalgic or numerous' (Guillery 2011, p. 1). Architecture in this chapter, by contrast, refers to well-known architect-designed buildings from the conventional 'canon' of architectural history, which includes those that are generally accepted to be the most important and influential.

2. Banham op. cit., Walkley op. cit.

3. Re-numbered as 14 in 1908.

In this fragment of history, the workhome emerges as a specific building type. This offers a new perspective on architectural history as a whole. Hundreds of well-known buildings, previously extensively written about as houses or workplaces, can be reclassified as workhomes and reconsidered in terms of their dual use. And the architectural merit of many lesser-known buildings that bring workplace and dwelling together in unexpected or innovative ways becomes apparent. Architects have been designing workhomes for hundreds of years, so a full history of these buildings would run into many volumes. This chapter discusses only a few, selected from the architectural canon[1] to identify a continuing tradition and to explore some different approaches architects have taken to bringing dwelling and workplace together in a single building.

With an inevitable focus on space, light and materiality, questions also arise about how these buildings work in practice. As with the vernacular buildings, two contrasting approaches emerge: one involves spaces carefully designed around a building's dual functions; the other involves the design of flexible spaces that can accommodate any function. Chapter One examined the developing traditions of building for home-based work in two contrasting cultures: England and Japan. This chapter takes a roughly chronological approach in exploring some cross-cutting themes and, while acknowledging the increasingly international influence of individual architects, largely ignores national boundaries.

The studio-house

The studio-house is a workhome with a long and distinguished (though not necessarily well-known) architectural history. Reyner Banham wrote briefly about Parisian examples; Giles Walkley unearthed hundreds in his study of London.[2] These buildings often have street elevations similarly quirky to the weavers' workhomes discussed in Chapter One. Characterized by large expanses of glass and the juxtaposition of double-height working spaces with conventionally scaled living spaces, the architecture usually

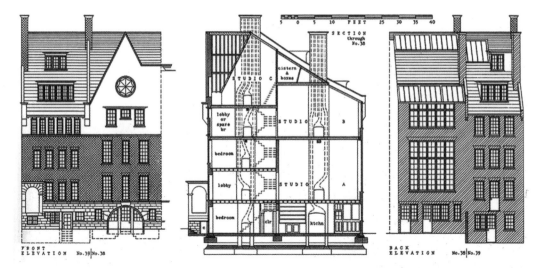

FIG. 2.1 *Artists' work-home, 33–39 Cheyne Walk, Chelsea, London. C.R. Ashbee, 1894*

deliberately reflects the dual functions of dwelling and studio [**Fig. 2.1**]. Many built for artists, such as Philip Webb's 1876 studio-house for Royal Academician Val Prinsep at 1 Holland Park,[3] were large and idiosyncratic. They provided a way for an artist to assert him/herself in the art world and, by implying success, impress their clientele [**Fig. 2.2**]. Many architects designed studio-houses for their own use as a form of calling card, to promote their work. A discussion of a few uncovers some underlying principles.

Huge, barrel-vaulted windows dominate the street elevations of a terrace of eight highly visible studio-houses, St Paul's Studios, on

FIG. 2.2 *Studio-house for Val Prinsep, 1 Holland Park, London. Philip Webb, 1876*

FIG. 2.3 *Street view, St Paul's Studios, Talgarth Rd, Baron's Court, London. Frederick Wheeler, 1890*

the Talgarth Road in west London [**Fig. 2.3**]. These were designed by Frederick Wheeler in 1890 'to suit the requirements of bachelor artists' which were not met by the purely residential buildings of the period.[4] Provision was made for a housekeeper rather than a family. In each, a large double-height north-facing studio, built into the roof to maximize space and natural light, sat above two floors of living space. A mezzanine provided extra working space, and a tall slit window made it easy to get large canvases out of the building. The artist's reception room, where they showed work to potential customers, and bedroom were on the ground floor. Kitchen and housekeeper's rooms were relegated to the basement, their separate front door reached via area steps. A further back door was for the sole use of the model who was not, at the time, considered very respectable. Designed to catch the eye of both the art world and potential clients, the flamboyance of the street elevations of these buildings contrasts with their plain rear. An artist inhabiting one of these buildings, like a weaver in a Coventry cottage factory, lived at their workplace rather than working in their home. Wheeler's workhomes lacked any shared space or sense of communality. Speculatively built, they were designed to create living and working spaces for artists who were not yet wealthy or successful enough to commission a studio-house to meet their own precise requirements.

C.F.A. Voysey took a different approach in his 1896 house, Hill Close. In this workhome, a ground-floor studio was incorporated into a conventional house [**Fig. 2.4**]. In contrast to the celebration, or even exaggeration, of the elements of Webb and Wheeler's buildings that identify them as studio-houses, an effort seems to have been made both to reduce the impact of the artist's studio on this modest building and to disguise its dual use. The house is cottage-like, with small-paned windows, tapered buttresses, dormers and sweeping hipped roof, the large window on the north-east elevation being the only clue that this is a workhome. The non-domestic height and volume of the studio are disguised both by sinking it into the ground and by reducing the height of the bedroom above. The study next door to the studio, in contrast, is the same height as the purely domestic dining room and hall. A conceptual distinction can be made between 1 Holland Park Road, where Prinsep lived at his workplace in a building which was dominated by its studio and did not have conventional living or reception rooms, and Hill Close, where the artist worked in his home surrounded by family and domesticity. This raises an important theme: dominant function, which will be discussed further in Chapter Three. Both Hill Close and St Paul's Studios were home and workplace for domestic staff, as well as for the artists who employed them. While the housekeeper's rooms were placed in the basement in Wheeler's building, in 1913, Voysey designed a separate combined cottage/garage, complete with car-repairing pit, for the chauffeur and his housekeeper wife at Hill Close.[5] This is neatly edited out of most publications about the building, presumably because it was not considered interesting or important. Such omissions have been a recurring theme in researching the history of the workhome.

Architects also designed blocks of smaller, cheaper artists' workhomes in the nineteenth century. R. Stark Wilkinson's 1882 block at 57

4. Walkley, op. cit.

5. D. Simpson, *CFA Voysey: An Architect of Individuality* (1979), p. 46.

FIG. 2.4 *Hill Close, Studland, Dorset. C.F.A. Voysey, 1896*

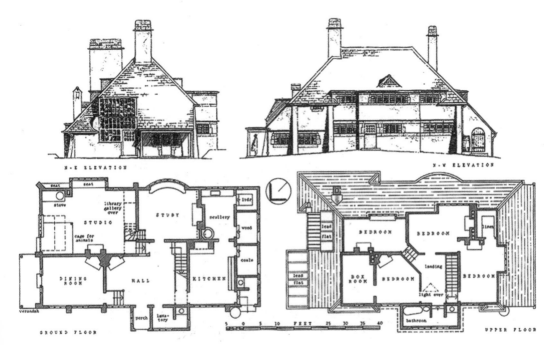

N-E ELEVATION   N-W ELEVATION

GROUND FLOOR   UPPER FLOOR

Bedford Gardens, Kensington, has four floors of studio-apartments above two ground-floor sculpture workshops [**Fig. 2.5**].[6] Ten units, each less than 30 square metres, are accessed from a common top-lit staircase big enough to get large canvasses in and out. Each has a double-height open-plan studio space and a gallery bedroom above a small scullery and WC. Large expanses of glass to the street provide the high levels of north light coveted by artists. They also make it clear that these are not ordinary apartments. The rear, once again, is nondescript. Generations of artists, including 1940s painters John Minton and Jankel Adler, the cartoonist Ronald Searle, science fiction author John Wyndham, and painter and author Wyndham Lewis, have lived and worked in the simple, cheap, well-lit spaces of this building. The 24-hour occupation of these unconventional dwellings has generated an on-going loose community of like-minded people – artists, friends and collaborators. This is a common characteristic of clusters of workhomes, especially when they are designed around a particular occupation, as with this building or the Coventry cottage factories. Common space is an important ingredient. Here the occupants all share a staircase designed to allow large pieces of work to be removed from the building. It is easy to see how struggling with unwieldy pieces of art could encourage neighbourly relationships.

The house and studio elements of the workhome that Belgian architect Victor Horta built for himself at 23/25 Rue Américaine,

6. Now re-numbered 77–79.

7. D. Dernie and A. Carew-Cox, Victor Horta (1995).

FIG. 2.5 57 Bedford Gardens, Kensington, London. R. Stark Wilkinson, 1882

FIG. 2.6 *Horta House and Studio, 23/25 Rue Américaine, Saint-Gilles, Brussels. Victor Horta, 1901*

FIG. 2.7 *Main stair and entrance to Horta's studio, Horta House and Studio, 23/25 Rue Américaine, Saint-Gilles, Brussels. Victor Horta, 1901*

Saint-Gilles, Brussels, in 1901, when he was 40 and married with an 11 year-old daughter, sit side-by-side [**Fig. 2.6**].[7] The house is the grander of the two, four storeys high and wider, with a larger entrance. A showy marble-clad stair leads from the front door up to a suite of formal reception rooms; a second, narrow servants' stair is tucked away out of sight. The workplace next door is only three storeys high and has a narrower front door. Inside, where there is space for five employees, the circulation is cramped and the stairs are steep. An internal door connects a half-landing on the grand staircase in the house, however, to the first-floor waiting room outside Horta's office in the studio building, making Horta's personal working spaces, in effect, a part of the house [**Fig. 2.7**]. He and his visiting clients entered his private working spaces via the lavish entrance of the house without coming into contact with his architectural staff or experiencing the more utilitarian parts of the studio building. Large areas of glass on the street façade and roofs provided high levels of natural light in the studios, which are supported on the upper floor by a steel frame. It is curious that this 'next door' arrangement has not been adopted more frequently in contemporary workhome design. Many home-based workers prefer a degree of physical and social separation between home and workspace. This will be discussed further in Chapter Three.

FIG. 2.8 *Own house and studio, Oak Park, Chicago. Frank Lloyd Wright, 1989*
FIG. 2.9 *Studio entrance, house and studio, Oak Park, Chicago. Frank Lloyd Wright, 1989*

Home-based work was also central to US architect Frank Lloyd Wright's career. In 1889, when only 22 years old, he built his own workhome in the Chicago suburb of Oak Park, shortly after marrying Kitty Tobin [**Fig. 2.8**]. For the first few years, while working for Louis Sullivan, he worked evenings and weekends on his own jobs in a first-floor studio that was surrounded by bedrooms and subservient to the domesticity of the rest of the building. Leaving Adler and Sullivan acrimoniously in 1893, Wright set up his own practice, which he ran outside his home for five years.

But by 1895, he and Kitty had four children; a fifth and a sixth were born in 1898 and 1903. Wanting to bring professional and home lives closer together in 1898, Wright added a substantial studio to their home. North-facing, connected to the existing building by a corridor and with its own entrance to the street, it had a large double-height workroom with a balcony where Wright's employees and collaborators worked. With an independent entrance, professional and domestic comings and goings could be kept separate [**Fig. 2.9**]. Academic Alice T. Friedman tells us:

The home and studio were crafted by Wright not only as a place for family life and education, but also for the practice of architecture in, as he put it, 'an environment that conspires to develop the best there is' in the person of the creative artist.[8]

Employee and colleague Marion Mahony (the first woman registered as an architect in the USA) saw the practice as

a hothouse world in which the boundaries between personal and professional life are clearly blurred ... Just as the home and studio were envisioned as a laboratory in which to test new ideas, combining the traditional functions of a suburban house with the more public functions of a kindergarten and an architect's office — to the mutual

FIG. 2.10 *Taliesin, Wisconsin. Frank Lloyd Wright, 1911*

8. A.T. Friedman, 'Girl Talk: Marion Mahony Griffin, Frank Lloyd Wright and the Oak Park Studio', in D. Van Zanten (ed.), Marion Mahony Reconsidered (2011), p. 42. The quotation is from Wright's 1898 announcement of his practice in Oak Park. For Wright's philosophy as expressed through the Oak Park studio, see G. Wright, 'Architectural Practice and Social Vision in Wright's Early Designs', in C.R. Bolon, R.S. Nelson and L. Seidel (eds), The Nature of Frank Lloyd Wright (1988), pp. 98–124, cited in Friedman, op. cit.

9. Friedman, op. cit.

10. Ibid.

benefit of both — so too were the relationships within the studio meant to be mutually enriching and collaborative.[9]

As well as providing space for home and studio, Wright's workhome at 951 Chicago Avenue, Oak Park, was an effective advertisement for his work. He built 24 more buildings in the area between 1889 and 1913.

In 1911, having fallen in love with his client and neighbour, Mamah Cheney, and left his family, Wright built a vast second workhome for himself, Cheney and a shifting population of employees and students in the Wisconsin countryside and named it Taliesin after a Welsh poet. Friedman describes it as 'a hybrid plan dedicated to work and community, a home and studio for artists based on principles of gender equality, a home embedded in and inspired by landscape'.[10] Roughly L-shaped, with living spaces in one wing and studio in the other [**Fig. 2.10**], it burned down and was rebuilt twice. Cheney and her two children died in the first fire, which was the result of an act of arson by a servant; the second was caused by an electrical fault. In 1929, after his third marriage and the birth of his seventh child,

FIG. 2.11 *Masters' houses in the woods, Bauhaus, Dessau. Walter Gropius, 1926*

11. *Ibid.*

Wright built a further workhome, Taliesin West in Phoenix, Arizona, as headquarters for his teaching programme. Between 40 and 50 architectural students spent April to November each year living, working and studying in Wright's Wisconsin workhome (renamed Taliesin East), and December to March in Arizona. All his life, Wright refused to separate the domestic from the professional. Friedman considers that this and his commitment to a collaborative immersion in architecture 'made a major contribution to the development of what is generally considered his individual genius'.[11]

Modernism

The international Modernist movement in architecture represented a radical shift away from traditional forms and methods of construction in response to major changes in technology and society. Its defining features are a rejection of historical precedent; the idea that form should be simplified (and generated from the inside out, by the functional spatial requirements of the building); an exploration of new materials (initially concrete, steel and glass) and a reduction of ornament. Despite the marginalization of home-based work in the twentieth-century, many iconic Modernist buildings, both institutional and for individual/ family use, were designed as workhomes, but scant attention has been paid to their dual use. Aalto's 1932 TB sanatorium at Paimio, for example, included housing for doctors and nurses, while Terragni's 1936 Casa del Fascio, Asplund's 1937 Gothenburg law courts and Scharoun's 1963 Berlin Philharmonic Hall all have integrated living spaces for a porter or caretaker. The overlapping of public and private, home and workplace raises architectural challenges that, because these buildings have previously been approached from a mono-functional point of view, have not been explored. To what extent can a nurses' home ever really be 'home'? Is this different for an individual doctor's house, even if they sit adjacent to each other and the hospital they serve? Does the collectivity of such an arrangement contribute to or detract from the working life of the institution? What sort of life does the caretaker or porter of a major cultural building have? What impact does living in such unusual circumstances have on the family, especially the children? And what is the impact on the cultural organization of having a residential member of staff? Why has this practice died out? Or has it? What relationship do the residential and workplace aspects of these workhomes have to each other, and what are the consequences of this?

12. Available at: www.breuer. syr.edu (accessed 9 May 2012).

Even the Modernist buildings known to combine dwelling and workplace elements are rarely analysed as workhomes. Walter Gropius's 1926 art and architecture school at Dessau, the Bauhaus, is typically described as consisting

of a glazed, three-storey workshop wing, another three-storey wing for the vocational school and a five-storey studio building with projecting balconies. A single-storey element connecting the workshop wing and the studios housed an auditorium and canteen.[12]

But the Bauhaus students and staff lived together as well as working together. This was central to the way the school ran, to its philosophy and success and to the design of the Dessau buildings. While the design community at Taliesin might be characterized as working in Wright's home, students and staff at the Bauhaus lived at their workplace and the architecture reflected this. It also reflected the power structure of the institution. The more senior the person, the more living space he or she had, and the more separate it was from the main teaching buildings. Gropius's detached house in the pinewoods was a short walk from the main buildings; the senior Bauhaus masters [**Fig. 2.11**] were a little closer, in three pairs of semi-detached houses. But students and junior masters worked and slept in individual studios at the heart of the teaching complex, seven to a floor sharing a single WC [**Fig. 2.12**]. Communal bathrooms, laundry and gymnasium were in the basement; on the ground floor were a centralized kitchen and a collective refectory whose environment and furniture were expressly designed for discomfort, as a way of encouraging students to get back to work.

FIG. 2.12 *Students' and junior staff's live/work studios, Bauhaus, Dessau. Walter Gropius, 1926*

Similarly, despite being almost universally written about as a solitary chapel, Le Corbusier's Notre Dame du Haut at Ronchamp in France is also a workhome [**Fig. 2.13**]. Built on what has been a pilgrimage site since the thirteenth century, it is part of an ensemble of buildings that includes two houses, one for the priest and one for pilgrims, all designed by Le Corbusier and built contemporaneously in 1955. The chapel sits on the top of the hill, visible for miles, with views all around, while the subsidiary residential buildings are tucked into the landscape, one on either side of the pathway down the hill, their green roofs (the first in modern architecture) reducing their

FIG. 2.13 *Notre Dame du Haut, Ronchamp, France. Le Corbusier, 1955*

FIG. 2.14 Grass-roofed Pilgrims' House, Notre Dame du Haut, Ronchamp, France. Le Corbusier, 1955

13. W.J.R. Curtis, 'Ronchamp Undermined by Renzo Piano's Convent, France', Architectural Review, 24 July 2012.

14. Banham, op. cit.

visibility from above [**Fig. 2.14**]. The priest, in traditional manner, is on site throughout the 24 hours, taking services, caring for his parishioners, hosting religious and architectural pilgrimages and, as his house overlooks the path to the chapel, providing security for the building. This aspect of Le Corbusier's design has tended to be ignored, reduced to ghostly outlines on site plans. Renzo Piano's much-criticized 2012 addition of a convent for 12 nuns, which includes space for visitors and a second small chapel, intensifies both residential and workplace aspects of the complex.[13]

Le Corbusier's workhome for his friend, the painter and sculptor Amédée Ozenfant, was built on an irregular corner site in the Parisian XIV arrondissement in 1923 [**Fig. 2.15**]. The 73-square metre,

FIG. 2.15 Atelier Ozenfant, Paris. Le Corbusier, 1924

FIG. 2.16 *Second floor studio, Atelier Ozenfant, Paris. Le Corbusier, 1924*

double-height, top-floor studio provided an all-purpose living and working space, even housing a painting school, L'Académie Ozenfant in 1932–35 [**Fig. 2.16**]. The floor below combined a small gallery space where Ozenfant showed his work and a 'museum' storage space for artifacts, along with a small amount of purely domestic space, limited to a tiny kitchen tucked into a corner of the entrance hall and an en-suite bedroom. Staff accommodation and a garage were on the ground floor [**Fig. 2.17**]. A cylindrical external stair marked the public route up to the studio, while a small internal stair between ground-floor garage/staff flat and first floor reflected the servants' and models' back stairs in earlier studio-houses. But while contemporaneous Arts and Crafts studio-houses used a familiar, domestic architectural language of brick, pitched roofs and timber windows, Banham observes that, by the late 1920s, architects in Paris had 'examined the existing vernacular elements of the studio-house tradition … and subsumed them in a new aesthetic whose formal discipline drew on the experimental painting of the post-Cubist epoch'.[14]

It also drew on the aesthetic of the factory. Extensive areas of glass on three façades and factory-style roof glazing lit Ozenfant's studio, while ground and first floors had ribbon windows. The combination of domestic and non-domestic scale volumes and windows produced an architecture that echoes earlier workhomes. White-painted render, steel industrial-style glazing and a flat roof with north-facing saw-tooth roof-lights set this building apart from its suburban residential neighbours. It is unclear how the studio/living space, with its large areas of uninsulated glazing, walls and roof, remained habitable through cold winters. It seems unlikely that its small stove and fireplace heated the space effectively. So, like many contemporary artists working in large studios, Ozenfant and

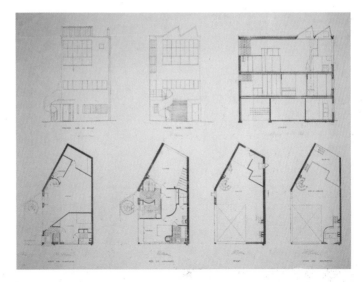

FIG. 2.17 *Plans, section, elevations, Atelier Ozenfant, Paris. Le Corbusier, 1924*

his students probably wore many layers of clothing when it was cold. Art school, gallery, studio, museum, staff quarters, garage and home combined in a single building in response to an unconventional lifestyle and, with its arresting street elevations, advertised Ozenfant's business as artist and teacher.

Nine years later in 1933, when he was 46 years old, Le Corbusier went on to design his own studio-apartment at the top of a nine-storey residential block at 24 Rue Nungesser-et-Colis in Paris. He lived and worked here with dressmaker and fashion model Yvonne Gallis until he died in 1965. Predictably, this was a groundbreaking building. It overturned an unspoken but previously almost universal convention in architect-designed workhomes, namely that the residential and non-residential spaces should be articulated differently to reflect the two functions. Spatially continuous, the studio, hallway and living room were 2.5m high and undifferentiated throughout in terms of materials; neither function was prioritized. Studio and living spaces were placed symmetrically around a central entry hall. A large pivoted door (minimally interrupting the space when it was open) allowed the studio to be closed off from domestic space or not. As this was a private workspace, where Le Corbusier painted each morning before leaving for his busy architectural office, the workhome did not need to accommodate visiting members of the public or a family life that involved bringing up children. This programmatic simplicity contributed to the development of a spatially undifferentiated workhome, an approach adopted subsequently by many.

The seminal Maison de Verre, designed by Pierre Chareau and Bernard Bijvoet in Paris in 1932 for Dr and Mme Dalsace, is not a *maison* at all, but a workhome combining family home with a suite of gynaecologist's consulting rooms. While doctors' workhomes were

common at the time, this building broke with tradition: its street elevation gave no clues to either of its functions [**Fig. 2.18**]. Inside, a vast double-height living room, flooded with light from the south-east-facing glass-block wall and reached by a generous, industrially detailed stair, was positioned above a ground-floor surgery that included a reception area, a waiting room, a consulting room, an examination room and a laboratory. The doctor also had a first-floor study next to the main living space, linked to his ground-floor consulting rooms by a narrow stair. Three en-suite bedrooms on a second-floor mezzanine overlooked the main living space. The service wing, overlooking the entrance courtyard and organized across the three levels, had a separate ground to first floor stair. Unusually for the period, family and domestic staff shared the main first-to-second floor stair.

This building has been extensively written about, mainly in terms of its innovative form and spatiality, its materiality and mechanisms, and its quality of light.[15] But a doctor's surgery is a public space, requiring a calm and quiet atmosphere, and this workhome was designed as a single open volume, without spatial or acoustic separation between the doctor's rooms on the ground floor and the private family home above [**Fig. 2.19**]. Family life can, as we know, be anything but calm and quiet. This building has been heralded as one of the great icons of modern architecture, but how did it work in practice, on a day-to-day basis? What constraints did it place on family life? How were the public and private functions of the building negotiated or reconciled?

FIG. 2.19 *Salon, Maison de Verre, Paris. Pierre Chareau and Bernard Bijvoet, 1932*

15. *The building contains many moving parts, particularly doors and windows that open in inventive ways; they often reference train or bus design of the period.*

16. *D. Vellay, La Maison de Verre: Pierre Chareau's Modernist Masterwork (2007), p. 7.*

17. *Ibid., p. 18.*

The building itself gives us some clues and family members' memories supplement them. It was organized by three circulation flows that did not mix. The single front door, used by family, patients and domestic staff alike, had a triple doorbell [**Fig. 2.20**]. The bells for 'doctor', 'visitors', and 'service' made different sounds, so the correct person could answer the door.[16] The doctor's bell indicated a patient was at the door. The receptionist, positioned so she could view simultaneously the access corridor from the front door, the bottom of the main staircase and the passage from the waiting room to the doctor's surgery, opened the door and showed patients to the waiting room. At the end of the appointment they left by the corridor to the front door. A pivoting glass and perforated metal screen at the bottom of the main staircase, always closed during surgery hours, discouraged them from absent-mindedly wandering upstairs into the private family home [**Fig. 2.21**].[17] The housekeeper or her

FIG. 2.20 *Triple doorbell, Maison de Verre, Paris. Pierre Chareau and Bernard Bijvoet, 1932*
FIG. 2.21 *Pivoting perforated metal screen, Maison de Verre, Paris. Pierre Chareau and Bernard Bijvoet, 1932*

husband, the chauffeur, answered the visitors' bell to guests. When the Dalsaces were entertaining, the pivoting screen at the bottom of the main stair would be left open. Children made their presence known by a specific number of rings on the service bell (two in the case of the Dalsace's grandson, Marc Vellay). The housekeeper would then answer the door and they would use the back service stair to go upstairs to the family home.[18]

Dalsace's granddaughter, Dominique Vellay, describes the Maison de Verre as 'an enormous sound box, I could hear the sound of my grandfather's study sliding open and shut and the rush of water through the pipes'.[19] This suggests a lack of acoustic separation between the functions of dwelling and workplace potentially as problematic as that of the Coventry cottage factory. Sound-absorbing materials, including rubber flooring, books and clothes-filled cupboards, mitigated against this to some extent. Sliding doors to the doctor's ground-floor consulting room and first-floor study, both spaces where confidentiality was crucial, had cork cores behind their perforated metal surfaces to provide acoustic insulation. Marc Vellay remembers that when they were closed 'one could make out the buzz of a conversation, but one could not make out the words or the content'.[20] A soundproofed telephone booth was retrospectively fitted in Dr Dalsace's study. The plan was also organized to limit sound transmission: three doors and three changes of direction prevent kitchen noises being heard in the waiting room.

But despite these measures, noise inevitably still circulated. That the building remained in dual use until 1997 suggests this was not a problem and Marc Vellay concurs with this, taking the view that it worked well for the Dalsaces. It was normal at the time for doctors' children to live with medical consultations and patients; they were taught early on not to make any noise so as not to disturb their parents' work, which took precedence over domestic life. Vellay's memory is that he generally met his friends in their homes rather than his, but that this was not problematic and that

if such noises are familiar and pleasant, they do not pose any problem. Better still, they convey the modes of use and goings on in the house (someone rings the bell, someone goes upstairs, the table is being laid, there's hoovering, there are guests in the little blue salon, X is playing the piano ...). At this level, they are reassuring and promote 'family living'. They thus allow one to adapt to, or to anticipate, an event taking place or about to happen, generally relating to movements of people that you care about.[21]

Vellay comments, however, that children's upbringing was strict between the 1930s and 1950s and that 'when the rules and working methods were no longer consistent or were no longer respected, noise became a problem'.[22] This suggests that particular forms of behaviour were necessary for the Maison de Verre to function effectively as a combined doctor's surgery and family home, and that these may have broken down when parenting became more liberal. A

18. Email correspondence between the author and Marc Vellay, April/May 2012.

19. Vellay, op. cit., p. 18.

20. Email correspondence between the author and Marc Vellay, April/May 2012.

21. Ibid.

22. Ibid.

parallel exists here with both traditional and contemporary Japanese workhomes, which also often involve similar lack of spatial, and therefore acoustic, compartmentalization between functions. This will be examined in more detail later.

Charles and Ray Eames took the design of their Modernist workhome a step further. The 1949 Eames House, built at Pacific Palisades, Los Angeles, consists of a pair of rectangular, flat-roofed buildings, one for home and one for studio, separated by a small courtyard. Designed around a standardized structural grid and constructional system, the dwelling and studio clearly make up two parts of the same building, with the same scale, aesthetic, floor-to-ceiling heights and internal spatial strategy. There is no attempt to distinguish architecturally between domestic and workspace [**Fig. 2.22, 2.23**]. The smaller element, closest to the road, contains the studio; a mezzanine darkroom and storage area that converts into a spare bedroom when necessary has a kitchen and bathroom tucked underneath it. The smaller building shields the larger, their home, from the street. This has a double-height living space, just one bay longer than the studio; mezzanine bedrooms and bathrooms have kitchen/dining spaces below them. But Charles and Ray Eames did not differentiate between the two functions; they engaged with all aspects of their lives with the same curiosity, moving seamlessly from design to childcare, or from cooking to model-making or film-making: life in work. On first impression, their workhome, with work and the rest of life formally separated into distinct buildings, does not seem to match this lifestyle. However, this is a building designed for the warm, dry Californian climate and the doors to both elements of the building were left open 11 months of the year, and the courtyard was used as a further, external room.[23] So the rear retaining wall provided spatial continuity between all the elements of the workhome and the Eameses moved fluidly between them, inside and out. This building has been extensively written about in terms of its delicate steel frame and constructional elements selected from an industrial catalogue (a radical approach for a house in the late 1940s). It is equally radical in the way it ignores conventional boundaries between work and home.

23. Interview with Eames Demetrios, March 2012.

FIG. 2.22 *Eames House, Pacific Palisades, Los Angeles. Charles and Ray Eames, 1949*
FIG. 2.23 *Plan/3D view, Eames House, Pacific Palisades, Los Angeles. Charles and Ray Eames, 1949*

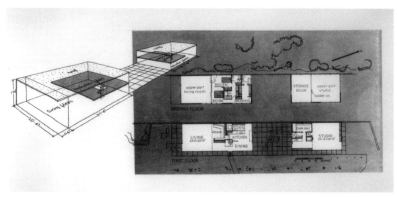

FIG. 2.24 *Hopkins House, Hampstead, London. Hopkins Architects, 1976*
FIG. 2.25 *Studio, Hopkins House, Hampstead, London. Hopkins Architects, 1976*

24. *See Chapter Three for a detailed discussion on architectural determinacy and indeterminacy.*

25. *Venetian blinds, installed to define different functions, were unused.*

26. *Interview with Patty Hopkins, February 2012.*

27. *Ibid.*

In London, Michael and Patty Hopkins' 1976 Hampstead workhome takes the Eames House logic even further. Similarly built from industrial materials throughout, with delicate steel frame, flat roof, fully glazed front and rear elevations and steel cladding, this workhome is completely indeterminate spatially [**Fig. 2.24, 2.25**].[24] There is no attempt to design differently for domestic or workplace use, with two notable consequences. The first is an unconventional attitude to the relationship of public workspace to private family home; the second is its flexibility in use over time. For eight years, the street-level first floor combined the Hopkins' architectural practice (four architects to start with, expanding to ten by 1984) and their sleeping space, open plan and undivided.[25] A bed in the office: Patty Hopkins remembers occasions when it was put out of the window (a wonderful image) before a client visited, to make the office look bigger and more professional.[26] Sadly no photographs have survived. The Hopkins' three children (aged 5–11 when they moved in, 13–19 when the practice moved to a separate building) played in the ground-floor living spaces and the garden while their parents worked above. In common with the Maison de Verre, child-noise did not disrupt the practice, despite a similar lack of acoustic separation between floors and functions. Reflecting on this, Patty Hopkins thinks the children were long-suffering and 'must have been terribly good'.[27] It is also possible, however, that the semi-public environment reinforced behavioural boundaries that are more difficult to achieve in the privacy of a nuclear family home. The indeterminate nature of the building's spaces and lack of internal divisions have accommodated family and practice growing and shrinking over time and allowed Hopkins to interweave her work and family obligations. By 2012, the children have left home and the architectural practice, now 70-strong, has long since moved to Marylebone. However, it still functions as a workhome. Patty and Michael Hopkins each have a working space on the first floor. Partners' meetings, requiring greater privacy than can be achieved at their main open-plan office, continue to be held there and clients come for dinner. The building still acts as calling card, home and workplace 37 years after it was built.

28. S. Zukin, *Loft Living: Culture and Capital in Urban Change* (1988), p. 42.

29. *Ibid.*, p. 11: $2.28 per sq ft per year.

FIG. 2.26 *47 Howard St, SoHo, New York, 1972*

Live/work

'Live/work' was a lesser twentieth-century architectural movement that also led to the construction of workhomes on both sides of the ocean. This term entered the English language in the 1970s, coined to develop and market loft-style apartments in New York. Before artists moved in and created an alternative lifestyle, the neglected and generally unoccupied buildings in the SoHo district of Manhattan had little value. Traditional manufacturing businesses had moved out of the area to premises on the outskirts of the city, in part because of planning blight due to a proposed freeway development. A local group of activists, led by Jane Jacobs, fought and defeated the proposal, thereby preserving a district of fine, nineteenth-century loft buildings [**Fig. 2.26**].[28] Artists gradually moved into these, as the vast open spaces made ideal studios and were cheap. By 1965, between 3,000 and 5,000 artists were living and working in Manhattan.[29]

FIG. 2.27 *Interior Canal St loft, SoHo, New York, 1972*

Initially this was illegal, as the area was zoned as light industrial not residential. However, after a sustained struggle, a 1964 Amendment to the Multiple Dwelling Law, known as Article 7-B, was passed, which allowed people certified as 'regularly engaged in the visual fine arts, such as painting and sculpture, on a professional basis and so certified by an art academy association or society',[30] to both live and work in the lofts. The new occupants approached with imagination the large scale (the average size of a living-loft was more than 200 square metres), open spans and high levels of natural light of the semi-derelict spaces they moved into. Often rejecting conventions such as kitchen, bedroom and living room, they combined studio workspaces and living spaces in the vast lofts in original and often eccentric ways [**Fig. 2.27**].

The neighbourhood gradually developed notoriety, with many of its inhabitants choosing to live unconventional lives (at subsistence levels, in vast unheated spaces, often with no more than a single cold tap and a toilet) in order to be able to work on their art. As a cluster of like-minded people living in challenging conditions, with many similar goals and needs, a strong collective life-style and spirit developed between the artists. Some well-known artists moved in and, with the help of the media promoting the idea of lifestyle, the fact that something new and exciting was happening became publicized. Property developers, financiers and politicians recognized the immense potential value of the central district's neglected buildings, and started to develop the area, initially as live/work apartments in order to meet the legal requirement for artists to both live and work there.

Market pressure led to the relaxation of the requirement that inhabitants of the new live/work spaces should be working artists: first, to include people who were in some way associated with the art world, and then to include people who were merely sympathetic to it. Finally, the condition was removed altogether. But no mechanism was put in place to ensure that people did, in fact, work in these spaces, and it soon became apparent that many of the new apartments were live/work in name only. Legalizing the lofts' usage as affordable living and working spaces in 1964 had appeared to be a great victory for the community of artists, but it set an important and dangerous precedent, the ramifications of which were not recognized at the time. Without an effective way to enforce their dual function as living and working spaces, the lofts were rapidly converted into what were, essentially, large and luxurious apartments. Property prices soared as a result of the live/work re-use of previously rundown light industrial properties. And within a decade the area had been transformed into a smart residential neighbourhood, inhabited largely by high-earning professionals.

The last remaining members of the traditional manufacturing population and the original artists were priced out of the area. A valuable commodity was created from the unpromising raw material of generally disused, semi-derelict factories and warehouses located in an area with minimal infrastructure, lacking schools, health facilities, shops and other local amenities. This was achieved through a process of branding; a new model of urban lifestyle emerged that was marketed energetically. The term 'live/work' was coined to sell apartments that were intended to embody the unconventional spatial qualities of the original artists' lofts and; by association, the promise of a bohemian, creative lifestyle. While the idea clearly appealed to the thousands of young professionals who bought these properties, in reality, many of them never worked in their live/work units. For an emerging young, middle-class, high-earning group, the ideal of the suburban house was swiftly overtaken by chic images of inner-city loft living. This pattern of development was repeated in old industrial cities across the Western world, encouraged by public policy and regeneration practice.[31] And fairly soon the live/work unit was being dismissed as a scam by planning authorities who saw developments inhabited in ways they had not predicted and achieving almost residential prices. Paradoxically, this was despite it being a building type needed as never before.

30. Ibid., pp. 52–3.

31. G. Evans, J. Foord and P. Shaw, Creative Spaces: Strategies for Creative Cities (2006); D.F. Bell and M. Jayne, City of Quarters: Urban Villages in the Contemporary City (2004), pp. 71–92.

FIG. 2.28 Corson-Heinser workhome, Zoe St, San Francisco. Tanner Leddy Maytum Stacey, 1990

32. Zukin, op. cit.

The live/work brand did, however, spark the architectural imagination. And, as well as producing a large number of highly marketable dwellings, it also spawned some good workhomes. A classic is the 1990 Corson/Heinser Live-Work building by Richard Stacey of Tanner Leddy Maytum Stacey [**Fig. 2.28**]. This building combines dwelling and workplace for a photographer and a graphic designer on a narrow site on Zoe St, in the South of Market district of San Francisco. This warehousing and light industrial area, close to the docks and with a substantial transient and working-class population, underwent a transformation similar in many ways to that documented by

FIG. 2.29 Top floor photography studio, Corson-Heinser workhome, Zoe St, San Francisco. Tanner Leddy Maytum Stacey, 1990

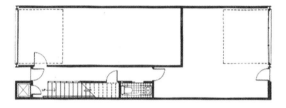

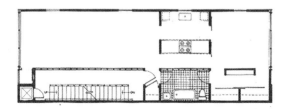

FIG. 2.30 *Plans,*
Corson-Heinser
workhome, Zoe St, San
Francisco. Tanner Leddy
Maytum Stacy, 1990

33. T.A. Hutton, The New
Economy of the City:
Restructuring, Regeneration
and Dislocation in the
Twenty-First Century
Metropolis (2008).

34. C. Melhuish, Modern
House 2 (2000).

Sharon Zukin in the SoHo area of New York.[32] The boom in live/work properties, many of which were dwellings dressed up as workhomes, changed the area beyond recognition and an Industrial Protection Zone was created in 1999 in an attempt to control gentrification, putting a moratorium on further live/work developments.[33]

The Corson/Heinser building follows the tradition of nineteenth-century weavers' workhomes by placing a double-height photography studio with vast areas of glass front and rear on the top floor [**Fig. 2.29**]. Open-plan first-floor living space is sandwiched between this and a ground-floor design studio and garage. A narrow circulation and service zone runs the full length of the building. The photographer works at the top of the building, the graphic designer at the bottom; they meet in the middle to relax, eat and sleep [**Fig. 2.30**].

Function and budget were determining factors for decision-making in the design of this building. Clare Melhuish suggests the materials used 'flag up the hybrid identity of the live/work typology',[34] but there are few concessions to the domestic. Industrial-scale steel glazing systems to front and rear combine with sheet metal panels on the side elevations to provide a tough, industrial-chic aesthetic. Internally the finishes are basic throughout, undifferentiated between the dwelling and workspaces: white-painted plastered walls abut particleboard or shuttering-ply floors.

So much architectural writing considers space, form and materiality, but ignores how buildings are used in everyday life. As workhomes often incorporate functions with conflicting programmes, a close scrutiny of their inhabitation can throw up unexpected issues. Seventeen years after Zoe St was built, the building is still occupied by the original clients, photographer Thomas Heinser and graphic designer Madeleine Corson. In the early 1990s they had recognized that what they were spending on renting three separate buildings in San Francisco (a photographic studio, a design office and an apartment) would be the equivalent to a mortgage on a single purpose-built workhome, and that the hour a day that they both spent commuting between these buildings could be better spent. Clear about the non-standard spaces they wanted, and working closely with Stacy, they changed the design of this building little from inception to realization. Heinser describes it, nearly two decades later, as their 'perfect space'.[35]

He refers to it as both their 'house' and their 'home'. But while it is a detached building of residential scale, it is unlike most contemporary houses. Once inside the front door, it is a building in three parts, office, apartment and studio, each with an entrance off what might be interpreted as a communal staircase and hallway. The use of the term 'house' here seems to refer back to a pre-industrial era when 'house' included workspace as a matter of course. 'Home' is entered not through the front door off the street, but through the internal door to the apartment off the staircase. It is used little; the couple work long hours, communicating by email between their separate workplaces during the working day. Physically, the functions of dwelling and workplace are kept separate; they go to work when they leave the apartment, without leaving the building. Corson employs a team of three in her design office five days a week, while Heinser has two full-time employees plus freelancers. Lunch is eaten in the separate workspaces and members of staff rarely enter the private apartment space. A triple doorbell on the street echoes that of the Maison de Verre. Its central, domestic button remains enigmatically unlabelled to protect their privacy.

Six years after the building was completed, a small three-storey rear extension was added. This tempers the initial open-plan intention of the building by adding a small, enclosed space on each level, in which the clients now spend most of their time. These include a proper bedroom (the original sleeping space was barely separated from the kitchen by a sliding screen), and a private working space each. Every weekend the household decamps to another workhome, a nineteenth-century farmhouse an hour outside San Francisco. There, work and life continue to intermingle, with a shift of emphasis to cooking and socializing. The original spaces of the farmhouse have been left intact, but a historic barn has been rebuilt, providing a vast open-plan space that is used both for Heinser's photographic work and large-scale entertaining. So while Zoe St is primarily a workplace where Corson and Heinser also sleep, the farm is primarily home, where they also work.

While undoubtedly also used in the UK as a brand to market loft-style apartments, the live/work movement has produced some good British workhomes. King's Wharf, built in 2001 on a semi-industrial canal-side site in east London by Stephen Davy Peter Smith, combines 57 live/

35. Interviews with Thomas Heinser, September 2009 and December 2012.

FIG. 2.31 King's Wharf,
east London. Stephen
Davy Peter Smith, 2001

work units with thirteen purely commercial units [**Fig. 2.31**]. Arranged
on five levels around a courtyard, these have deck-access from two
staircases and a domestic-scale lift. Each unit employs the by now
hackneyed spatial formula of a double-height space and mezzanine
with a further small, enclosed space and bathroom. In some,
mezzanine and/or a small rear room provide distinct workspaces or
combined sleeping and working spaces; in others the main space
combines living and working space. Internally white-painted plaster
walls, exposed concrete frame and steel-framed double-height

glazing contribute to an aesthetic neither conventionally domestic nor commercial, neither cosy nor austere, equally suited to domestic life or business entertaining.

Confusion about the rules surrounding live/work initially led to difficulty between the local authority (the London Borough of Hackney) and the inhabitants of this building, raising difficult-to-answer questions that will be discussed in Chapter Five. Is it compulsory to work in a live/work unit? Does computer-based work count as work in these circumstances, if it could just as easily be carried out in a bedroom? Should home-based workers have to double up on their property tax, paying business rates as well as the residential council tax? Despite the controversy, however, a home-based working community has quietly developed that eight years on includes people working in a range of different occupations including accountancy, fashion, design, music, architecture, film and photography. Some are freelance, some employees. Others are involved in start-up businesses: one, selling a device that provides on-tap boiling water, turned over £80,000 in its first year and six years later has a £2,000,000 turnover.[36] Collaborations are common. The 24-hour inhabitation of Kings Wharf encourages the development of local social networks. Neighbours meet in the circulation areas, and a bicycle on a balcony overlooking the central courtyard or peripheral canal signals a neighbour is at home. It is a true creative cluster.

Today

Workhomes are not just a thing of the past. These buildings appear regularly on the pages of contemporary architectural journals, often disguised as houses or in the form of live/work developments. However, the dual-use nature of these buildings is rarely given more than a passing mention. A full discussion of the contemporary architect-designed workhome will, like that of the Modern Movement workhome, have to take place elsewhere. Those included here, from the USA, the UK and Japan, explore a few of the different approaches architects are taking to bringing dwelling and workplace together in a single building. They increase our awareness of a continuing tradition and a developing architectural language.

USA

As Agelio Batle grew up, his mechanic father worked out of the basement of their family home in a working-class district of San Francisco. So, comfortable with home-based work, when he finished art school, he set up a studio in the basement of his own house. Because the area he and his father inhabited was residentially zoned, the work was illicit.[37] Playing with the idea that it was his hand he drew with, not a pencil, Agelio invented a process to produce a small hand, crafted from graphite. Painstakingly making one a day, the first gallery he approached sold his entire stock of 30 in a couple of weeks. He rapidly built up a staff of eight producing 100 pieces

36. Available at: www. firstclasswater.com (accessed 2 October 2013).

37. The issue of governance systems that are an obstacle to home-based work will be discussed in Chapter Five.

FIG. 2.32, 2.33 Home and Workplace, Batle Studio, Potrero Hill, San Francisco. McCoppin Studios, 2007.

a day to 40 different designs; the basement studio soon became cramped and delivery lorries jammed the cul-de-sac. But Agelio and his wife Delia, who was also by then working in the business, enjoyed the close relationship between work and home. With two small children, they did not want to move their business to a commercial unit. Instead they found an old, light industrially zoned warehouse in the Potrero Hill district of San Francisco, where an upstairs office had been converted, legally, into a flat in 1980. They commissioned McCoppin Studios to design them a workhome.

Completed in 2007, their first-floor home sits above the front third of a 95 square metres open-plan workspace combining gallery, shop and office with top-lit clean and dirty studios. An internal door connects home and workplace. The distinctly domestic apartment has a 2.5m high ceiling, crisp white-painted walls, timber furniture, and cork/carpet floors. But, light and airy, the generous kitchen/ living/ dining area doubles as a meeting room for employees and clients [**Fig. 2.32**]. And two compact bedrooms provide private space for sick or breast-feeding employees to rest or express milk. Similarly, the positively industrial ground floor, with its 3.5m ceiling height, exposed ceiling joists, high-specification extract system that contains the dust in the 'dirty' studio, industrial lighting systems and polished concrete floor, provides space for teenage boys to hang out with their friends, for bicycle storage, for cello practice and a piano [**Fig. 2.33**]. A fold-away TV room is in the pipeline. Agelio relaxes by drawing and painting downstairs late into the night.

Flat-roofed and clad in profiled steel sheet, however, this building's identity is unclear, and its dual use is not explicit. The distinct ground- and first-floor functions and volumes are only subtly marked; horizontal cladding to the ground-floor workplace is rotated to run

FIG. 2.34 Exterior detail, Batle Studio, Potrero Hill, San Francisco. McCoppin Studios, 2007

38. One of Le Corbusier's five principles of modern architecture, pilotis are ground-level columns that lift a building up a storey, thus freeing the spaces under the building for circulation.

vertically for the first-floor home [**Fig. 2.34**]. The entrance gives the game away, though. A domestic-scale apartment door with a marble threshold step sits next to the commercial-scale studio entrance, under a common cantilevered canopy. A marble block, intended to carry signage but still blank after five years, separates the two, while well-tended welded steel planters unite them.

This is a workhome designed around the needs of a family with two homeworking parents involved in a business organised around a dirty manufacturing process with eight employees. Modest in its conception and execution, it provides a flexible living and working environment in which domestic space is designed to a different scale and uses a different palette of materials to the workspace, but, in use, work and home migrate constantly between the two.

UK

The workhome that architect Sarah Wigglesworth, running a dozen-strong architectural practice, and her architect and academic partner Jeremy Till designed for their own use in 2004 in north London takes a different approach. At 9–10 Stock Orchard Street, public workplace and private home are raised on pilotis[38] and separated into the two arms of an L-shaped building. A formal meeting room is placed at the pivot-point between the two. Wigglesworth describes it as a 'pompous space'. Devoid of personal possessions, it separates living space from office. A sliding wall, locked shut during the working day, slides open at night, allowing this intermediary space, which doubles as a formal dining room, to create an internal route between living and working spaces. Unlike the Batle Studio, employees never pass into the private zone of home. And the two functions have deliberately distinct architectural expression, inside and out, both experimental. The exterior of the largely timber-clad 'straw-bale'

FIG 2.35, 2.36 *Quilted office and Strawbale home, 9-10 Stock Orchard Street, Islington, London. Sarah Wigglesworth Architects, 2004.*

home is chaotic and fragmented, while a more ordered approach is taken to the 'quilted' office [**Fig. 2.35, 2.36**].

Inside, home combines a generous, double-height, non-orthogonal kitchen/living/dining space with tiny enclosed spaces designed around particular functions. These include Wigglesworth's history-filled study, a treetop perch where Till writes his books and the main bedroom, located as far from the office as is possible, a level below and at the opposite end of the building. The workplace, in contrast, consists of two levels of business-like rectilinear white-painted office space linked by a perimeter double-height slot. Small windows with restricted views keep the workforce on task [**Fig. 2.37**].

FIG. 2.37 *Office interior, 9–10 Stock Orchard Street, Islington, London. Sarah Wigglesworth Architects, 2004*

FIG. 2.38 Gate to the street, 9–10 Stock Orchard Street, Islington, London. Sarah Wigglesworth Architects, 2004

Entrances reflect the different attitudes to home and workplace. A single gate, with double doorbells again reminiscent of those of the Maison de Verre, gives home and workplace equal status onto the street [**Fig. 2.38**]. Inside the gate, the office door is on an axis with, and immediately in front of, the street gate. Boldly painted, it is approached across crunchy gravel through a formal colonnade created by the structure of the office above. Reaching the more domestic house entrance, tucked away at the far end of the building, however, involves taking a meandering route through the vegetable garden, past chickens and bicycles. Only people in the know, or with an express invitation, are likely to venture into what is clearly such private territory.

The potentially conflicting programmes of private dwelling and public workplace are elegantly resolved in this workhome. But despite being written about in 20 different languages, architectural commentary has largely ignored this central achievement, focusing only on the form, materiality and environmentally sustainable design of the building.

Japan

Despite excellent examples in the UK and the USA, Japan leads the field in contemporary design for home-based work for three main reasons. First, because its tradition of home-based work is unbroken from feudal times to the present day, generations of Japanese architects have had plenty of experience of designing workhomes. This has resulted in a sophisticated and well-developed architecture of home-based work. Following on from and underpinning this, Japanese governance systems, such as planning and property tax, enable design for home-based work rather than obstruct it. This critical issue will be discussed in Chapter Five. And, finally, the Japanese approach to building is different to the European approach, and second-hand houses, like second-hand clothes, are not generally valued. Domestic architecture in Japan is, as a result,

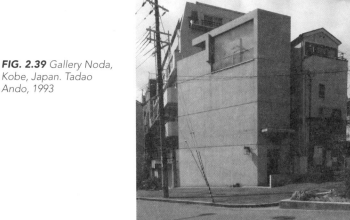

FIG. 2.39 *Gallery Noda, Kobe, Japan. Tadao Ando, 1993*

39. GA Houses, 37 (March 1993), p. 32.

viewed as a product and houses have, on average, a life of less than 30 years. Large numbers, therefore, are designed around the specific requirements of their often homeworking inhabitants.

The Japanese master-architect Tadao Ando designed a number of little- known workhomes, some radical and some beautiful in their ordinariness. His 1993 Gallery Noda in Kobe, a diminutive four-storey wedge-shaped, largely windowless, corner building with a narrow entrance façade, was conceived as a single open volume [**Fig. 2.39**].[39] Only the bathrooms are enclosed. All other spaces are continuous, a series of inhabited landings including a first-floor double-height studio, accessed from a circulation route that starts at the street entrance and winds around the shell, with a ladder short cut between ground-floor gallery/bar and tiny top-floor living quarters. Cast concrete inside and out, each space is lit via a central void by a large roof-light [**Fig. 2.40**]. Ando's 1988 Yoshida House,

FIG. 2.40 *Interior, Gallery Noda, Kobe, Japan. Tadao Ando, 1993*

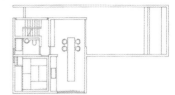
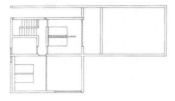
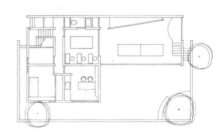

FIG. 2.41 Plans, Yoshida House, Osaka, Japan. Tadao Ando, 1988

40. The shop-house is a workhome with a long and distinguished history. See H. Davis, *Living Over the Store: Architecture and Local Urban Life* (2012).

in a city south of Osaka, takes a different approach. Here a single-storey clothes shop, built into a slope and with a modest window onto the street, is entered from a sunken courtyard [**Fig. 2.41, 2.42**]. A glass wall separates shop and courtyard, but gives no clue that this building also conceals a home for a woman and her younger brother and his family.[40] A workroom, where clothes are made and altered, is sandwiched between shop and apartment; the living spaces are entered from a parallel street at the opposite end of the building to the shop. The upper-level maisonette includes a kitchen/dining room overlooking and opening onto the shop-top roof garden, and bedrooms above them with balconies. In contrast to Gallery Noda's spatial continuity, public and private are skilfully separated and concealed from each other in this building. Domestic spaces do

FIG. 2.42 Shop courtyard, Yoshida House, Osaka, Japan. Tadao Ando, 1988

FIG. 2.43 *Vegetable Seller's House, Tokyo, Japan. Atelier Knot, 2001*

41. Shadow restrictions limit the height of buildings so as to ensure sufficient sunlight in residential Land Use Zones, etc. in Japan. The minimum number of hours per day that the shadows of building sites must fall outside the area are specified by the bylaws of the local governments according to the Japanese Building Standard Law.

not overlook public spaces nor vice versa. Dwellings and workplace interlock, and the aesthetic of the building is consistent throughout. There is a single rear entrance for owners and residents and a public courtyard entrance for employees and customers.

A miniscule (3m x 6m) site meant the shop-house that Yoko Inoue of Atelier Knot designed for the third generation of a family of Tokyo greengrocers in 2001 had to have as many storeys as the city's shadow restrictions allowed.[41] Even with six (82 square metres in total), space is in short supply for both dwelling and workplace [**Fig. 2.43, 2.44**]. The building, for a family of five, is entered through the shop, which is run during the day by the grandmother, who lives in an adjacent building. Boxes of produce sit on the pavement all day, and in the very early morning the vegetable seller appropriates the road in front of the shop to organize his day's purchases from the market into orders to be delivered to his restaurant- and bar-owning customers. The security shutter, front door to both shop and home, is closed before the evening meal each day. Customers ring the

FIG. 2.44 *Plans, Vegetable Seller's House, Tokyo, Japan. Atelier Knot, 2001*

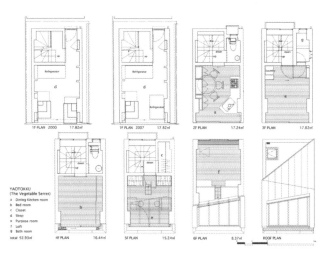

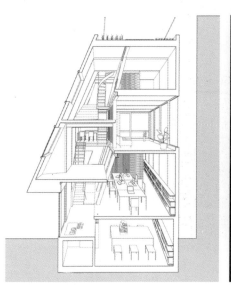

FIG. 2.45 *Sectional perspective, House and Atelier Bow-Wow, Tokyo, Japan. Atelier Bow-Wow, 2005*

FIG. 2.46 *Indeterminate pivot space, House and Atelier Bow-Wow, Tokyo, Japan. Atelier Bow-Wow, 2005*

bell if the shop is closed, and family coming home late have a key. The entrance to the family home is at the back of the shop, reached by squeezing past goods, fridges and the till. A tiny; almost spiral staircase links atomized living accommodation, spread over the five floors above the street-level shop. Household items are stored in crevices between structural elements, and finishes are omitted to gain a few extra internal millimeters. The first-floor kitchen/dining room is the main communal family space. An all-purpose living room above houses washing machine and computer, sewing machine and television. The fourth-floor bedroom gives a degree of privacy to the parents, while children's beds are shoehorned into the fifth and mezzanine sixth. This building can, to some extent, be read as a vertical interpretation of the traditional *machiya*: the shop is entered directly from the street; a service space, rising behind it and containing the bathrooms, connects a sequence of living spaces. Unlike the *machiya*, however, each space is determinate, meticulously designed around a particular function that is fixed because each floor is so tiny.

In direct contrast to the fixed functionality of the Vegetable Seller's House, the workhome that Atelier Bow-Wow principals, Yoshiharu Tsukamoto and Momoyo Kaijima, built for themselves is organized around a shifting tide of home and work. With a teaching job each and a sixteen-strong architectural practice, all at different locations, they found they were spending only a few hours each week in their home. By combining home and practice in a single building, they aimed to make their lives more efficient and enjoyable. They realized that creating separate compartments for private home and increasingly public workspace would not give them the flexibility they needed, so House and Atelier Bow-Wow, built in Shinjuku-ku, Tokyo, in 2005, takes the form of a single open volume over four floors. Only the bathrooms and a small sleeping compartment are enclosed [**Fig. 2.45**]. Two lower floors of studio space are separated from the more private upper spaces by an indeterminate pivot space [**Fig. 2.46**]

FIG. 2.47 *Extended stair landing, House and Atelier Bow-Wow, Tokyo, Japan. Atelier Bow-Wow, 2005*

42. Interview with Yoshiharu Tsukamoto, July 2008.

similar to that in the Wigglesworth/Till Strawbale House, by turns meeting room and dining room. In fact, the whole building transforms according to use. In the evenings after employees have left and at the weekends, the entire building becomes home. And when the owners are working to a major deadline, like an architectural competition, the whole 211 square metres building becomes a workplace. A single entrance is used by everyone. The open, irregular stair has extended landings that provide model storage, entrance lobby and relaxation space as well as a minimal cooking area, informal eating space, and a washing machine tucked into a corner [**Fig. 2.47**]. A simple aesthetic has been adopted, neither homely nor corporate, but with a softening materiality as the building progresses from more public to more private. White-painted open-tread steel stair and polished concrete floors are replaced with timber on the upper floors of the building. The uppermost and most private space in the building is a cabin-like bedroom. It is the only space, apart from bathrooms, with a door.

The overlap of public and private functions and the lack of acoustic separation between most spaces in the workhome require a traditional Japanese sensibility that Tsukamoto considers is being lost.[42] And despite the tight urban site, there is a sense of indifference to neighbouring buildings and functions. The neglected side elevation of the building next door, just a few metres away, faces directly, like wallpaper, onto the central pivotal space through a large and unexpectedly placed picture window. Privacy between spaces and adjoining buildings is addressed through what Tsukamoto describes as 'a deep, and beautiful, relationship between behaviour and space'. He explains: 'You can see and hear, but don't.'

Ikushima Library, Atelier Bow-Wow's 2008 workhome for a couple of writers and their three children, is conceived as two interlocking volumes, one for people and one for books, with space flowing freely

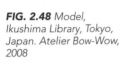

FIG. 2.48 *Model, Ikushima Library, Tokyo, Japan. Atelier Bow-Wow, 2008*

between them [**Fig. 2.48**]. The only enclosed rooms are child-sized sleeping alcoves and bathrooms. The materially rich 'book house' dominates the building: the library lines two levels of working space. An open staircase separates it from the 'people house', which is defined by changes of level, scale and materials [**Fig. 2.49**]. Dividing the space vertically into these two pavilions creates a dramatic piece of architecture, but a central question about its effectiveness in use is raised. Despite the conceptual division into two separate houses, this building is a single spatially continuous volume, like House and Atelier Bow-Wow. But this building is built around a family with three small children, and how does the often noisy business of running a family mesh with the need for a quiet space where a writer can concentrate? The Maison de Verre, also a single open volume combining family life with a workplace that demanded a calm, quiet environment, raised the same question. In 1930s France, children's education was strict and house rules regarding noise during surgery hours firmly applied. In twenty-first-century Japan, a parallel formality

FIG. 2.49 *View through stair, Ikushima Library, Tokyo, Japan. Atelier Bow-Wow, 2008*

FIG. 2.50 *Klarheit, Tokyo, Japan. Koh Kitayama + architecture WORKSHOP, 2008*

43. Interview with Koh Kitayama, July 2008.

44. Le Corbusier's Unité d'Habitation at Marseilles, completed in 1952, was designed as a mixed-use building. It has 337 apartments over 18 storeys, accessed via internal corridors. These are interrupted at the seventh level by a double-height shopping 'street' with shops and other facilities, including a bakery, a hairdresser and a 24-room hotel and bar-restaurant. There is a crèche on the eighth floor and a roof-top gym.

and containment in the family make successful a spatial arrangement that might be uninhabitable by an equivalent UK family.

Leading Japanese architect Koh Kitayama estimates that half the buildings he designs are this 'important contemporary building type'.[43] Two, one a speculatively built cluster and the other designed around the specific requirements of a client, provide contrasting approaches to workhome design. Klarheit, completed in 2008, is a mixed-use building with six workhome units sandwiched between a ground-floor commercial space and a fourth-floor bar/ restaurant [**Fig. 2.50**]. The units are arranged, Unité-like, on either side of an internal corridor that has been designed as a semi-public street.[44] Floor-to-ceiling glazed 'shop-fronts' make the workspaces public, light the internal access way and create transparency between units [**Fig. 2.51**]. Inhabitants are therefore aware of each other's movements. Each workhome is entered through its workspace. Larger units have a spiral staircase up to their protected private living spaces while

FIG. 2.51 *Transparent 'street', Klarheit, Tokyo, Japan. Koh Kitayama + architecture WORKSHOP, 2008*

FIG. 2.52 *Top floor bar, Klarheit, Tokyo, Japan. Koh Kitayama + architecture WORKSHOP, 2008*

the smaller ones have ladder-like stairs down to theirs. Materials and floor-to-ceiling heights are consistent throughout, with no concessions to ideas of home or workplace. The flexibility of Tokyo's governance systems means that, though designed as workhomes, these units can also be inhabited purely as workspace or purely as dwellings. The public bar/restaurant and terrace on the top floor provides space for inhabitants to meet their clients and each other, as well as being accessible off the street by members of the public. Stylish design and panoramic views across Tokyo ensure its commercial success [**Fig. 2.52**]. This building neatly addresses the issues of social isolation among home-based workers, the acknowledged benefit of creating clusters of similar workers, and the reluctance of some home-based

FIG. 2.53 *Music room, House at Kamakura, Japan. Koh Kitayama + architecture WORKSHOP, 2009*

FIG. 2.54 *Buffer space, House at Kamakura, Japan. Koh Kitayama + architecture WORKSHOP, 2009*

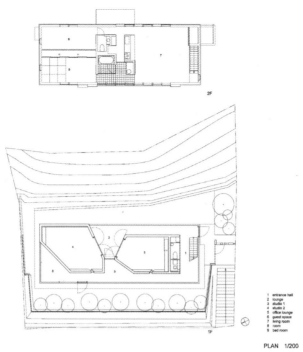

2F

FIG. 2.55 *Plans, House at Kamakura, Japan. Koh Kitayama + architecture WORKSHOP, 2009*

1F

1 entrance hall
2 lounge
3 studio 1
4 studio 2
5 office lounge
6 guest space
7 living room
8 room
9 bed room

PLAN 1/200

workers to meet members of the public in their premises. The combination of workhomes, shop and bar in a single building creates a fine-grained mixed use that increases the 24-hour inhabitation of the city and the development of local social networks, and stimulates the local economy.

In contrast to this speculatively built development, Kitayama's 2009 House at Kamakura is a workhome for two musicians, a violinist and a pianist, designed meticulously around the spatial and environmental requirements of both occupations and family. Acoustic considerations (including the need for sound insulation between spaces, minimization of breakout and a professional acoustic for music practice and performance) were primary generators of the design. But the brief was also to provide a beautiful family home. The two distinct functions have generated a building in two radically different halves. Ground-floor music rooms provide space for practice and chamber music concerts [**Fig. 2.53**]. Non-parallel, inclined reinforced concrete walls provide acoustic separation and create the required acoustic inside the music rooms. A fully glazed buffer space around these provides space for members of the public to congregate before performances, increases the efficiency of the air-conditioning in the music rooms and reduces acoustic breakout [**Fig. 2.54**]. Perched on a ledge across a steep slope, the music rooms support the timber-framed home that nestles in the treetops above [**Fig. 2.55**]. A single entrance leads past them and up to the flexible open-plan living space. Radically different from the dark, heavy, enclosed, irregular, air-conditioned working spaces below, this light, open, rectilinear living space has views on all sides. Designed so that the wind can blow freely through it, full-height glazed panels slide open, leaving

FIG. 2.56 Home interior, House at Kamakura, Japan. Koh Kitayama + architecture WORKSHOP, 2009

a delicate, almost imperceptible balustrade in place [**Fig. 2.56**]. This workhome is an inventive response to the potentially conflicting programmes of public/private, noisy/quiet, family/workplace.

This overview of the different approaches taken in these examples gives us an idea of the extent to which the dual use of these buildings underpins their design. It also brings into focus two distinct approaches: buildings that are designed specifically to meet the needs of a particular home-based worker, and those that are designed to be flexible and adaptable and so can accommodate a range of different occupants. This will be explored further in the next chapter.

Everyday realities

Everyday realities

1. Unusually for architectural research, this study was equally interested in the people and the buildings. This was because the dual functions of home and work are often legible only through a study of buildings in use. As a result, methodologies from both social science and from architecture were used. Data retrieved through interviews informed the architectural analysis, while visual techniques, including photography, orthogonal drawing and diagrammatic mapping, contributed to understanding informants' working practices and life-worlds.

2. This research formed the basis of a doctorate. See F. Holliss, 'The Workhome... A New Building Type?', PhD, London Metropolitan University (2007).

Chapter Two gives us a glimpse of how a few architects have approached the design of the workhome. But most contemporary home-based workers do not live and work in purpose-designed premises. Instead, they squeeze home into workplace or work into home. We do not know much about this. Who are they? What work do they do? Who do they work for? How do they organize their work? How do they combine work and home spatially? What are the buildings they inhabit like? And, crucially, how can we design better, at both the urban and the building scale, to meet their needs?

These questions set a challenge. Home-based workers in different contexts in England, let alone different cultures across the world, have radically different lives, occupations and workhomes. Is it possible to generalize from the lives and premises of a limited number of culturally similar home-based workers? Starting close to home, but with the aim of finding answers that apply universally, I interviewed home-based workers from across the social spectrum in a socially and culturally diverse London borough. I quizzed them about their lives, and measured, drew and photographed their buildings.[1]

I repeated the process in a London suburb, and then in a rural village. An analysis of the amassed information resulted in the development of a series of typologies and design considerations.[2] These were then tested against eight US home-based workers in diverse occupations and buildings. The resultant four typologies and nine design considerations provide a set of tools for use when designing for home-based work.

Workhome user-group typology

Rich and poor, skilled and unskilled, old and young, the 76 UK home-based workers studied include men and women in equal numbers, of different ethnicities, with and without caring responsibilities. They are employers, employees and self-employed people working in a wide range of occupations. Some occupy purpose-built workhomes, either historic buildings from a time when home-based work was common or contemporary architect-designed buildings, generally studio-houses or live/work units. Most, however, have appropriated domestic or industrial spaces for the dual functions, adapting them to fit home into industrial buildings or work into a house or flat as best they can.

Home-based workers are usually considered as individuals rather than as a workforce, but to see them as a workforce is both useful and necessary when thinking about designing for this working practice. It is difficult to design good buildings without understanding their future use. An analysis of those interviewed for this book, taken as individual members of an, albeit disparate, overall home-based workforce, uncovered eight sub-groups with distinct spatial and environmental needs. As so little is known about the contemporary home-based workforce, it is not possible to estimate what proportion of the total working population falls into each category, and it is also likely that other sub-groups exist. These eight, however, give us an idea of the different sorts of home-based workers that exist in even a small sample and an indication of their distinct spatial and environmental requirements.

3. London Borough of Hackney, Live/Work Supplementary Planning Guidance (1996), revoked in 2006.

Family care-givers

Many people work at home or live at their workplace so that they can look after their children or elders. This fact has commonly been ignored: in 1996, a pioneering UK live/work local authority determined, in its guidance for building for this working practice, that 'no more than two bedrooms should be included in each unit, as live/work uses are not considered suitable for family accommodation'.[3] But the evidence is clear. Family care-givers interviewed for this book combine family home with workplaces that include office, studio, shop, workshop, consulting room, salon and kitchen. One started a home-based business so he could contribute to the care of his severely disabled child [**Fig. 3.1**]. Another, a hairdresser, set up a

FIG. 3.1 Family care-giver's workhome, UK, MD of business making electronic components

FIG. 3.2 Family caregiver's workhome, UK, hairdresser
FIG. 3.3 Family caregivers' workhome, US, landscape architect and kinetic sculptor

4. See Charles Booth Online; C. Booth and J. Steele, *The Streets of London: The Booth Notebooks* (1997).

home-based salon when she became a single parent [**Fig. 3.2**]. A kinetic sculptor and a landscape architect combine the chaos of three children under the age of 4 with their two home-based occupations [**Fig. 3.3**]. And the two Batle boys, now teenagers, have lived in the flat above their parents' studio and workshop and run in and out of them all their lives [**Fig. 3.4**]. The environmental and spatial needs of this group are distinct. Combining workspace with a family home raises issues about physical, emotional and psychological boundaries that can be resolved through good design.

Backbone of the community

Charles Booth's notebooks identify home-based workers who inhabited beer-houses and corner shops, funeral parlours and lodging houses, as well as vicarages and teachers' houses next door to churches and schools. Embedded in every area of nineteenth-century London, these people made an important social contribution to their immediate communities.[4] This tradition continues today. A fifth of the people interviewed for this book, from school caretaker to baker and

FIG. 3.4 Family caregivers' workhome, USA, designers and makers of graphite sculptures

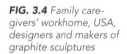

FIG. 3.5 *Backbone of the community's workhome, UK, funeral director*
FIG. 3.6 *Professional's workhome, UK, architect*

funeral director to fish and chip shop proprietor, are the backbones of their local community. All are visible, well-known members of it, and generally work long hours in some form of public service. These home-based workers are so familiar that we no longer see them, and rarely design for them [**Fig. 3.5**].

Professional and managerial

Many of those interviewed are professionals or managers. They include architects and photographers, academics and writers, translators and psychotherapists, a dietician and a senior manager of a large corporation as well as a director of a not-for-profit organization. Their spatial and environmental requirements differ depending on the nature of their work. Some have highly visible public roles that involve daily interactions with clients and employees, banks of computers, meeting rooms and a library [**Fig. 3.6**], while others, working in an intensely solitary way, need silence and privacy supported only by a mobile phone signal and an Internet connection [**Fig. 3.7**]. Architects often inhabit buildings they have

FIG. 3.7 *Professional's workhome, UK, BT manager*

FIG. 3.8 *Professional's workhome, UK, architect*

designed for themselves and these act as living, breathing business cards, advertising their skills to potential clients [**Fig. 3.8**]. Other professionals and managers can find it harder to create appropriate space for their home-based work. This can raise problems with occupational identity that will be discussed in Chapter Six.

24/7 artists

A fourth group consists of artists, who do not generally differentiate between their work and domestic lives. One photographer thinks nothing about stopping in the middle of a working day to cook lunch for a few friends or watch a football match [**Fig. 3.9**]. He works intermittently from 8 a.m. until 7 p.m., starts again at 9.30 p.m. and often does not finish until 1 a.m. He says:

I don't see any borders between my private and professional life at all. I find it very difficult to build them, and really there aren't any, if I look at my tax return, it's blurry … I can travel all over the place, and stay on a bit longer … is it holiday or work? I'm still working, still taking pictures. I can't say that personal time is not work time … it just never happens.[5]

FIG. 3.9 *24/7 artist's workhome, UK, photographer*

FIG. 3.10, 3.11 *24/7 artists' workhome UK, studio and gallery*

Many home-based artists inhabit collective buildings. A group of London painters rent a floor of an industrial building. It has a central gallery space, flanked on one side by seven small studios and on the other by four bedrooms and an office, with a large communal kitchen/living room, and a bathroom at the far end [**Fig. 3.10, 3.11**]. And in the USA, a contact juggler lives with 350 other artists of all ages in a disused smelting works divided into 60 or so living/working units. Circus artists, inhabiting eight of these, have created vast triple-height mirrored rehearsal spaces rigged with trapezes, with communal kitchen/living spaces and cabin-like bedrooms accessed from ladders [**Fig. 3.12**]. This collectivity counters one of the central disadvantages of home-based work: social isolation. It links back to historic collective forms, like the weavers' cottage factory, and has considerably wider potential application that will be discussed later.

FIG. 3.12 *24/7 artists' workhome USA, circus artists' collective, studio*

FIG. 3.13 *Craftworker's workhome, UK, garage proprietor*

Craftworkers

A fifth group was found to be making or mending in a range of trades. These people include a furniture-maker, a costume-maker, a mechanic, a carpenter, a caterer/preserves-maker, a plumber, a market gardener and a curtain-maker. Their workhomes respond to the nature of the work, family structure and location. A rural mechanic's detached house, workshop and petrol station have provided home and workplace for this family-run business since his grandfather started selling petrol in 1912 [**Fig. 3.13**]. A carpenter lives and works in an adapted industrial unit. While unexpected, this combination of dirty, noisy, potentially dangerous work and family life is relatively common. Other members of this group adapt domestic environments: a preserves-maker works in a much-extended domestic kitchen and a curtain-maker in an under-used garage [**Fig. 3.14**].

Top-up

A sixth group uses home-based work to supplement a low household income. Some top up UK benefits; others top up low wages earned outside the home. Some, but not all, members of this group work in the informal sector and as a result hide their home-based work, even

FIG. 3.14 *Craftworker's workhome, UK, preserves-maker*

FIG. 3.15 *Top-up workhome, UK, childminder*
FIG. 3.16 *Top-up workhome, UK, website designer*

from their neighbours. One person reaching the end of her working life has retrained as a child-minder in order to add to her pension in her retirement [**Fig. 3.15**]. Another, a young website designer, has a disabling illness. He hopes to be well enough at some point in the future to sign off from his benefits and build up his business. In the meantime he works informally to top up his benefit, keep physically and mentally active and ward off depression [**Fig. 3.16**]. The group also includes a person selling children's clothes and women's underwear, a piece-working manufacturer and a newspaper distributor.

Live-in

A seventh, often overlooked group consists of people with live-in jobs. They include a school caretaker, the manager of a historic building and a residential care-worker. In each case their home is embedded in the institution for which they work, the security of the building being an intrinsic part of the job [**Fig. 3.17**]. One of the perks is the private use of public facilities: the school caretaker's children have the run of the playground out of hours, while the historic house manager enjoys the elegant spaces she inhabits.

FIG. 3.17 *Live-in workhome, UK, care-worker*

Start-up

Most businesses in the UK start up at home to reduce overheads and to lessen the impact of the long hours involved in getting a new enterprise off the ground. Two people in the process of establishing new businesses were interviewed. A needlewoman struggles to work in the spare bedroom of her terraced cottage: the work is dusty and the cat leaves hairs on her finished pieces. And a financial advisor inhabiting an affordable live/work unit finds it difficult to create a life for himself outside his work.

This sample is too small to represent all UK home-based workers, let alone those of other countries or cultures. However, identifying an expandable range of radically different home-based workers with distinct spatial and environmental requirements highlights the fact that this is a diverse field. This typology provides a warning against the one-size-fits-all approach that has plagued the design of many live/work developments, and can be used to design buildings and cities to accommodate this increasingly popular working practice.

The first principle of workhome design therefore is that home-based workers can be categorized into a range of different, culturally specific groups, each with distinct spatial and environmental requirements.

Workhome typologies

So what are the underlying design issues? How is the workhome or urban quarter that is designed around the needs of the freelance computer-based social policy researcher with two young children different to that designed for the single metalworking sculptor or the school caretaker?

The aim has been, through an analysis of the disparate sample of UK buildings, to develop a series of widely applicable principles that can support design for home-based work. The work of two North American architects provided a springboard for this. Penny Gurstein pioneered research in this area in her groundbreaking 1990 doctoral study of electronic homework in the US detached suburban house, which was consolidated in two subsequent publications.[6] Thomas Dolan's architectural practice has specialized in the design of live/work buildings since 1998 and he has published his accumulated expertise on a website and, more recently, in a book.[7] Gurstein's work identifies the spatial relationship between the dwelling and workplace aspects of this building type as a central issue. Dolan develops this and identifies the further issue of dominant function.

However, when the less homogeneous UK sample was tested against the work of Gurstein and Dolan, rather than confirming the typologies they had developed as universally applicable, disparities were found. Some buildings did not fit their categories, and there seemed to be some important categories missing.[8] So, taking their work as a starting point, a process of visual analysis was used to develop three

6. P. Gurstein, 'Working at Home in the Live-in Office: Computers, Space and the Social Life of Households', PhD, University of California, Berkeley, (1990), published in a report: P. Gurstein and D. Marlor, Planning for Telework and Home-Based Employment : A Canadian Survey on Integrating Work into Residential Environments (1995), and a sole-authored book: P. Gurstein, Wired to the World, Chained to the Home: Telework in Daily Life (2001).

7. See www.live-work.com and T. Dolan, Live-Work Planning and Design: Zero-Commute Housing (2012).

8. A detailed discussion of this can be found in Holliss, op. cit. (2007).

new typologies that, when tested against thousands of workhomes old and new, have so far been found to be universally applicable.[9]

Perhaps a small digression would be useful here to unpack the idea of architectural typology. The eighteenth-century French politician, art critic and philosopher, Quatremère de Quincy, made one of the earliest. In his contribution to the Encyclopédie Méthodique (1788), he classified all buildings into three basic categories according to their form, material and structural system: 'hut', 'cave' and 'tent'. He acknowledged the spatial consequences of the different systems, connected them to social systems (hut = farmers, tent = shepherds, cave = hunters) and traced their influence on much later architectural traditions (hut = Greek, cave = Egyptian, tent = Oriental). In this typology, de Quincy identifies what might be considered a universal truth about architecture, which can still be applied. In the final volume of the Encyclopédie Méthodique, he made a clear and much-quoted distinction between the 'type' and the 'model':

9. A detailed discussion of this process can be found in F. Holliss, 'Space, Buildings and the Life-Worlds of Home-Based Workers', (2012).

10. A-C. Quatremère de Quincy, in Encyclopédie Méthodique, vol. 3 (1788), p. 544: inexpert translation from the French by author.

11. A. Tyng, Beginnings: Louis I. Kahn's Philosophy of Architecture (1984), p. 31.

12. Ibid., p. 76.

The word 'type' presents less the image of something to be copied or imitated completely than the idea of an element which should itself serve as a rule for the model … The 'model', as understood in the practical execution of art, is an object that one must repeat such as it is. The 'type' is, on the contrary, an object from which one can conceive works that do not resemble each other. Everything is precise in the 'model', everything is more or less vague in the 'type' … Thus we can see that in the imitation of types one can recognize spirit and feeling, and nothing that cannot be questioned in its prevention and ignorance.[10]

This distinction was important in the development of the following workhome typologies.

In the 1960s, Louis Kahn developed another useful spatial typology in his recognition of two fundamental types of space: 'served space' and 'servant space'.[11] Served space was defined as the space used by humans, while servant space was that taken up by mechanical facilities such as pipes and boilers. Over time this idea expanded to encompass the major and minor spaces in any building, living spaces being served spaces, and bathrooms, hallways, staircases, as well as such spaces as plant rooms, being servant spaces. Kahn believed that this typology represented a universal truth about architecture.[12]

An early, clear example of the architectural consequences of working with this spatial typology can be seen in the design of medieval castles, where service rooms and staircases are contained in hollows in the massive walls that surround the great halls. Equivalent architectural typologies have been sought that clarify the important principles underlying design for home-based work.

1 Dominant function

The first and most basic, but also potentially most useful workhome typology that emerges from an analysis of the UK buildings in the

FIG. 3.18 *Home-dominated workhome*
FIG. 3.19 *Work-dominated workhome*

sample was triggered by noticing that some workhomes are mostly workspace, while others are mostly dwelling. In other words, some home-based workers work in their homes [**Fig. 3.18**] while others live at their workplaces [**Fig. 3.19**]. This simple observation identifies two radically different types of workhome, which I call 'work-dominated' and 'home-dominated'.

The home-dominated workhomes in the sample include flats, houses, cottages, a bungalow and a live/work unit. Some have a dedicated working space [**Fig. 3.20**], while others use a spare bedroom [**Fig. 3.21**], their living room or work on the kitchen table [**Fig. 3.22**]. The work-dominated workhomes in the sample include industrial units, live/work units, work/live units, a funeral parlour, two pubs, a pub converted into a mechanic's workshop, a historic house and a residential care-home [**Fig. 3.23**].

FIG. 3.20 *Home-based translators' dedicated workspace*

Some of the 76 buildings, however, do not fit into either of these categories. An adjacent village gallery/framing workshop and family

FIG. 3.21 *Home-based social policy researcher's spare bedroom workspace*

FIG. 3.22 *Home-based curator's dining room table workspace*

FIG. 3.23 *Work-dominated work/live units*

FIG. 3.24 *Equal-status workhome*

house have separate front doors but link internally [**Fig. 3.24**]. An architect's house faces onto a London square; her separate but connected office (for eight employees) is at the bottom of the garden with its own entrance onto a parallel non-residential mews. As neither home nor work dominates, these buildings fall into a third, equal-status category.

A second principle of workhome design is therefore that all workhomes can be categorized according to their dominant function as home-dominated, work-dominated, or equal-status.

Each of the eight workhome-user groups aligns broadly with one of these categories. Artists who work 24/7 and craft workers tend to prefer their workhomes to be work-dominated, while many family care-givers and start-up businesses prefer home-dominated. More developed businesses, including many professional ones, like the equal-status type best. As each provides a radically different life-world for their associated home-based workers, this typology provides a tool

FIG. 3.25 *Social policy researcher's live-with kitchen table workspace*

13. See Holliss, op. cit. (2012).

14. More than half the 76 UK buildings studied were live-with. They included six industrial units, three purpose-built studio-houses, three purpose-built work/ live units, five purpose-built live/work units, 16 terraced houses or cottages, four terraced houses converted into maisonettes or flats, five purpose-built flats, five detached houses, one residential care-home, one purpose-built funeral parlour with living accommodation above, one historic house with integral manager's living accommodation, and one purpose-built shop with attached living accommodation that had been converted into an office with attached living accommodation.

for architects designing workhomes to suit a wide range of different occupations and situations.[13] As home-dominated, work-dominated and equal-status workhomes generate urban conditions with radically different characteristics, it can also contribute to the design of the city.

A lack of understanding of the distinction between home-dominated and work-dominated workhomes has led to confusion in policy-making on both sides of the Atlantic. Permission was granted for many live/work developments in run-down light-industrial areas in both the London Borough of Hackney and the San Francisco South of Market Area, with the expectation that the work function would be dominant. But this was not explicit: the local authorities did not distinguish between the workhomes they wanted (work-dominated) and those they did not want (home-dominated). The resultant buildings were often inhabited as loft-style apartments by people working at home in IT-based work. Incensed by the unwanted change in urban character as well as by the disproportionate profit developers made from converting light-industrial land to quasi-residential use, the authorities have placed ongoing moratoriums on workhome development in both these city neighbourhoods. This is despite a rapidly growing home-based workforce and demand for such buildings. The influence of regulatory frameworks on design for home-based work will be discussed later.

FIG. 3.26 *Graphic designers' live-with attic workspace*

2 Spatial design strategies

Establishing these categories of dominant function raises questions about the relationship between work and home in these dual-use buildings, often involving very different activities. For example, how does the organization of 10 Downing Street to accommodate family and running the country compare to that of the doctor's surgery and family home in the Maison de Verre? Can the vast pool of existing workhomes be analysed to form a typology that, following in the footsteps of Quatremère de Quincy and Louis Kahn, presents an essential architectural truth about the relationship between home and workplace in the workhome? By testing and developing Gurstein and Dolan's work through a visual pattern-making process as before, three basic degrees of spatial separation between work and home were identified: none, some and total.

No spatial separation

'Live-with' is the most common but not necessarily the most popular or desirable arrangement. In this type, dwelling and workplace are contained, either as part of or as an entire building, in a single compartment with one front door.[14] In some live-with models, home and work are literally in the same space: people work at the kitchen table in their house [**Fig. 3.25**] or live on a mezzanine above their studio or workshop. In others, a distinct space is created for work in the home or for living in the workspace. It can be a whole floor or just a room [**Fig. 3.26**]. But in every case the functions overlap, to a greater or lesser degree, as a result of the single entrance.

Some spatial separation

In 'live-adjacent' workhomes, the two functions are contained in separate compartments next door to each other, above, below or side by side, each with its own entrance to the street [**Fig. 3.27**]. This provides a degree of spatial separation between work and home

FIG. 3.27 Licencees' live-adjacent pub work-home

FIG. 3.28 Fish and chip proprietor's live-adjacent workhome: home

15. The live-adjacent buildings included a semi-detached house with a salon, a purpose-built school caretaker's house embedded in a primary school building, a terraced house with a door knocked through into an adjacent terraced shop, four terraced shops with living accommodation above, a detached shop with living accommodation on both the ground and upper floors, an industrial building of which the upper two floors had been converted into residential accommodation, two pubs, and a disused pub converted into a car repair workshop, with living accommodation on three floors above.

that many home-based workers like, particularly where interactions with members of the public are involved.[15] There is often an internal linking doorway, which allows movement between the two worlds without going out onto the street. But some people, like this fish and chip proprietor [**Fig. 3.28**], prefer not to have this link:

There is no connection between downstairs and upstairs. It's good because when we're upstairs we don't feel part of the shop, and don't get bothered. The bad point is that I have to go out into the street with the takings each night, which can be up to £700. I also have to chase upstairs and downstairs. I've got a head like a sieve so I'm always leaving stuff downstairs; it's a pain having to go round to open the door and go upstairs. I have thought about opening an internal door up, but at the moment I prefer it as it is. The benefit of separation is more important than the inconvenience.

The live-adjacent arrangement is particularly useful where the two functions have conflicting design constraints. It allows a home-based furniture-maker, for example, to keep work-generated dust and noise out of his home, and his children safe from potentially dangerous machines [**Fig. 3.29**].

FIG. 3.29 Home-based furniture-maker's live-adjacent workhome

FIG. 3.30 *Architect's live-nearby workhome home*

16. *The live-nearby buildings included: a terraced house with a Portakabin in the back garden, a terraced house with a mews-style studio built at the bottom of its garden accessed by a subsidiary road, a terraced house with commercial greenhouses on adjacent land accessed by a different road, a terraced house with a bakery in an adjoining yard, a terraced house with a nearby church, a terraced house and shop with a workshop at a short distance, a semi-detached house with a shed in the garden, a semi-detached house with a substantial 'homechalet' in the back garden, a detached house with a petrol station and workshop in an adjoining yard, a detached house (bungalow) with a workshop in the garage and a detached house with a nearby church.*

17. *It is debatable how far apart 'live-nearby' can be before it counts as going out to work: a walk of 2 minutes or less is taken as the cut-off point here.*

Total spatial separation

In the third type, 'live-nearby', dwelling and workplace elements are detached and at a small distance from each other.[16] For many people, especially family care-givers and professionals, this is the ideal arrangement, as it helps them to create separate domains for home and work.[17] In Georgian London, large houses were often built with mews stables and coach-houses at the bottom of their gardens, accessed by a subsidiary road, where stable boys, grooms, coachmen and their families worked and lived. These buildings make good contemporary live-nearby workhomes, particularly for home-based workers with a public profile, as the two functions can be kept completely separate and presented to the world in different ways. A London architect found it difficult combining her roles as principal in a practice with eight employees and as mother of four children in her Georgian terraced house [**Fig. 3.30**], so she redeveloped the mews building at the bottom of her garden. The resulting crisp, modern office provides a professional workplace accessed from a narrow commercial road and is an effective advertisement for her practice [**Fig. 3.31**]. Home and work are separated from and linked to each other by the garden:

FIG. 3.31 *Architect's live-nearby workhome: workplace*

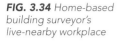

FIG. 3.32 Walt Disney's first workspace in his uncle's garage, a live-near-by workhome
FIG. 3.33 Home-based soft-furnishings designer/maker's live-nearby workplace

I like having two front doors; it creates two different worlds. It's a good model … a public entrance for work; employees need a separate entrance. It also makes a showpiece for prospective clients. I like the formality of the entrance off a different street.

'Working in the garage' is a live-nearby model made famous by Walt Disney, who started his film empire in his uncle's garage [**Fig. 3.32**]. The 'shed at the bottom of the garden' is another, popular in suburbia where gardens are larger [**Fig. 3.33**] as well as in tight urban situations. A building surveyor has a sick wife, in and out of hospital, and needs to work at home in order to care for their children. Finding himself distracted when he tried working in his house, he had a Portakabin craned into the garden of his modest terraced house, just a few yards from its back door [**Fig. 3.34**].

I can walk out of the house, shut the door and completely forget about my house. When the children come home from school, I can open the door and just watch them doing their homework. It's very convenient that way.

FIG. 3.34 Home-based building surveyor's live-nearby workplace

FIG. 3.35 *Roald Dahl's live-nearby writing hut*

FIG. 3.36 *Baker's live-nearby workhome*

FIG. 3.37, 3.38 *Market gardener's live-nearby workhome: home and workplace*

Many writers, including Virginia Woolf, Roald Dahl and Philip Pullman, have adopted this model [**Fig. 3.35**].

People in traditional home-based occupations often also inhabit live-nearby workhomes. In a rural village, bakery and shop sit across a yard from the baker's house [**Fig. 3.36**]; a forecourt separates the garage proprietor's house from petrol pumps and workshop. And a market gardener, like the mews-working architect, has cottage and glasshouses accessed off parallel roads. Few of her customers are even aware she is a home-based worker [**Fig. 3.37, 3.38**].

A third principle, therefore, for workhome design is that workhomes fall into one of three categories depending on the degree of spatial separation between dwelling and workspace: live-with, live-adjacent or live-nearby.

Historically all three types were purpose-built. Contemporary workhomes, however, tend to be conceived as live-with buildings, despite the fact that this is not the ideal arrangement for most home-based workers. The potentially substantial demand for live-adjacent and live-nearby workhomes raises urban design issues, and problems with current governance frameworks in the USA and the UK at least, that will be discussed in Chapters Four and Five.

3 Patterns of use

Regardless of the buildings they inhabit, different people use space in distinct ways. Some home-based workers use all the spaces in their workhomes for both their work and domestic lives, no matter what space they have. A photographer works in bed, in the bath, on the WC and on the sofa in his kitchen/living room, as well as in his studio. The team of seventeen or more other people involved on a shoot will also use his WC, kitchen and dining room and, when necessary, his bedroom, not just the studio. Other home-based workers prefer to contain the functions, and combine dedicated living space with dedicated workspace [**Fig. 3.39**]. Work is never carried out in domestic space, and vice versa. Most people lie somewhere between these two extremes, combining dedicated workspace, if there is room, with dual-use space and dedicated living space. These preferences override the spatial arrangement of the building. Many artists, for example, will use all the space available to them as both home and workspace, whether they live and work in a bungalow, a semi-detached house with a shed at the bottom of the garden or an industrial unit. However, professionals inhabiting the same buildings are likely to organize their two worlds into dedicated, separate spaces if they can.

This final typology, therefore, identifies three ways people use space in their workhome, no matter what form their building takes: 'dual-use space', 'dedicated workspace' and 'dedicated living space'. Home-based workers combine these differently, depending on their personality, the work they do and who they live with, as well as what space they have available to them and how they want to present themselves to the world. The more closely this pattern of use aligns with the spatial design strategy employed in their workhome, the better for all concerned.

FIG. 3.39 *Building surveyor's Portakabin dedicated workspace*

Synthesis

These typologies provide some universal principles that can help us to make sense of a vast range of past and present workhomes and to design buildings and cities better to accommodate and support home-based work. **Figure 3.40** shows the wide range of effective options. For example, a home-dominated workhome can be arranged around any of the spatial design strategies and involve any of the patterns of use, but some combinations are more compatible than others. For example, if all the spaces in an artist's workhome are in dual use, then separate entrances for work and home may be more of a nuisance than a boon. Conversely if a psychotherapist does not want her clients to have any contact with her private world, then live-adjacent or live-nearby will be a more suitable approach than live-with. And so on.

FIG. 3.40 *Diagramatic synthesis of workhome typologies*

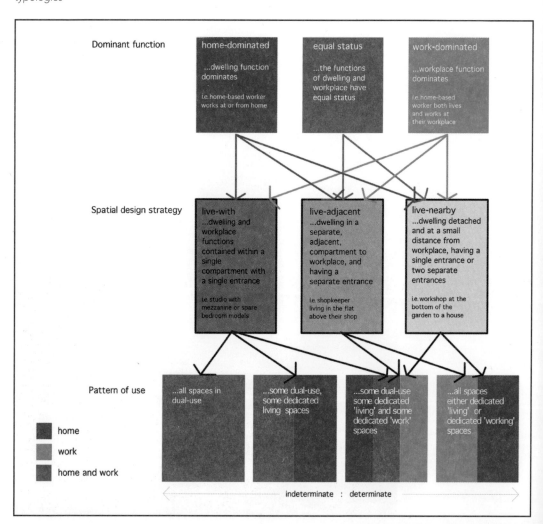

Further design considerations

This section will briefly discuss nine primary considerations, all affecting the design of the workhome, which were distilled from the study of 86 contemporary home-based workers' premises.

1 Flexibility

Flexibility is a core idea. Schneider and Till's definition of flexible housing as 'housing that can adapt to the changing needs of users' can equally be applied to the workhome; their arguments in its favour are compelling.[18] Socially, it empowers the users to take control of their space. Demographically, it means buildings can be adjusted over time to new living and working patterns, to different configurations of users, and even to complete changes of use. Economically, it avoids obsolescence and the cost of reconfiguration or refurbishment.[19]

18. T. Schneider and J. Till, *Flexible Housing* (2007), p. 4.

19 Ibid., p. 5.

But what is flexible for one home-based worker is inflexible for another. The open-plan Hopkins House has adapted elegantly to changes in the way the Hopkins family and practice have used it over more than 35 years. But add a troubled teenager or a career change to psychotherapy by one of the partners and the lack of acoustic separation between spaces and the single entrance off the street could make the building unworkable. The cellular nature of an eighteenth-century Welsh farmhouse, in contrast, inhabited by an artist working with flowers and printmaking, has proved enormously flexible, enabling her to move studio, flower room, office and living space for herself, her partner and two children around like a sliding tile puzzle [**Fig. 3.41**]. When the situation changes, depending on the number of people living in the house, whether or not she is employing anyone, and how much printing/flowers she is doing, she shifts functions from room to room. The Hopkins House, flexible for the Hopkins household, would make an inflexible and indeed uninhabitable building for her, as hers would for the Hopkins.

FIG. 3.41 Artist's flower room in eighteenth-century Welsh farmhouse

So what does it mean to design a flexible workhome? Trying to solve this problem by analysing the lives and premises of the 76 UK home-based workers in this study proved difficult. The evidence contradicted each potential answer. A child-minder's flexible use of the tiny spaces in her 49 square metres, 1950s council maisonette counters the hypothesis that size, then structural flexibility and the ability to extend are critical factors [**Fig. 3.42**]. The difficulty a costume-designer/maker's boyfriend has sleeping while she works through the night to meet a deadline disproves any direct relationship between open-plan indeterminacy and flexibility [**Fig. 3.43, 3.44**]. While ideal for her on her own, the space is inflexible when shared with someone not involved in the same work. And so on.

It finally became apparent that flexibility in workhome design means different things in different situations. There is no simple equation that can guide us in the design of the flexible workhome, no silver bullet. What shines out from the research, however, is how adaptable and flexible people themselves are. Most of the interviewees have appropriated a single-use building, either dwelling or industrial unit, for their home-based work and organized it to accommodate their changing living and working patterns as best they can. While most have gripes, some major, about design issues, the inflexibility that causes them the biggest problem is the rigid web of government-generated rules that determine what buildings we can build where, and how we can inhabit them. The negative impact this has on home-based work in the UK and the USA will be discussed, and compared to the highly flexible Japanese system, in Chapter Five.

2 Determinacy/indeterminacy

The second consideration, relating to the determinacy or indeterminacy of the design approach, has cropped up in relation to a number of buildings already discussed. The term 'determinate' is used architecturally to refer to buildings designed around a

FIG. 3.42 *Childminder's cellular workhome*

fixed use. A determinate workhome, therefore, combines distinct, purpose-designed dwelling and workplace elements or spaces. The two functions are often expressed architecturally and legible from the street [**see Fig. 1.15**]. 'Indeterminacy', in contrast, refers to buildings that are designed around an indefinite or uncertain use. Indeterminate workhomes can be enigmatic buildings, neither home nor workplace [**see Fig. 2.18**]. They are designed to accommodate changing patterns of living and working, rather than to distinguish between the two functions in a fixed way.

Most of the purpose-designed determinate workhomes in the sample are nineteenth-century buildings still in use for their original function.[20] On moving to the city, a car mechanic struggled to find a building he could live and work in:

20. Some 40 per cent of the 86 buildings in the study are purpose-designed workhomes; the rest are dwellings or industrial buildings appropriated for dual use.

I grew up in the country, and you had a little house, with a garage alongside it, a shed in the garden or a greenhouse, and everyone, including all the kids, fixed their own scooters and cars and motorbikes on the drive or in the garage outside the house ... when I moved to London I couldn't do that because all you get is something you can live in, go home, close the door and can't do anything with it. I've always found that really frustrating, so I first got a railway arch, lived upstairs, worked downstairs and then I got this pub that was in receivership.

While living upstairs, he converted the bar into a workshop by installing soundproofing, garage doors, an extractor system and seals round internal doors to prevent dust migrating. Purpose-designed dual-use buildings like this are comparatively rare and much sought-after in the UK. Their recognizably distinct dwelling and workplace elements can be adapted to a wide range of home-based occupations and family structures. But Koh Kitayama's House at Kamakura, an example of a determinate workhome meticulously designed around the needs of two musicians and their family [**see Fig. 2.53–2.56**], brings into focus a problem relating to such

FIG. 3.43, 3.44 *Costume designer/maker's open plan workhome: home and work ends*

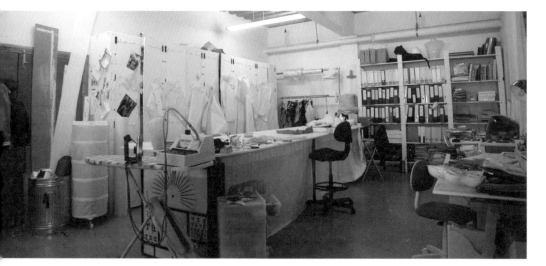

FIG. 3.45 *Architect's indeterminate workhome*

buildings. If the design is too specific, then the building may not be sufficiently adaptable for use by a different occupant. In Japan, this often leads to buildings being demolished when their owners move.

Indeterminate buildings, on the other hand, suit home-based workers with less compartmentalized or specific spatial requirements. Although indeterminacy is not a new concept,[21] the examples in the sample are all contemporary buildings. An architect's office is an open-plan rectangular concrete and brick space with large windows on two sides, dominated by a technical library, desks and computers. There are no clues that anyone lives here [**Fig. 3.45**]. Employees and members of the public are in and out of the office every day, generally unaware of the tiny personalized space with a narrow bed hidden behind the technical library and rotating storage unit [**Fig. 3.46**]. The materiality of Atelier Bow-Wow's own workhome softens slightly as it leads up to the bedroom, but the other parts of the building are indeterminate, allowing workspace to become home and home to become workspace as desired.

3 Public/private

Although often perceived as a solitary way of life, many home-based occupations, from publican to shopkeeper, child-minder to rector, or hairdresser to teleworker whose supervisor visits at intervals, involve

FIG. 3.46 *Architect's private snug in his indeterminate workhome*

FIG. 3.47 *Home-based hairdresser's public 'hair room'*

22. *In an architectural plan, adjacent spaces are separated only by the thickness of the wall between them. In these topographical diagrams, spaces (drawn to scale) are reorganized on the page to communicate potential patterns of movement or direct communication between spaces. A thin black line joins only those spaces that are connected to each other by a door or opening. For a more detailed discussion of the use of visual research methods in this research, see Holliss, op. cit (2012).*

interactions with members of the public, either as employees, people with appointments or passing trade [**Fig. 3.47**]. This important issue is generally ignored, but it has major implications for the design of the city as well as the workhome. This will be discussed in Chapter Four.

Diagrams of the 76 UK buildings, with areas in public use overlaid in yellow, reveal the different ways home-based workers engage with members of the public [**Fig. 3.48**].[22] They also highlight the extent and impact of the public/private interaction.

A curtain-maker says: 'I have no problem with customers coming into my house; I have an open door.' But interaction with members of the public raises complex social and spatial issues for many other home-based workers. A social policy researcher and mother of two says:

I never have meetings at home. I always offer to go out, partly because the house is hard to get to, partly because it doesn't feel like a proper workspace and partly because I like to get out. I would have to clear up a lot if I had meetings with clients at home. I often have meetings in cafés.

FIG. 3.48 *Topographical diagram of artists' collective workhome*

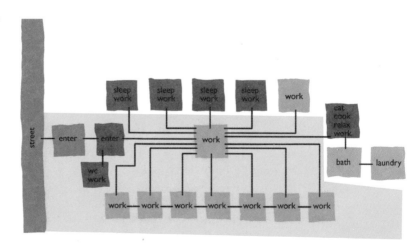

FIG. 3.49 *Public workhome, the rectory*

This is common. An artist says: 'I don't really like meeting here [at home], as you have to look at the children's laundry, or the uneaten cornflakes …'.

Some home-based workers negotiate public access to their inherently private workhomes. A music teacher allows pupils to use her kitchen and bathroom but, anxious to protect her privacy, keeps the bedroom door shut at all times. Others find it compromises their normal inhabitation of the home. A bed-and-breakfast proprietor does not like the position of the stairs in her seventeenth-century thatched cottage because it means guests have to pass through her private lounge when they go to their bedroom. A psychotherapist, similarly, feels she has to keep the bathroom spotless and personal possessions out of sight because members of the public come into her workhome. She would prefer a second entrance off the street, straight to her consulting room, so that clients did not have to come into her home. A graphic designer with a purpose-built attic studio would also prefer to have a second entrance:

It is too intimate walking through the house, bringing a new client, especially a man, upstairs past our bedroom … it doesn't feel right. But it's OK when we enter the workspace. We get very anxious about keeping bedroom doors shut to protect our privacy. A client comes in once a fortnight. We do a big clear up before they come, make sure the bathroom's clean. If we've had lots of kids in over the weekend we'll have to work hard to make sure it looks presentable.

Despite the fact that they are beautiful, open-plan and double-height, an architect is concerned that his private spaces (and therefore his domestic detritus) are in public view. He sometimes wishes he could screen off certain areas and that the office was not next to his bedroom. A costume designer/maker inhabiting an industrial unit does not like the fact that the units are arranged off an internal corridor with their doors opposite each other, because it compromises her privacy when they are open.

Other workhomes, however, are public buildings, and legible as such from the street; these present a different set of issues. A rector speaks of his constant anxiety about who will turn up at the door of his rectory in need of help [**Fig. 3.49**]. Security is an on-going issue for him, and he has a hefty chain on the front door, a panic button and a lockable door between house and workroom.[23] An artist inhabiting a collective workhome with six others has a slight sense of being in a 'Big Brother household'. Since it is run, in part, as a gallery, members of the public walk through the studios and comment on work, so the artists have a continuous sense of being on display (**see Fig. 3.10, 3.11**]. Although it is not a big issue, he suffers when his work is going badly. A baker says: 'It's a very public job. I do like people, but not on Saturday afternoons and Sundays.' She locks the gate to her yard when the bakery is closed; family have keys but members of the public are excluded [**Fig. 3.50**]. And everyone in the village knows not to ring the house doorbell, as bakers sleep unconventional hours because they work at night. A school caretaker in a busy London borough does not find it so easy, however, to make it known when he is off-duty; parents often knock on his door during out-of-school hours (**see Fig. 1.26**). Urban design solutions that address such issues will be discussed later.

23. Church of England vicarages are built to a standard layout that pays careful attention to the relationship between workspace and home.

4 Visibility/invisibility

Many UK and US home-based workers are deliberately invisible. They work covertly in their home or live secretly at their workplace, usually either because they fear they are or because they actually are

FIG. 3.50 Public workhome, the bakery/ baker's shop

FIG. 3.51 Workhome that appears to be a house
FIG. 3.52 Workhome that appears to be a workplace

breaking some regulation or other. And as a result, many buildings that appear to be houses are also workplaces [**Fig. 3.51**], while others that appear to be workplaces are also homes [**Fig. 3.52**]. The negative impact this can have on home-based workers' occupational identity will be discussed in Chapter Six. Here, however, we can consider the need to design workhomes that deliberately hide their dual function. These can be either home-dominated, like those of the watch-makers in Coventry, or work-dominated, like that of the architect whose tiny private space is concealed behind his technical library. Other workhomes are deliberately visible, advertising the work of the occupant, and incorporating it and them into neighbourhood social and commercial networks. Many examples have been discussed in earlier chapters, but they are generally historic. Contemporary workhomes often have enigmatic exteriors that do not recognize the value, to the occupant or the neighbourhood, of making the occupation being carried out explicit. Even a name-plate, which was common in Victorian times and still occasionally occurs today, helps to make the home-based occupation visible, and therefore part of the local economy [**Fig. 3.53**].

5 Noisy/quiet

Acoustics present a major issue for home-based workers. It was the design issue mentioned most consistently: nearly half the people interviewed had a problem of one sort or another. Buildings are often designed with little acoustic separation between spaces, between each other and between inside and outside. This is not a problem for those who have the spatial sensibility identified by Tsukamoto of Atelier Bow-Wow when he said: 'We can see and hear, but we don't.' But it presents a major problem for other home-based workers who, inhabiting the same building through the 24 hours, are susceptible to noises over which they have no control.

A psychotherapist, whose terraced-house living room doubles as her consulting room, is concerned about protecting her clients from domestic noises:

FIG. 3.53 *Signage makes a workhome explicit*

It is difficult for my daughter and my lodger when I have clients … she and the lodger have to keep quiet. I give my lodger a timetable of clients, and ask them to be very careful coming and going. It needs much better sound insulation. It has an impact on both clients and psychotherapist.

Family and friends disturb an artist who inhabits a live/work unit with mezzanine living spaces above his studio:

There is very little spatial separation; when my girlfriend is watching TV, I find it really distracting. I can hear it downstairs. Friends live in the area but visit for a limited time. If people come and stay, they have to go out when I am working.

And a home-based British Telecom senior manager is disturbed by his daughter clattering about in her bedroom above his office in their detached modern executive home [**see Fig. 3.7**].

Many home-based workers are disturbed by their domestic appliances. A dietician working in the kitchen of her eighteenth-century cottage is typical: 'I'll put the washing machine on, but that drives me mad during the day because of the noise of it … if I am on the phone and have the washing machine going, I just can't hear.'

A curator is so distracted by the noise of her dishwasher that she often does not put it on, and then has no clean dishes in the evening. A costume designer/maker, who flexibly inhabits a single open-plan industrial space for work and home and whose work dominates her life (her friend says 'she virtually sleeps under her bench'), has the same problem. She says: 'You need a separate sound-proof room for the washing machine … I can't get away from the noise.'

While a seventeenth-century thatched cottage appears to be an ideal bed-and-breakfast workhome [**Fig. 3.54**], its poor acoustic qualities make life difficult for the proprietors. With only floorboards between guests' bedrooms and the kitchen and dining room below, sound is easily transmitted:

FIG. 3.54 *Bed and breakfast proprietor's workhome with poor acoustic qualities*
FIG. 3.55 *Academic's workhome with poor acoustic qualities*

We have the washing machine running a lot of the time; I put it on during the day when guests are not there. I wouldn't put it on during the night. I also always lay the breakfast table the night before so I don't crash about underneath the guests in the morning.

And a graphic designer does not want her clients to be aware of 'all the domestic stuff': 'If I go down to the kitchen to make a cup of tea and the phone rings while the washing machine is on, I'll always turn it off before I answer the phone.'

Home-based workers are also often disturbed by their neighbours. An academic hears his neighbour shouting at her children all day through the party wall, and is aware every time her shower and WC are used [**Fig. 3.55**]. A soft-furnishings designer/maker working in a shed-studio in her suburban garden is distracted by children playing next door. And a collective of artists living and working in an industrial unit [**Fig. 3.56**] above an experimental musician has a similar problem: 'Horrible noises come up, from any instrument. She sometimes plays

FIG. 3.56 *Artists collective workhome with poor acoustic qualities*

FIG. 3.57 *Photographer's workhome with poor acoustic qualities*

three notes on her piano for nine hours. It is challenging, so bad that it is funny.' A photographer in a light industrial unit 'jumps out of his skin' when someone upstairs drops something [**Fig. 3.57**]. A costume designer/maker in similar premises expects it to be noisy during the day, but is annoyed by unnecessary noise at night. She can hear the squeaky wheels of her upstairs neighbour's chair when she is in bed and bangs on the ceiling with a broom to stop it [**see Fig. 3.43, 3.44**]. She also has a problem with the noise of her own washing machine. As she inhabits a single open-plan space, it is difficult to get away from and she thinks all workhomes should have a sound-insulated utility space for the washing machine as well as 'all the crap you don't want to look at, like the ladder and your bicycle'.

This is not just the case in home-dominated workhomes. A school caretaker's house embedded in a primary school building [**see Fig. 1.26**] has living spaces next door to classrooms:

When my older kids come home I have to tell them to turn the noise down and not jump across the floor. And when the play-centre used to have drumming downstairs we were on tenterhooks. It sounded like it was in the room ... it had to be moved elsewhere.

Similarly a live-in historic house manager, whose top-floor flat is sandwiched between one of the public show rooms and a staff office, has to be careful about noise when she is off-duty. So do her colleagues:

Staff and members of the public walk right past my door ... I am concerned that the sound of the TV travels; I don't want visitors to hear it. But my colleagues are very good, they are very quiet, they creep along on a Sunday morning ... if I was truly asleep it wouldn't wake me.

In contrast, an architect in a development of 27 purpose-built work/live units says: 'This building has good sound insulation. I can turn the music up loud and the concrete walls mean it doesn't disturb anyone. We home-based workers work when we want and it doesn't affect anyone.'

Generally a priority only in such buildings as performance spaces, acoustics emerge as an important consideration in all workhome design, as a result of 24-hour inhabitation of buildings that often combine functions with radically different requirements. Most home-based workers prefer a high level of acoustic separation between the living and working spaces in their workhomes, whether home- or work-dominated, and also between the workhome, the neighbours and the outside world. Like drainage, this is an invisible area of design that has immense impact, positive or negative, on the way a building functions. High-specification acoustic separation adds to the cost of a building and its lack of visibility means it is often a low priority.

6 Clean/dirty

Home-based occupations can be dirty and/or smelly. In this study, furniture-making, costume/props-making, car mechanics, carpentry, art (two painters and a kinetic sculptor), catering, fish and chips, market gardening, baking, sewing, floristry, hairdressing, picture-framing and product manufacture, amounting to a quarter of the overall sample, all fall into this category.

For some, the smell (or the dirt) does not present a problem. A preserves-maker, for example, processes industrial quantities of vegetables in her extended domestic kitchen, producing a spicy, vinegary smell that both she and her neighbours enjoy [**Fig. 3.58**]. In contrast, a hairdresser hated the impact her work had in her home: 'I used to work in an upstairs bedroom, washing hair in the bathroom. I couldn't stand the hair everywhere … especially upstairs; and I couldn't stand the smell of the perming chemicals.' Wanting to remain home-based as a single parent, she built a salon, separated

FIG. 3.58 Preserves-maker's workhome produces a spicy, vinegary smell

FIG. 3.59 *Mechanic lives nearby his dirty, and sometimes smelly, work*

from the house by its own entrance lobby, in a rear extension to her semi-detached house. The live-adjacent design of this workhome keeps the mess and smell out of the home.

A furniture-maker worries about the impact of the dust from his workshop on his family: 'The kids don't hang around downstairs; it's too dusty. I've stopped working in ordinary MDF and now use environmentally friendlier material that has zero formaldehyde. The very fine particles are a bit of a worry.'

Some people adopt the live-nearby approach, separating clean home from dirty and smelly work in separate buildings a short distance from each other. The baker lives across the yard from her bakery; two car mechanics' workshops are across the way from their homes, while another has a yard next door to his home [**Fig. 3.59**]. A fourth, obsessive about keeping the dirt in his workshop, follows an elaborate set of procedures, including washing, taking off his overalls and blowing all the dust off his clothing with a compressed airline, before he 'goes home' upstairs. Others, like the fish and chip shop owner and the product manufacturer, have double defences against dusty or smelly processes: they have installed expensive equipment to remove pollutants in the workplace element of live-adjacent workhomes.

The fact that artists' studios are often dirty, smelly and, in some cases, dangerous places is generally ignored, even in purpose-designed buildings. A painter [**Fig. 3.60**] finds: 'It's fumey. It can be a nightmare in the studio in the summer. Turps hangs in the air; I get nauseous after ten minutes. There's no ventilation at all.' Even in a purpose-designed work/live unit, another painter finds paint fumes a problem because of inadequate ventilation.

This issue can usually be resolved with little difficulty when designing for home-based work. For example, a lobby separates a kinetic sculptor's home and three children under the age of 4 from a workshop full of toxic chemicals, metal-filings and sawdust [**Fig. 3.61**]. Timber and metalworking machines have powerful extractor systems and both realms have through ventilation and their own entrances. It simply requires careful thought.

7 Hot/cold

Heat is also often an issue for home-based workers. Some freeze, either because their workspace is unheated and uninsulated or because, conscious of the bills, they do not want to heat a whole building when they are using only one space. A journalist, not wanting to heat her house in winter just for herself, wears layers of jumpers and a hat while she is working and takes little 'fire breaks' from her work, warming up in front of an electric heater. An academic with a purpose-built study, does not put the heating on during the day unless it gets really cold, because she worries about the heating bills. Instead she too puts on more jumpers and gets up and walks about. Her study is open-plan with the rest of house and she regrets not having a way of heating it separately. The artists' collective keep only the bedrooms, kitchen and bathroom warm. They tried heating the studios, where everyone had electric heaters, but their electricity bill in the first quarter came to £4,000, so they had to stop that.

We don't heat the studios and it gets cold in there, really cold. We put on two jumpers, two trousers and two pairs of socks to go to

FIG. 3.60 *The painter's unventilated studio makes him nauseous*
FIG. 3.61 *The kinetic sculptor's workshop is separated from home by a lobby*

FIG. 3.62 *The bakery is too hot in the summer*

work … *the bathroom is lovely and warm, but we have to go through the freezing gallery space to get to our bedrooms.*

A member of the clergy sits in a draught from the window next to her desk. Not wanting to heat the whole property, she used to put a duvet around her feet and shiver. A gas fire in her workroom now means she can heat the one room. This is not a new problem. In 1902, Scott of the Antarctic, when frozen in by sea-ice for many weeks on the ship *Discovery*, worked at the desk in his cabin with his feet in a hay box. It seems that little has changed in the intervening 110 years.

A few keep the heating on around the clock in winter. Two child-minders find this very expensive. Others, however, overheat, either because their work produces excess heat, or because of solar gain and inadequate ventilation. A baker's ovens are a comfort in the winter, but make the bakery too hot in the summer [**Fig. 3.62**]. Waste heat from fridges and freezers has the same effect for a village shopkeeper who lives above his shop [**Fig. 3.63**]. Similarly, a preserves-maker who has her Aga cooker on all year round finds this cosy in winter, but it gets too hot in summer. She has an extractor but does not use it because the noise gets on her nerves. She would like more opening windows. This should be a simple issue to resolve in purpose-built workhomes. But again it is not a glamorous aspect of design and is often missed. An architect's own highly glazed south-facing spaces get too hot in summer: 'I don't want to spend too much time up there – even with the roof lights open.' And two live/

FIG. 3.63 *Waste heat from fridges and freezers make the village shop too hot in summer*

FIG. 3.64 *The garden provides important playspace for childminder*

work units I encountered in London, with non-opening south-facing clerestory lights, get intolerably hot in summer: up to 50°C.

Environmental design is important in the workhome because it is inhabited throughout the 24 hours. High levels of thermal insulation, well-designed ventilation and protection from solar gain would solve most of the issues raised about this by the people interviewed for this book, in some cases combined with heating systems that can heat distinct parts of a building at different times of day. This is not difficult to achieve, but it is currently expensive. Sarah Wigglesworth has installed a system at 9–10 Stock Orchard St that is programmable to allow different spaces to be heated or unheated throughout the day or the week.

8 Inside/outside

Echoing nineteenth-century East End yards and courts, a garden or yard provides a primary home-based workspace for some, including a US mechanic [**see Fig. 3.59**], and an additional working space for others, including a UK carpenter and a child-minder [**Fig. 3.64**]. Many others, including an academic, an architect, a writer, a social policy researcher, a photographer and a curator, enjoy pottering in their gardens or hanging their laundry out to dry when they break from their work. Some, like a graphic designer and a translator, like to open double doors and work half-outdoors when it is warm. For others, like the architect with the mews-style office, an outside space

FIG. 3.65 *The yard provides a place for home-based creatives to meet*

FIG. 3.66 *Collective courtyards provide space for artists to meet*

creates a buffer zone between public work and private home. For a few, like the school caretaker, work-associated exterior space offers an unparalleled amenity [**see Fig. 1.26**].

Outdoor space can give home-based workers a place to meet like-minded people. Every night when it is warm, a community of young creative people, including a graffiti artist, a photographer and a carpenter, gather on old sofas set up around a bonfire in a yard behind the London industrial buildings where they live and work, to put the world to rights and dream up ideas for new collaborations [**Fig. 3.65**]. Similarly, US artists inhabit the scattered courtyards of the old smelting works where they live and work [**Fig. 3.66**]. A home-based photographer, a painter and others share a beer on a neutral slice of land between car park and workhome at the end of the working day. Rarely specifically designed for the purpose, such pieces of appropriated land can be crucial to the well-being of the home-based worker, for whom social isolation can be a major issue.

9 Storage

And finally the seemingly trivial issue of storage can have a disproportionate effect on the home-based worker when neglected in the design of the workhome. Very few of the people interviewed for this book had enough storage space. Even architects designing their own workhome found within a year that they had underestimated how much they would need [**Fig. 3.67**]. For most people, work and home both involve a lot of clobber. While many prefer to be able to put work items out of view once their working day is over, few have this option [**Fig. 3.68**].

Design solutions

FIG. 3.67 Home-based architects underestimate the amount of storage they will need
FIG. 3.68 Most home-based workers do not have enough storage space

Many of the problems home-based work presents, spatially, environmentally and even socially, can be solved through design. The live/work 'double-height space and mezzanine' and the speculative house 'desk under the stair' emerge as lazy, stereotypical solutions that do not meet the needs of most home-based workers. These four typologies and nine design considerations provide prompts that can help improve design for home-based work.

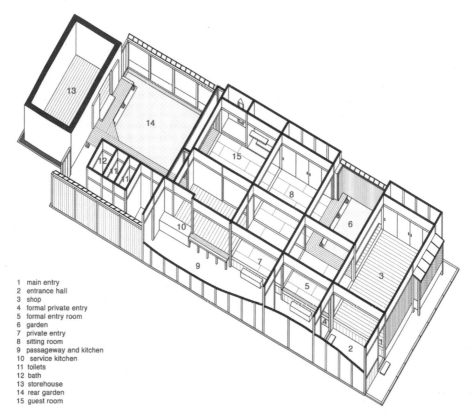

1 main entry
2 entrance hall
3 shop
4 formal private entry
5 formal entry room
6 garden
7 private entry
8 sitting room
9 passageway and kitchen
10 service kitchen
11 toilets
12 bath
13 storehouse
14 rear garden
15 guest room

FIG. 3.69 Axonometric of a machiya

The Japanese *machiya* provides a traditional precedent that addresses many of the issues that have been discussed in this chapter. Paired spaces that can be combined into a single larger space are separated, and naturally lit and ventilated, by small gardens or courtyards and connected by a linear service and circulation space [**Fig. 3.69**]. They can have radically different qualities from each other: public/private, noisy/quiet, dirty/clean, hot/cold. Each includes a large floor-to-ceiling storage area, often somewhere between a quarter and a third of the overall floor area of the space, so furniture and artifacts can be taken out and replaced as it transforms from one use to another through the day.[24] *Machiya* elevations are enigmatic, neither home nor workplace, and can be open or closed [**Fig. 3.70**]. Traditional signage, in the form of the *noren* or half-curtain taken down at the end of the working day, indicates what the business is and when it is open. There are also exemplary modern precedents. Koh Kitayama's House at Kamakura, discussed in Chapter Two, meticulously addresses the issues of public and private, hot and cold, noisy and quiet, visible and invisible [**Fig. 3.71**]. However, most contemporary buildings that claim to be designed for home-based work fail in one or more of these areas.

There remains an unanswered question about the relative merit of designing determinate and indeterminate workhomes. Both approaches bring benefits and disadvantages. It is important to

24. Bedding would be put away in the morning, and replaced by a table and chairs for use during the day, for example.

25. See www.theworkhome.com/introducing-pattern-book/

recognize that the field is vast, and that workhomes of different shapes and sizes and design approaches suit different occupants. While people have tried to be prescriptive about what constitutes real live/work, in fact, the workhome is an extremely diverse building type with many possible forms. Some of these have recently been explored in an online Workhome Pattern Book.[25]

Too often, however, people approach this field with a restricted view, considering only one small corner of the whole. This is, in part, because governance frameworks, such as planning regulations and property taxation, are organized around mono-functional building types; the difficulty this places on building and inhabiting workhomes will be discussed in Chapter Five. But first let us have a look at the implications of home-based work and the workhome for the city.

FIG. 3.70 Machiya street elevation

FIG. 3.71 House in Kamakura, Japan. Koh Kitayama + architecture WORKSHOP, 2009

The city

The city

1. E. Howard, To-Morrow:
A Peaceful Path to Real
Reform, original (1898)
edition with a new
commentary by P. Hall, D.
Hardy and C. Ward (2004),
p. 3.

2. This was written
by Congregationalist
clergyman, Andrew Mearns.
See A. Mearns, The Bitter
Cry of Outcast England: An
Inquiry into the Condition of
the Abject Poor (1883), p. 4,
and quoted by P. Hall, Cities
of Tomorrow: An Intellectual
History of Urban Planning
and Design in the Twentieth
Century (1998, reprint 2002),
p. 16.

3. Booth's document
D6, 'Homeworkers', LSE
Booth Archive (1886–1903).
Charles Booth Online
Archive, available at: www.
booth.lse.ac.uk (2004). It is
unusual in that it is a typed
document attributed to Ada
Heather-Biggs; all the other
documents in the Booth
archive are unattributed,
hand-written by different
authors.

Most historic cities grew up around some form of home-based work: a castle or palace, a church or monastery, trade at a crossroads or a clustered manufacturing or farming community. The modern city, in contrast, tends to ignore this working practice, despite the fact that a rapidly increasing number of people, rich and poor, skilled and unskilled, are engaged in it. This chapter will discuss why this shift happened and explore how cities might once again benefit from being designed around home-based work.

The English medieval city teemed with home-based work. Surveyor Ralph Treswell's plans of London, drawn just before London's Great Fire in 1700, give us a glimpse of the intricate urban grain that supported this [**see Fig. 1.2**]. Blocks, delineated by main streets lined with shops and workshops, were hollowed out by both semi-public courts, entered through narrow entrances, and semi-private yards, accessed through a shop, workshop or warehouse. These courts and yards provided flexible indeterminate space where work was carried out in association with adjacent workhomes until the end of the nineteenth century.

The combined forces of industrialization and the Enclosure Acts changed the English city beyond recognition in the nineteenth century. London's population grew six-fold during the century and almost doubled (from 3.9 to 6.6 million) between 1871 and 1901. This rapid expansion stretched the resources of the city to beyond breaking point, and led to intolerable urban conditions.[1] Poverty and deprivation were commonplace, a result of the punitive conditions of employment imposed by early industrialists. Crime was widespread. And, because until 1859 the Thames was London's makeshift sewer as well as its main source of drinking water, disease was widespread. The elderly, sick and disabled had to fend for themselves as best they could, and families often inhabited a single dangerously insanitary room:

Walls and ceilings are black with the accretions of filth which have gathered upon them through long years of neglect. It is exuding *through cracks in the boards overhead; it is running down the walls; it is everywhere. What goes by the name of a window is half of it stuffed with rags or covered by boards to keep out wind and rain; the rest is so begrimed and obscured that scarcely can light enter or anything be seen outside.*[2]

The 'evils' of home-based work

The polluting fumes of coal-powered factories covered neighbouring workers' houses in grime, and home-based work was carried out under appalling conditions:

awful, work done in living room, everything thick with fur. Two women working, one had bad cough … Filthy home, small, horrible, fur choking up all the staircase … Work done in the bedroom. Filthy. Six children … Dreadfully dirty. Smell of skins simply sickening. Two women working in one tiny room. Window wouldn't open. Work not done in living room, but fluff got everywhere … Husband out of work. She complained of work as being very unhealthy and bad for the chest. It ought to have a separate room set aside for it but they cannot afford it.[3]

Sweated labour, the exploitation of unregulated and poorly paid, usually home-based, pieceworkers, was considered one of the scourges of the East End slum. Condemnation came from all sides. Trades unions, campaigning for a male family wage, argued that when women earned, often at home because of caring responsibilities, employers were let off paying men a living family wage.[4] They also objected to home-based work because its lack of regulation led to the exploitation of some of the weakest and most vulnerable members of society.[5] Employers opposed home-based work because the increased degree of control they had over factory- or mill-based workforces resulted in greater profits.[6] The prevalent conservative idea that a woman's place should be in the home, her role restricted to domesticity and motherhood, reinforced opposition to this working practice.[7] Even the social reformers of the time opposed it on account of the horrific physical conditions of the buildings that many of the poorest homeworkers inhabited.[8]

Flight to the suburbs

During this period, Britain was expanding its empire. Once the French had been defeated at the Battle of Waterloo in 1815, Britain became the dominant military power globally. With the strength to control safe trade routes and colonies, British merchants traded freely all over the world, growing wealthy and through their consumption habits enabling London's shopkeepers and suppliers to grow wealthy too. The financial institutions of the city, supporting much of this international trade, grew to dominate global financial affairs. Nathan Rothschild commented in 1832 that London had become the bank for the whole world. Armies of clerks were needed to keep these financial cogs turning and a new employment class emerged: the city

4. The aim of trade unionism, according to Henry Broadhurst, Secretary of the TUC, speaking in 1875, was 'to bring about a condition … where wives and daughters would be in their proper sphere at home, instead of being dragged into competition for livelihood against the great and strong men of the world'. TUC Congress Report (1875), p. 14, cited in M. Davis, 'An Historical Introduction to the Campaign for Equal Pay'.

5. D. Bythell, The Sweated Trades: Outwork in Nineteenth-century Britain (1978), p. 214.

6. Ibid., p. 235.

7. See Victoria and Albert Museum article: J. Marsh, 'Gender Ideology and Separate Spheres in the 19th Century'.

8. S. Pennington and B. Westover, A Hidden Workforce: Homeworkers in England, 1850–1985 (1989), p. 98.

FIG. 4.1 *'Model Housing' at Katherine Buildings, Aldgate, London, 1885*

9. A. Power, Hovels to High Rise: State Housing in Europe since 1850 (1993), p. 172.

10. B. Webb, My Apprenticeship, vol. II (1938), p. 310.

11. G. Stedman Jones, Outcast London: A Study in the Relationship between Classes in Victorian Society (1971, reprint 1984), pp. 193–6.

12. The impact of this has been far-reaching and will be discussed in Chapter Five.

office worker. Swathes of countryside around London were developed as quiet, low density, largely residential suburbs, mainly to house these many clerks. As the city came to be seen as the embodiment of everything evil and dangerous, the middle classes relocated to the suburbs, the newly invented tram, omnibus and railway making living at a distance from the workplace possible.

The birth of social housing

Social reformers, appalled by the conditions of the poorest in the overstretched city, were driving forces in the clearance of the London slums. Octavia Hill, a leading progressive, opposed the demolitions, arguing instead for renovation and firm housing management,[9] but was still involved in determining the nature of the dwellings that replaced the slums in the second half of the nineteenth century.[10] Organizations such as the Metropolitan Association for Improving the Dwellings of the Industrious Classes, the Peabody Trust and the East End Dwellings Company were set up to provide what was then considered to be good-quality housing for the poor, with an underlying agenda of reform for the 'immoral and dissolute' lifestyle of the working classes.[11] On the basis of evidence of occupations like fur-pulling being carried out in the home, they equated home-based work with overcrowding and poor sanitation.[12] And so the intricate jumbles of buildings, sheds, courts and yards that had supported myriad different home-based occupations were cleared and replaced by austere blocks of high-density 'Model Housing'. These were expressly designed to discourage home-based work, and managed by tenancy agreements that prohibited it. Sparse but hygienic environments, generally arranged vertically and often with deck access, replaced the complex but squalid layers of public, semi-public and private space where home-based work had flourished [**Fig. 4.1**]. Deliberately ironing out the urban nooks and crannies, ostensibly to improve the morals of the poor, removed the territory in which many of the most deprived made their living. This continues today. The 1961 Parker Morris report *Homes for Today and Tomorrow* established national housing standards that were mandatory until

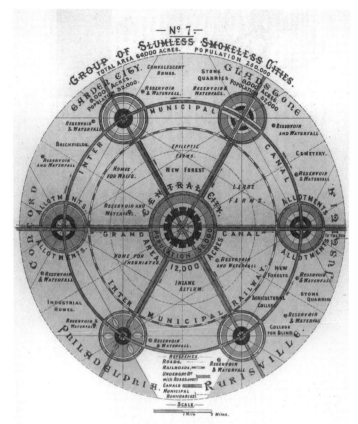

FIG. 4.2 *Ebenezer Howard's Diagram no. 7 'Town-country Garden City', 1902*

13. Hall, op. cit. (1998, reprint 2002).

14. Introduced in Howard's hugely influential (1898) book, To-Morrow: A Peaceful Path to Real Reform, re-worked and re-issued as E. Howard, Garden Cities of Tomorrow: Being the Second Edition of 'To-Morrow: A Peaceful Path to Real Reform' (1902).

Margaret Thatcher's government stopped council housing in the 1980s and housing associations started to build to a lower standard. There is no mention of, or allocation of space for, home-based work anywhere in this report. But it remains the starting point for such discussions: the Mayor of London's new housing standards are discussed in terms of Parker Morris plus 10 per cent.

A solution?

As well as inspiring the development of model housing for the poor, the 'plight of the millions of poor trapped in the Victorian slums' was also a central concern for pioneering urban planners throughout the twentieth century.[13] In 1898, a shorthand typist, untrained in urban design or planning, proposed a solution to the problem of both urban and rural poor that was subsequently adopted and adapted worldwide. Ebenezer Howard's 'Town-country Garden City' offered a third way of living, neither urban nor rural, that aimed to bring together the benefits of town, including employment and social opportunity, and country, including the beauty of nature, clean air and water, while eliminating their individual, substantial disadvantages.[14] In Howard's diagrammatic layout for the Garden City, a compact settlement organized in concentric rings was surrounded by a large green belt combining agricultural land with institutions like convalescent homes that could benefit from rural surroundings [**Fig. 4.2**].

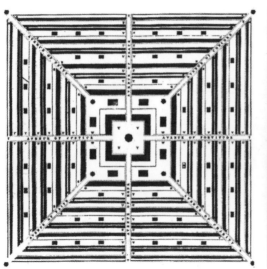

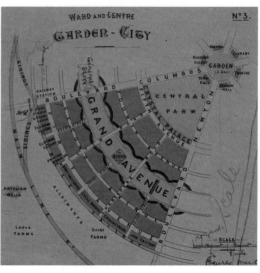

FIG. 4.3 *James Silk Buckingham's plan for a model city, 1849*
FIG. 4.4 *Ebenezer Howard's Diagram no. 3 'Garden City', with original annotations, 1902*

Many aspects of this diagram were drawn from a plan for a model town developed 50 years earlier by Member of Parliament, James Silk Buckingham [**Fig. 4.3**].[15] Both schemes included radial boulevards which were intended to create

an economy of distances in communicating by diagonal lines of streets, and the effect of these diagonal lines by their allowing the free sweep of the winds from different quarters, the most perfect external ventilation, and the most general distribution of benefits of exposure to the rays of the sun.[16]

Buckingham's plan initiated the spatial separation of dwelling and workplace. Dwellings and workplaces were interleaved in concentric streets. Small multi-occupancy houses for the many poor were sandwiched between streets of workshops and heavy industry. Superintendents' houses were placed between 'public edifices' and a 'crystal palace' shopping arcade, while detached mansions for the wealthy few overlooked a grand central square with churches, university, gallery and town hall. Noxious work was relegated to the outskirts:

In these workshops, which would thus be in immediate proximity to the dwellings of the workmen and their families, no kind of labour would be carried on which would be in its nature offensive to the inhabitants ... all such being removed to some distance from the Town: such as steam-worked factories, slaughter-houses, chemical works, forges and furnaces, glass-works, &c.[17]

FIG. 4.5 *Ebenezer Howard's 'Three Magnets' diagram, 1902*

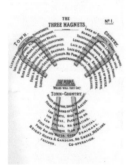

Howard's Garden City plan took a radical step further by creating completely separate zones for dwellings, civic buildings and employment. Employment was placed on the periphery and public buildings in the centre; a purely residential zone was sandwiched between the two [**Fig. 4.4**]. This was effective in reducing pollution in people's homes. But it simultaneously, and not altogether accidentally, wiped out home-based work: Howard's much-published diagram, 'The Three Magnets' lists 'no sweating' as one of the advantages of the 'Town-country' [**Fig. 4.5**].

FIG. 4.6 *Mixed-Use Residential Zone, Berkeley, CA, USA*

15. Howard, op. cit. (2003), p.141.

16. J.S. Buckingham, *National Evils and Practical Remedies, with the Plan of a Model Town ... Accompanied by an Examination of Some Important Moral and Political Problems* (1849), p. 197.

17. Ibid., p. 185.

Universally adopted, but a disaster in the making

Functional zoning was zealously adopted by urban planners, with some unexpected and unwelcome consequences. In the nineteenth century, a great deal of home-based work was, in fact, socially accepted, respectable and beneficial, providing a fine-grained mixed use that encouraged the development of neighbourhood social networks and stimulated the local economy. Shopkeepers lived above their shops, clergy next to their churches, headmasters and teachers in their schools. Doctors' and dentists' homes incorporated surgeries, while those of the upper classes included a gentleman's study. Booth's notebooks reveal an infrastructure of 'live-in' members of the community, including police officers, firefighters, shopkeepers, caretakers, clergy, restaurateurs, funeral directors, company managers and school-teachers, who kept a watchful eye on their immediate neighbourhoods. Inevitably well known and often well respected, these visible and responsible home-based workers made a positive contribution to social cohesion in the neighbourhoods they served and provided an intermediate, invisible but firm layer of security. But both factors were sacrificed to functional zoning, under which cities were organized according to colour-coded plans that separated out residential, industrial, educational and retail uses. This deliberately eroded, indeed tried to eliminate, the intricate fine-grained mixed use of the historic city that planners are now trying to reintroduce, generally unsuccessfully in the UK, where mixed-use zones often result in supermarkets with flats over them. In the USA, experimental mixed-use residential zones are more successful [**Fig. 4.6**]. Both will be discussed later.

Removing the means to earn a living for the poorest

A further side effect was to remove the means for some of the poorest of making a living. Booth's notebooks reveal hundreds of different home-based occupations (see Appendix). Very few, in fact,

posed any health hazard, apart from making existing overcrowding worse. Some involved employees coming into the home, as well as home-based outworkers:

The (clothing) trade may be divided into two sections a) large workshops sometimes deserving the name of factories, in which all parts of the work are done on the premises, b) shops in which all the machine work is done while the finishing is given to women working in their own homes. No special buildings are required but private houses or parts of houses are adapted so far as may be by the requirements of the trade.[18]

Others just involved family members: 'One elderly cabinet maker worked with his son, their workshop being at the rear while the shop in front [was] occupied by his wife who is a milliner.'[19]

From school-keeper to landlord, baker to tailor, umbrella-repairer to bicycle-maker, and hair-cutter to flower-seller, most were simply doing their job or exercising the trade they knew. Working at home or living at their workplace was normal. Legitimate concern about home-based work exacerbating overcrowding or causing minor pollution could have been resolved by the design of the buildings that replaced the slums, had the will to do so existed. But it did not, despite the work of organizations such as the Women's Industrial Council, which supported women's right to be home-based workers and campaigned for effective regulation of the home-based workspace.[20]

Imposing a rigidly gendered division of labour

Discouraging and then prohibiting this working practice imposed a radical change of lifestyle on the many re-housed slum-dwellers who had been used to working at home. The family economy model was replaced by one of dependence on a male chief earner, who 'went out to work', leaving the wife to care for children and home. While a few occupations were fundamentally incompatible with a domestic setting, in general, this working practice had helped families stay above the breadline and allowed those with caring responsibilities, mainly women, to earn.

Howard's ideas and the subsequent Garden City movement had a huge influence on early twentieth-century housing. Massive estates appeared, such as Becontree, where the London County Council (LCC) built 27,000 'homes for heroes' around a small Essex village between 1921 and 1932 to house many of those displaced by slum clearance.[21] This was built as a model 'cottage-estate':

… two-storey cottages, [were] built in groups of four or six, with medium or low pitched roofs and little exterior decoration, set amongst gardens, trees, privet hedges and grass verges and often laid out in cul-de-sacs or around greens.[22]

The houses were generally semi-detached or terraced, at a density of only twelve dwellings per acre, compared with 40 per acre for by-law

18. Booth's notebook, B350, 'Bethnal Green': 'walk on Jan. 3, Briersley, Glawber, Wharncliffe, Hunslett and Stainsbury St', (1898); B351, 'Bethnal Green': 'walk on March 28, Sealbright St, Viaduct St', (1898).

19. Booth's notebook, A6, 'Cabinetmakers', (1886–1903), p. 253.

20. B. Harrison, Not Only the 'Dangerous Trades': Women's Work and Health in Britain, 1880–1914 (1996), p. 97.

21. T. Young and S.B.E. Baldwin, Becontree and Dagenham (1934), pp. 37–65.

22. M. Swenarton, Homes Fit for Heroes: The Politics and Architecture of Early State Housing in Britain (1981), p. 1.

FIG. 4.7 Becontree, later known as Dagenham, 1970

23. The UK Public Health Act of 1875 required local authorities to implement building regulations, or by-laws, which insisted that each house should be self-contained, with its own sanitation and water. This change in the design of housing complemented the public investment in sewers and water supply.

24. S.M. Gaskell, Slums (1990), p. 198.

25. A. Rubenstein, Just Like the Country (1991).

26. R.K. Home, A Township Complete in Itself: A Planning History of the Becontree/Dagenham Estate (1997), p. 30.

27. Conditions of tenancy for the Beconsfield Estate, 1933. See Young and Baldwin, op. cit, p. 373.

housing[23] or 80 per acre in the slums being demolished [**Fig. 4.7**].[24] Spatially and in terms of amenity, they were far superior to those of the East End courts. Families used to the poor conditions of the East End were relocated on the clean and spacious Becontree estate, one family per fully serviced dwelling, with gas, electricity, hot and cold running water, an inside flushing WC and a fitted bath. Vera Andrews, resident of Downham, an LCC estate contemporary to Becontree, says:

My parents were happy to move out here because they'd got a home at last, their first actual home. They'd been married God knows how many years and they'd got five children at that time. They'd lived in rooms, sharing cookers and water, so it was absolutely fantastic that here at last was this beautiful house.[25]

Although the physical conditions in the new 'council' housing were fabulous, the social impact of the move was seismic. The LCC's cottage estate building programme was 'about much more than just the building of houses. It sought to create new habits among its tenants, shaping the behaviour of an emerging nation of suburban house-dwellers.'[26] This was achieved in part through strictly applied draconian conditions of tenancy that included the prohibition of home-based work, continuing the Victorian tendency for social control through housing management:

The tenant shall not use the premises or any part thereof as a shop or workshop, or for the carrying on or the storage of any implements of any trade or business … or exposing in the premises or any part thereof any goods or materials for sale or hire or for keeping lodgers.[27]

This regulation was aimed, in part, at making a more salubrious home environment, in response to concern that working at home was unhealthy and dangerous. But it imposed a rigid separation between dwelling and workplace and, as a consequence, male breadwinner and female housewife. East End families were used to operating in a family economy to which all members of the household contributed.

Work and life were often carried on in a largely undifferentiated way in or at least close to the home. On moving to the new Becontree/Dagenham Estate, this way of life became impossible. The resultant gendered division of labour transformed many lives and something of great value was lost. Having been part of complex multi-functional spatial and social networks in the densely populated East End of London, on moving to Dagenham, people found themselves isolated in their palatial new homes and living routine lives. While the men went out to their often repetitive and boring work in the Ford factory, the women became housewives, spending time with their children and tending their homes, the notion 'house-proud' gaining currency as women strove to find meaning in their newly restricted lives.[28]

Loss of social capital

As well as imposing gendered roles that largely removed women from the workforce, the shift to functional zoning also had a detrimental impact on the life of the city. Home-based work was one of the ingredients that had created busy, lively, sociable neighbourhoods. Although by no means a socialist, Booth expressed sympathy for the working-class way of life: 'I see nothing improbable in the view that the simple natural lives of working-class people tend to their own and their children's happiness more than the artificial complicated existence of the rich.'[29]

His notebooks record that, despite poverty and deprivation, women in the poorest areas chatted at open doorways and their children appeared happy despite dirty faces or ragged clothes. In among descriptions of severe overcrowding and insanitary conditions, Booth's researchers comment on the liveliness of working-class areas where home-based work flourished and on the dull sterility of the quiet suburban districts where husbands were away working in the city, while women were inside behind closed doors:

Duncrieve Rd brings us to the beginnings of the St German's estate,

28. See H, Marchant, 'Feature Family: The Braggs', Ford Family, 1 (April 1952), p. 6; H. Braverman, Labour and Monopoly Capital: The Degradation of Work in the Twentieth Century (1974, reprint 1998).

29. C. Booth, Life and Labour of the People in London (1902), p. 160.

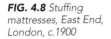

FIG. 4.8 *Stuffing mattresses, East End, London, c.1900*

which is rapidly being laid out according to the general plans of a large speculative builder, Corbett ... It is said that when all has been built over there will be something like 3,000 houses ... It is a rather weary wilderness and in the daytime hardly anyone is about. The heads of the households go mainly Citiwards for work.[30]

Booth found the tidy, well-scrubbed middle-class areas lifeless and impoverished, despite their affluence:

All the roads round here are fat and well liking. Life in them must be very dull and respectable ... a dull respectable street with generally a grown-up daughter sitting with needlework on her lap in the front bay window, just behind or to one side of the usual evergreen plant in an ornamental china pot; some piano strumming.

30. Booth and Steele op. cit. p. 228.

31. W. Seccome, 'Patriarchy Stabilized: The Construction of the Male Breadwinner Norm in Nineteenth-Century Britain', (1986).

32. Booth's notebook, A19, op. cit. p. 188.

In the twenty-first century we can reject out of hand the ideas that women's role in society should be restricted to motherhood and domesticity and that working women impact negatively on the male working wage. Widespread legislation supports women's right to both employment and equal pay. But the dominant ideology in Victorian Britain was that a woman's place was in the home[31] and many mothers, as a result, turned to home-based work so they could simultaneously earn a living, tend the home and care for their dependants. Booth describes the structure of the predominately home-based juvenile branch of the clothing industry:

The finishing ... will be given to homeworkers, usually married women who, unable to come to the factory, are glad to earn the poor pittance paid for this work ... One man said that he had over 80 women call one day when he put up a notice for workers and all of those wanted homework. He was compelled to alter his notice.[32]

Employment and entrepreneurship were carried out in the indeterminate courts and yards of Victorian London [**Fig. 4.8**]. But the tightly designed and regulated Model Dwellings [**Fig. 4.9**], and the 'bright homes and gardens, no smoke, no slums' of garden cities

FIG. 4.9 *Plan, 'Model Housing' at Katherine Buildings, Aldgate, London, 1885*

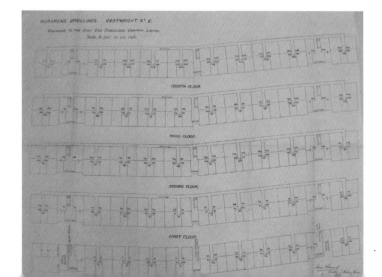

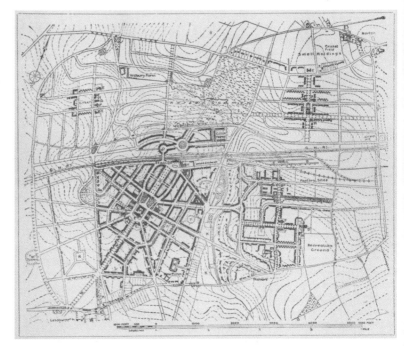

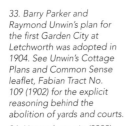

FIG. 4.10 *Parker and Unwin's original plan of Letchworth Garden City, 1904*

33. *Barry Parker and Raymond Unwin's plan for the first Garden City at Letchworth was adopted in 1904. See Unwin's Cottage Plans and Common Sense leaflet, Fabian Tract No. 109 (1902) for the explicit reasoning behind the abolition of yards and courts.*

34. *Howard, op. cit. (2003), p. 10.*

35. *Hall, op. cit. (1998, reprint 2002), p. 88.*

36. *Holliss, op. cit. (2007).*

like Letchworth [**Fig. 4.10**] that replaced the slums and re-housed their populations removed this possibility.[33] While hugely improving environmental conditions and reducing overcrowding, the urban forms and governance structures that followed slum clearances had serious but hidden repercussions that continue to reverberate in the twenty-first century.

Howard's vision that 'town and country *must be married*, and out of the joyous union will spring a new hope, a new life, a new civilization' was immensely influential in twentieth-century urban planning and design.[34] He imagined garden cities as 'vehicles for a progressive reconstruction of capitalist society into an infinity of cooperative commonwealths'.[35] Sadly this was not to be. Instead, one of his primary legacies has been the widespread adoption of functional zoning.

The spatial separation of dwelling and workplace emerges as a basic and apparently little questioned premise for urban planning and design. Although housing conditions were improved for the poorest of the population, home-based work, a valuable social, economic, architectural and urban practice, was driven underground.

Men and women today often work at home so that they can combine domestic and breadwinning roles. Cities designed to reflect and accommodate this would take a radically different form.[36] While a response to the plight of nineteenth-century slum-dwellers was urgently needed, the primary problems of the slum were overcrowding, poor sanitation and poverty, not home-based work. But, because on the one hand it contravened the conservative ideology of the time regarding women's role in society and, on the other, as an unregulated working practice, it provided a breeding ground for the exploitation of the weakest and most vulnerable, home-based work was banned. And cities have been designed to separate home from workplace ever since.

Back to the past

The first rift in this orthodoxy appears in the work of radical urban analyst Jane Jacobs, another important player with no formal training in the field. As urbanist Alan Ehrenhalt wrote in 2001:

When an entire field is headed in the wrong direction, when the routine application of mainstream thinking has produced disastrous results – as I think was true of planning and urban policy in the 1950s – then it probably took someone from outside to point out the obvious. That is what Jane Jacobs did 40 years ago.[37]

37. A. Ehrenhalt, 'Inspired Amateurs', (June 2001), p. 24. Jane Jacobs was not trained as a planner or urban designer; her work was based on observations of the neighbourhood where she lived in New York.

38. J. Jacobs, The Death and Life of Great American Cities (1961, reprint 1993) p. 285.

39. Ibid., pp. 352–3.

40. Ibid., p. 197.

41. Ibid., pp. 196–7.

In her seminal book, *The Death and Life of Great American Cities*, Jacobs fiercely opposed planners' attempts to beautify the city: she condemned the ideas of Ebenezer Howard among others, and accused him of looking at the slums of London and deciding that, to save the people, city life must be abandoned.[38] She argued that modernist urban planning rejects the city because it rejects human beings living in communities characterized by layered complexity and seeming chaos. And, crucially for this narrative, she considered that zoning (i.e. into residential, industrial and commercial areas) destroys communities and innovative economies.[39] She rejected the vast, functionally zoned urban renewal programmes advocated by mainstream US urban planners and economic developers in the 1950s and 1960s and in their place proposed a place-based, community-centred approach to urban planning and design.

Jacobs identified four generators of 'exuberant diversity in a city's streets' that she considered indispensable, saying: 'in combination, these conditions create effective economic pools of use … All four in combination are necessary to generate city diversity; the absence of any one of the four frustrates a district's potential.'[40]

First, she said that the district, and indeed as many of its internal parts as possible, must serve more than one primary function; preferably more than two. These ensure the presence of people who go outdoors on different schedules and are in the place for different purposes, but who are able to use many facilities in common. Second, she said that most blocks must be short; that is streets and opportunities to turn corners must be frequent. Third, she stipulated that the district must mingle buildings that vary in age and condition, including a good proportion of old ones so that they vary in the economic yield they produce, and that the mingling must be fairly close-grained. Fourth, she insisted on a dense concentration of people, for whatever purposes they might be there. This should include a dense concentration of people who live there.[41]

Home-based work, involving people living at their workplace or working in their home, creates a fine-grained mixed use that meets Jacobs' first condition: 'Intricate minglings of different uses in cities are not a form of chaos. On the contrary, they represent a complex and highly developed form of order.'[42]

Her second condition, short blocks, increases the permeability of the city, offers more choices to the pedestrian and creates more corners and connections between streets. Home-based micro-businesses, when visible from the street, provide reasons for people to take different routes through the city; corner sites have long been key positions for home-based shopkeepers, publicans and restaurateurs.[43]

Long blocks, in their nature, thwart the potential advantages that cities offer to incubation, experimentation, and many small or special enterprises, insofar as these depend on drawing their customers or clients from among much larger cross-sections of passing public.[44]

Jacobs' third condition, that buildings in any neighbourhood should be of varied age and condition, also encourages home-based businesses, which are often economically marginal and unable to support the cost of a new building:

Hundreds of ordinary enterprises, necessary for the safety and public life of streets and neighbourhoods, and appreciated for their convenience and personal quality, can make out in old buildings, but are inexorably slain by the high overhead of new construction.[45]

And finally, echoing Booth in her identification of 'The Great Blight of Dullness',[46] she sets out the importance of high density, which is not to be confused with overcrowding. She distinguishes the positive impact of high residential densities, which she sets at more than 125 dwellings per acre (50 dwellings per hectare), from the negative effect of overcrowding, measured by the number of people per room.[47] Jacobs observed that: 'For centuries, probably everyone who has thought about cities at all has noticed that there seems to be some connection between the concentration of people and the specialities they can support.'[48]

High density, combined with mixed uses, short blocks and variety in the age and condition of buildings, creates fertile conditions for successful home-based work. And, when overt, this working practice in return contributes to vital, safe, diverse city neighbourhoods. These ideas were radical in the 1960s, as journalist Adele Freedman notes:

Jane Jacobs' observations about the way cities work and don't work revolutionized the urban planning profession. Thanks to Jacobs, ideas once considered lunatic, such as mixed-use development, short blocks, and dense concentrations of people working and living downtown, are now taken for granted.[49]

42. Ibid., p. 235.

43. Davis, op. cit. (2012), p. 110.

44. J. Jacobs, Ibid., p. 238.

45. Ibid., p. 245.

46. Ibid., p. 235.

47. US census definition of overcrowding in 1961 was 1.5 persons per room or more. Ibid., p. 268.

48. Ibid., p. 261.

49. A. Freedman, 'Jane
Jacobs', Globe and Mail,
June 9, 1984.

50. Holliss, op. cit. (2007).

FIG. 4.11 *Bryant and
May factory, Bow,
London, 1921*

The current rapid growth of the home-based workforce is generating
a profound shift in the way we inhabit our towns and cities.[50] These
are no longer legible in the way they were in the 1920s and 1930s.
Then one could predict with a fair degree of certainty which buildings
were dwellings and which workplaces [**Fig. 4.11, 4.12**]. But, as we
have seen, in the early twenty-first century, a high proportion of
dwellings and workplaces is used as workhomes.

Despite a substantial shift in UK planning policy towards encouraging
mixed-use, discussed further in the next chapter, the 'intricate
minglings' created by home-based work generally remain hidden,
their contributions to the city are subtle and unacknowledged. Cities
designed around home-based work could be made up of buildings
that openly accommodate people living at their workplaces or
working in their homes, side by side with single-use and purpose-
designed mixed-use buildings. Those who plan and design our cities
have yet to recognize the huge potential value of such 'intricate
minglings'.

FIG. 4.12 *Kensal Rise,
London, 1921*

Precedents

While the Industrial Revolution tended to separate dwelling and workplace, the digital revolution and the shift to having more women in employment than ever before, among other factors, seem to be bringing them back together again. This has major implications for the city, which would take a different form if it were organized and designed around home-based work rather than, as is still implicitly the case, around a male wage earner and female housewife.[51]

While not specifically focused on home-based work, recent research into the relationship between urban forms and grassroots economic activity provides insights into one aspect of this. An analysis of the 'micro-urban' through a survey of 2,000 buildings in East London looked at relationships between buildings, the use of buildings, and the mobility of people in the local economy. It found small new businesses being established in a wide variety of building types, sometimes involving the physical subdivision of both large and small buildings. It also found that there were synergies between adjacent and nearby businesses of different sizes and types, and that a strong hierarchy of streets, alleyways and quasi-public spaces supported a variety of locations and rents. Davis writes: 'Making this ordinary daily life visible, and beginning to understand its spatial structure, is a first step toward its legitimization and toward the understanding of how designers, policy-makers and entrepreneurs might support the inclusive city.'[52]

A few almost-forgotten precedents demonstrate how the city has been organized around home-based work in the past. These and many others can help us imagine cities that, by responding to the needs of the home-based worker, are more resilient and sustainable.

51. Holliss, op.cit. (2007).

52. H. Davis, 'Making the Marginal Visible: Micro-Enterprise and Urban Space in London', (2013).

53. For a discussion of the value of such historic photographs as evidence in contemporary research, see Holliss, op. cit. (2012).

FIG. 4.13 Child sack-making in a court, London, 1899
FIG. 4.14 Matchbox-making, 1900

FIG. 4.15 *Making firewood, c.1900*
FIG. 4.16 *Backyard blacksmith, c.1900*

We have seen how the intricate densely packed English medieval city swarmed with home-based work. By penetrating deep into the urban block, courts and yards provided access, natural light and ventilation to a large number of small and therefore cheap buildings. These workaday spaces, in which sheds and shelters were constructed as necessary, allowed a wide range of different sorts of home-based work to flourish. Eleven workhomes, multi-storey work-dominated buildings, fronted onto Treswell's Phelant Courte, a space just eighteen feet across and 82 feet long [**see Fig. 1.2**]. Where these intricate, intimate yards and courts have survived, for example, in the George Inn Yard in Southwark, London, they are highly valued. This urban form has contemporary relevance for home-based workers who want small, cheap, probably work-dominated workhomes, built as a cluster to avoid social isolation and to encourage collaboration.

The courts and yards of the Victorian East End of London similarly provided low-cost flexible space where a variety of different home-based occupations were carried out. **Figure 4.13**, taken in 1899, shows a child sack-making in a court; a woman walking past takes notice of the child's activity while three more children play outside the next door house in front of a seated woman. **Figure 4.14**, taken in 1900, shows a woman and a child making matchboxes at a table outside their home in a yard or court. And **Figures 4.15 and 4.16**, also taken at the turn of the century, show men, surrounded by family members, at work in yards next to their homes. One shows piles of reclaimed timber protected from the weather by a ramshackle shelter, waiting to be processed into firewood on a sawhorse. In the other, a backyard blacksmith is making a shovel; there is a shed built against the tall rear wall.[53] Work is carried out surrounded by neighbours and family as an ordinary daily activity. The contrast with the contemporary housing estate could not be greater.

Workhomes in the form of coach-houses and stables were built behind large seventeenth- and eighteenth-century London houses. These mews developments were separated from the dwelling by a courtyard or garden, but also accessed separately from a subsidiary road or court. Coachmen and their families, grooms and stable boys lived above the household's horses and carriages [**Fig. 4.17**]. Ernest Shepard, the illustrator of *Winnie the Pooh*, recalled childhood visits to a nearby mews:

It was a most interesting place, with plenty going on – horses being groomed and harnessed, carriages being washed or polished, the grooms hissing and whistling at their work. Strings of washing hung from the upper windows, whence the womenfolk leaned out and chatted to the men below.[54]

The mews provided modest live-with accommodation for the coachmen, grooms, carriages and horses, in a live-nearby relationship to their employers' large townhouses. This urban form offers two potentially interwoven contemporary possibilities. The first is live-nearby workspaces at the bottom of the gardens of well-established home-based workers, with distinct entrances from the mews for employees and customers. The second is a cluster of small live-with or live-adjacent workhomes accessed from the mews.

The Japanese *machiya* also burrows deep into the urban block. But in contrast to the system of London courts, which enables public access right into the middle of the block, the *machiya* has a public crust to a private inner world. Its public spaces front onto the street, and when the façade is open become an extension of the street. And, vice versa, the street becomes an extension of the internal space, where people can meet and interact. Small courtyard gardens bring light and air into spaces that become progressively more private the further they are from the street, shifting from public to semi-public to private. Although generally only two-storeyed, *machiyas* create high densities by combining narrow frontages and deep plans. Combined with the 24-hour inhabitation that comes with home-based work, this ensures lively neighbourhoods.

Machiyas can be organized to create a variety of different urban forms. In historic Edo,[55] they often squeezed together around the perimeter walls of the 'spread out houses' of the ruling classes

54. Cited in B. Rosen and W. Zuckermann, *The Mews of London: A Guide to the Hidden Byways of London's Past*, (1982), p. 24.

55. The original name for Tokyo.

56. Jinnai, op. cit. p.30

FIG. 4.17 Upper Montague Mews, London, c.1900
FIG. 4.19 Workhome Pattern-Book machiya with workwing, plans

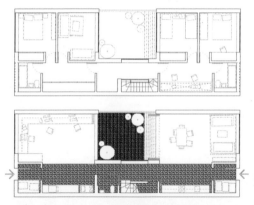

FIG. 4.18 *Machiya court, 2008*

who patronized their businesses.[56] In other parts of the city they surrounded areas of tightly packed artisans' *nagayas*, as described in Chapter One, where goods sold in the merchants' *machiyas* were made. And sometimes they were built in small self-contained developments to meet the needs of a particular manufacturer. [**Fig. 4.18**] shows one such group of *machiyas* in Kyoto, built by a master silk-weaver who inhabited the end workhome, with smaller *machiyas* on either side of the court for the silk-weavers he employed. A cluster of home-based artists, working in a range of different disciplines, including pottery and painting, inhabit these *machiyas* today. The open/closed nature of their façades, the intimacy of the development, with building frontages only 2 metres apart, and their 24-hour inhabitation, contribute to a close sense of community.

This urban form has substantial contemporary potential. Traditionally organized around multi-generational families, it can easily be adapted to meet the needs of different household structures. **Figures 4.19, and 4.20**, which show front and rear 'houses' opening onto a primary street and a secondary yard, court or roadway, give an idea of one flexible contemporary application. With entrances onto parallel streets, the building can adapt to the expansion and contraction

FIG. 4.20 *Workhome Pattern-Book double machiya with workwing, plans*

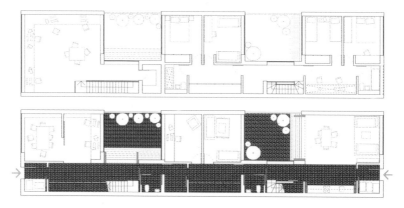

FIG. 4.21 *Suburbia*

57. *Davis, op. cit. (2013).*

58. *For the New Urbanism movement, see E. Badger, 'Mixed-Use Neighborhoods May Be Safer, Too', (2013).*

59. *Available at: www.pullensyards.co.uk/category/open-studios/*

of family and/or home-based work over time. Home or work can expand to dominate the building; the front and rear elements of the building can combine to make a large building or can separate to make two smaller ones. Elevations can be layered to be read as home or workplace or neither. With minimal alteration, this traditional workhome form can therefore be manipulated to provide any of the types discussed in Chapter Three: live-with, live-adjacent or live-nearby workhomes that can be home-dominated, work-dominated or equal-status. It offers real flexibility to its inhabitants and a shifting domestic- and work-generated vitality to the city.

Short blocks constructed in the London districts of Spitalfields and Bethnal Green, designed and built around the needs of the silk-weaving industry, generated a close-grained mixed use. These contained workhomes of different sizes and quality in which the well-off silk-masters and merchants, the journeymen, and the poorest pieceworking weavers lived and worked. Jane Jacobs would have approved.

Historically, streets of smaller work-dominated workhomes and larger home-dominated ones were interwoven and interleaved. Today there is evidence that this hierarchy of streets and semi-public spaces promotes urban resilience and sustainability.[57] The juxtaposition of residential and commercial (often light-industrial) functions with home-based work providing 24-hour inhabitation has enlivened neighbourhoods for generations. It goes against many current planning policies, however, that, still clinging to Victorian ideas of home as a feminine refuge from the dirty, noisy, male world of work, insist on residential neighbourhoods being as quiet as can possibly be arranged. These have spawned many soul-destroying built landscapes [**Fig. 4.21**]. Mixed neighbourhoods provide busier, livelier and safer environments, generally preferable to the residential deserts that have been created by generations of zoned planning policies.[58]

The south London Pullens Estate, built between 1887 and 1901, provides an unusual precedent. From the street it looks like any other tenement housing development of the period. Its original

FIG. 4.22 Pullens estate, Elephant and Castle, London, 1901
FIG. 4.23 Iliffe Yard, Pullens estate, Elephant and Castle, London, 1901

684 one-bedroom flats were built in twelve austere four-storey blocks across six streets, accessed off common stairwells [**Fig. 4.22**]. Each of the ground- and first-floor flats, however, extended into a contiguous workspace that backed onto one of four yards [**Fig. 4.23**]. This apparently unique arrangement developed the mews model around the needs of the manufacturing poor: blue-collar workhomes. Combining workers' housing with industrial units, it allowed artisans, small traders and their families to live and work on the premises [**Fig. 4.24**]. The trades carried out in these workspaces included a stationer, industrial clog-making for the Fire Service, manufacture of ships' fans, manufacture of X-ray machinery, hat-making, brush-making, bookbinding and printing as well as furniture-making and restoration. Ground-floor shops on either side of the entrance to each yard face outwards onto the street, creating the short blocks recommended by Jane Jacobs [**Fig. 4.25**].

FIG. 4.24 Unit, Iliffe Yard, Pullens estate, Elephant and Castle, London, 1901
FIG. 4.25 Entrance, Iliffe Yard, Pullens estate, Elephant and Castle, London, 1901

In 2010, just 360 flats and three yards of workshop/studios remain, their light industrial nature protected. The trades have evolved to include design, fine art, craft, publishing, film-making, furniture-making and restoration, musical instrument-making, photography, printing, shoe-making and yoga. Pullens has a strong collective culture: the three yards open to the public twice a year to show

the occupants' work and promote their enterprises.[59] And one of the shops functions as a community centre: fundamentally a café, it also provides a meeting place and a space where Pullens artists can display their work. The owner says:

Being part of this community means the world to me and my business. It's an honour to be told on a daily basis that we are the hub of the community. I love introducing people to each other who will get on and many friendships and useful partnerships have been forged here.[60]

Wider residential streets alternate with narrower light industrial/commercial yards and, though only a few are still live-adjacent workhomes, the close association of homes and studio-workshops means that this dense development is inhabited throughout the 24 hours of each day. Each yard has a population small enough for its inhabitants to know each other, at least by sight. And architecturally the estate is distinct, giving its inhabitants a sense of identity. Unlike many other London housing estates, residential deserts notorious for their unemployment and deprivation, the combination of dwelling and workplace in the Pullens Estate contributes to an extraordinarily positive sense of neighbourhood identity and to an ongoing development and enjoyment of local social capital. This key condition for successful community development is currently generally ignored.

Coventry's cottage factories provide a further urban precedent with contemporary relevance. They provide an intriguing model for community/neighbourhood development focused around home-based work. These terraces of live-with workhomes were often arranged in triangular blocks around allotments, a collective power source and a clock [**Fig. 4.26**]. Each unit consisted of a floor of dedicated workspace above a small two-up, two-down dwelling. A continuous driveshaft passed through each workspace, powering all the looms. Public, semi-public and private space was layered. At Cash's, front doors opened, without intermediary front gardens, directly onto a pathway. This was used by all members of the

60. R. Batchelor, 'The Pullens Story', p. 34. Available at: http://iliffeyard.co.uk/gallery-view/guest-gallery---the-pullen-s-story (accessed 7 Oct. 2013).

61. R.I.M. Dunbar, 'Neocortex Size as a Constraint on Group Size in Primates', (1992), pp. 469–93.

FIG. 4.26 *Triangular block of Eli Green's cottage factory, Coventry, 1858*

FIG. 4.27 *Cash's One Hundred cottage factory, Kingfield, Coventry, 1857. From across the canal*
FIG. 4.28 *Entrance to block, Cash's One Hundred cottage factory, Kingfield, Coventry, 1857*
FIG. 4.29 *Rear, Cash's One Hundred cottage factory, Kingfield, Coventry, 1857*

community but overlooked by ordinary passers-by only from the other side of the canal [**Fig. 4.27**]. While each workhome had its own front door, the block itself had few entrances, discouraging public access [**Fig. 4.28**]. A small area of semi-private open space outside each workhome's back door mediated between private interior and public space at the centre of the block [**Fig. 4.29**].

The numbers of workhomes, and therefore inhabitants, in each cottage factory development were limited. The often triangular blocks were generally approximately half the size of their conventionally rectangular counterparts. The widely accepted 'Dunbar's number', proposed by British anthropologist Robin Dunbar in 1992, sets the limit to the number of individuals with whom a stable inter-personal relationship can be maintained at between 100 and 230.[61] It seems that Coventry's cottage factories kept within this theoretical limit. At Cash's, 100 units were planned but only 48 were built; Eli Green's comprised 67 top-shops.

As well as reducing the numbers of people on the block, the triangular form also gave a sense of enclosure and intimacy. In the twenty-first century, going out to work is seen to offer important opportunities for social interaction and social isolation is one of the top disadvantages cited by contemporary home-based workers. But this is not inevitable. The urban form of these cottage factories encourages constant interaction between members of the community generated within each block.

It is symbolic and ironic that the central allotments at Cash's cottage factory, converted to social housing in the 1980s, are now in use as a car park that reduces the potential for such interaction. If contemporary home-based workers could be encouraged and enabled to rely on car clubs or similar, or just not to have a car, such parts of the street or public realm could be released from parked cars. The intrinsic form of the development appears, however, still to encourage social interaction. At both the front and the back of the terraces, neighbours were found standing outside chatting. Eli Green's cottage factory also had a corner shop that served the immediate community [**see Fig. 1.13**], probably selling basic foodstuffs and maybe silk-weaving supplies as well. The shopkeeper lived above and would have been known to everyone in the development, providing a further mechanism for neighbourly interactions.

Where cottage factories were developed over an entire urban block, this was enclosed but not gated. Openings midway and at the end of perimeter terraces allowed, and even encouraged, movement through the block, creating short-cuts across the site that were overlooked from all sides. This permeability was characteristic of smaller top-shop developments too. Terraces were often broken by an alleyway leading to a back passage that linked the rear yards of half a dozen or more workhomes [**Fig. 4.30**]. This form was particularly effective where manufacture was a collective enterprise such as watchmaking, where each small workshop made a single element that was worked on by successive neighbouring craftsmen. Breaking the street down into groups of workhomes with linked external space is an effective strategy in creating more intimately connected neighbourhoods.

62. J. Gehl, *Cities for People* (2010).

These precedents, and there are many others, have renewed relevance today as urban forms designed specifically to accommodate and support home-based work. Maybe unsurprisingly, each of them meets the four conditions Jane Jacobs identified as essential to creating exuberant diversity in a city's streets and dispelling the Great Blight of Dullness.

Historic precedents are plentiful because designing for home-based work was the norm before the Industrial Revolution. There are also many modern precedents involving multiple workhome units. But these, designed to fit into contemporary planning frameworks, tend to be designed as large rectangular blocks rather than as complex hierarchies of public, semi-public and private space.

Jan Gehl identifies the importance to the neighbourhood of active building façades:

The words 'soft edge' mean a facade where a lot of things happen. It

FIG. 4.30 Rear of watchmaker's topshop, 18 Norfolk St, Coventry

FIG. 4.31, 4.32
Residential and studios sides, Zomerdijkstraat Atelierwoningen, Amsterdam. Zanstra, Giesen and Sijmons, 1934

could be many doors, niches, or the vegetable seller putting out his tomatoes on the street. Soft edges could be the front yard where the kids are playing and grandma is sitting knitting just behind the hedge. We have found that the ground floor is where the communication between building inside and outside occurs. That's what you see. So if the ground floor is rich, the city is rich and it doesn't matter what you do further up.[62]

Courts and yards maximize the surface area of the urban block, creating a rich interface between the interior and exterior spaces of the city. But this is minimized in large rectangular blocks like the Dutch studio-apartment scheme, Zomerdijkstraat Atelierwoningen. And as a result the connection to the street is weakened [**Fig. 4.31, 4.32**]. Although south-facing living spaces and north-facing studios overlook parallel streets, only the eight ground-floor units have doors opening onto the street. All 32 units are entered through two doors on the residential side, like a block of flats [**Fig. 4.33**]. This simple shift privatizes most of what goes on in the building and deadens its interface with the street and consequently with the neighbourhood. In the early days of the building's life, the artists who lived and worked there organized an annual exhibition on the street to counteract this, so members of the public could access their work [**Fig. 4.34**].

FIG. 4.33 *Entrance to block, Zomerdijkstraat Atelierwoningen, Amsterdam. Zanstra, Giesen and Sijmons, 1934*

FIG. 4.34 *Early exhibition, Zomerdijkstraat Atelierwoningen, Amsterdam*

FIG. 4.35 Klarheit, Tokyo, Japan. Koh Kitayama + architecture WORKSHOP, 2008

63. J. Moran, 'Defining Moment: Streets in the Air Arrive on Britain's Housing Estates, 1961', (2010).

64. They are taught in urban design courses worldwide. Professor Sir Peter Hall (Bartlett Professor of Urban Regeneration and Planning) describes Death and Life of the Great American Cities as 'a book on cities that is surely the most influential in the entire history of 20th century town planning', Planning, 3 June 2011.

Koh Kitayama's Klarheit has a similar footprint. A single major retail space at ground-floor level 'kills' the façade, in Gehl's terms [**Fig. 4.35**]. Kitayama tries to mitigate the loss of public interface by including a rooftop bar, reached by a public stair and lift on the side of the building. He also lays the six third- and fourth-level workhome units out on either side of an internal 'street', each with a plate glass 'shop' window, making visible the people at work in each unit [**see Fig. 2.51**]. But, as with Alison and Peter Smithson's 1952 idea of streets in the air, it is a poor substitute for a real street, lacking both the numbers and the diversity of people passing and restricting the occupants' immediate interactions to only five other units.[63]

Such developments fail to meet three of Jane Jacobs' four criteria: short blocks, a mix of ages of building, and high density. While Klarheit attempts to offer an intricate mingling of uses, at the last count, four of the six intended workhomes were inhabited solely as workplaces. We can only speculate why people are choosing not to live there.

Howard's ideas still have currency in contemporary urban planning. And cities across the globe continue, albeit as a by-product of other concerns, to be planned, designed and governed to prevent or restrict home-based work. In the twenty-first century, however, there is growing support for Jacobs' principles.[64] This, logically, should lead to the home-separate-from-workplace orthodoxy being abandoned, and to us starting to plan the city around this popular, family-friendly, environmentally sustainable working practice, which is both good for the city and good for the economy.

Governance

Governance

1. 'Silos of governance' is a phrase used to describe a contemporary difficulty: government departments (at all levels) are confined to narrow areas, such as 'housing', 'work and pensions', 'business and industry', etc. Problematic regulations are a symptom of this bigger problem: government is structured in such a way that 'cross-silo' ideas (like home-based work) rarely emerge and, if they do, are extremely difficult to implement.

2. UK local authorities have a similarly polarized approach. The London Borough of Hackney has the following quite separate departments: Advice & Benefits; Business; Community & Living; Council & Democracy; Education & Learning; Environment & Planning; Health & Social Care; Housing; Jobs & Careers; Leisure & Culture; Transport & Streets.

3. Of the 76 UK participants, home-based workers across a wide range of occupations and building types, and from diverse socio-economic backgrounds in urban, suburban and rural settings, two-thirds were working covertly or illicitly in some way.

Some major obstacles remain in place, however, before cities can be imagined and planned in this way. In the twentieth century, governance structures were developed across the world (with Japan as a notable exception) that insistently kept dwelling apart from workplace. Housing and employment are regulated by separate 'silos',[1] i.e. governmental departments that do not work effectively together. The UK departments of Work and Pensions, and Trade and Industry, with housing buried in Communities and Local Government, continue to be organized around mutually exclusive areas of concern.[2] Their equivalents in the USA are Commerce, Labor, and Housing and Urban Development. These bodies generate rigid webs of rules that determine what sort of buildings can be built where, and how they can be inhabited. Barely acknowledging the existence of home-based workers or the buildings they inhabit, these regulatory frameworks are at best unsupportive and at worst punitive to this sector, despite its growth and modernity.

An unexpected finding in the research that underpins this book is that two-thirds of the people interviewed operate covertly – 'under the radar' – in some way.[3] Almost without exception this is because, although otherwise law-abiding (and tax-paying) members of their communities, they either fear they are, or actually *are*, breaking some regulation or other. Considering the rules that govern home-based work to be out of date and unnecessarily restrictive, they just ignore them.

Many are anxious talking about this. A social policy researcher, whose home-based work is legitimate in every aspect, says: 'I don't want to get caught out. I don't even want to ask as I don't want to fall foul of the regulations.' The areas that are most feared and contravened in the UK include planning, property taxation and tenancy agreements. While detailed discussions of policy issues can be difficult to digest, especially when they apply to another country, it is worth taking a look at the muddle that the UK is in, because aspects of it are echoed in many other countries. And, when the rules obstruct home-based work, it goes underground, triggering a raft of negative consequences that will be explored in Chapter Six.

Planning is the first area. UK development control is organized around a mono-functional building classification system, the Use Class Order, which does not easily accommodate dual-use buildings.[4] This contributes to the fact that most of the home-based workers interviewed, despite being ordinary, respectable, working people, either live secretly in their workplaces ('we hid the bath when the planners came') or work covertly in their dwellings for fear of being 'caught'. Many had applied for residential planning permission for an additional bedroom, for example, when they really wanted a workplace addition to their dwelling: 'It's a residential area; we didn't think we would be able to get commercial use.'

In fact, UK planning law accommodates dual-use buildings without difficulty:

'The lawful uses of a building can be mixed uses where there are two or more primary uses, or where there is a primary use and an ancillary use.[5]

When applied to the workhome, this produces three sorts of buildings: (1) dwellings with ancillary work use; (2) workplaces with ancillary residential use; and (3) buildings that combine dwelling and workplace as primary uses. This dovetails neatly with the dominant function typology of home-dominated, work-dominated and equal-status workhomes discussed in Chapter Three. So, on the surface, there would appear to be no problem from a planning perspective with people working in their homes, living at their workplaces or choosing to inhabit buildings where work and home are equally balanced.

But policy and law are separate issues. And national and local planning policy overrides the law in relationship to individual buildings. While many local policies attempt to accommodate home-based work in the guise of live/work, which will be discussed later, the overall system continues to separate dwelling from workplace through Local Policy Plans based on land use. UK cities are therefore still largely organized into zones by function and, as a result, people who work in their homes or live at their workplace often find themselves outside the law or operating covertly because they think they are.[6]

For example, a suburban hairdresser started working at home, using her bathroom and spare bedroom, when she became a single parent. But she disliked that 'hair got everywhere' and that the smell of chemicals permeated her semi-detached house. So she set up a fully-equipped 'hair room' in a back extension, separated by a door from the rest of the house and with its own side entrance and lobby [**see Fig. 3.2, 3.47**]. Convinced that this would not be permitted, she made a successful planning application for a domestic utility room. The small salon was built and is run covertly, despite the fact that her business is registered and she pays income tax. Providing a personal service to a clientele of local women, who are driven to and from

4. Based on the Abridged Building Classification (ABC), devised by the International Building Classification Committee (Geirtz and Hughes, 1981), which divides buildings into four main groups by function: (1) Public, civil, commercial and industrial buildings; (2) Ecclesiastical architecture, religious and funerary architecture; (3) Buildings for education, scientific and cultural purposes; and (4) Residential buildings. Each of these groups is divided into seven or eight sub-groups, to give 30 classes for all buildings. This system is primarily used for governance purposes, and is incorporated into planning law and building regulations.

5. Email exchange between author and Pat Thomas, OBE, planning lawyer, May 2008.

6. This has changed a bit in the twenty-first century to accommodate some mixed-use districts, but these generally produce buildings with flats above often unlet commercial premises or (rarely) small developments of live/work units.

FIG. 5.1 *Furniture-maker's apartment above his workshop*

7. See, for example, the London Borough of Hillingdon's 28-page Supplementary Planning Guidance for Live/work Accommodation. Many forward-looking local authorities have produced equivalent policies in an attempt to resolve an inherent difficulty with building for home-based work.

their homes when they are no longer able to make their own way, her business causes no nuisance in the neighbourhood. Although officially an archetypical residential suburb, with commerce restricted to other zones, in reality, it teems with such hidden home-based work.

Similarly, an urban furniture-maker has made an illicit apartment for his young family above his workshop on a light-industrial estate [**Fig. 5.1, 5.2**]. A farmer's son, he is passionate that his children should be brought up with the visceral understanding of work that he himself gained from watching his father driving a tractor across the fields around his childhood home. The hum of machinery below, a fine layer of sawdust, daily family lunches with dad at the table, and excursions into the workshop to find scraps of wood to play with provide a constant reminder of the labour being carried out in the workshop and an understanding of its value. The children's mother enjoys touching base with her partner in the middle of the day and the fact that the immediate surroundings are busy and sociable during the working week when she is looking after the children, but quiet and peaceful in the evenings and at weekends. Health and safety issues have been thoughtfully resolved: workshop and dwelling have separate entrances. But unfortunately no conventional UK planner would consider a light-industrial estate to be an appropriate place to raise a family, despite the fact that farms, also work-dominated home-based working situations, are generally regarded as ideal.

The 1980s and 1990s live/work movement challenged the inherently mono-functionally based UK planning system. Presented as a new phenomenon, however, rather than as a fresh incarnation of an age-old building type, it appeared to require new rules. In the absence of national guidance, these were generated piecemeal at a local level by numerous planning authorities in response to an influx of requests for permission to build live/work units.[7] These

8. *London Residential Research, Review of Live-Work Policy in Hackney* (2005), p. 42.

9. *Ibid., p.1.*

10. *In the UK, residential sites and buildings are generally considerably more valuable than light-industrial ones.*

11. *London Residential Research, op. cit.*

12. *Ibid.*

FIG. 5.2 *Furniture-maker's home-based workshop*

Supplementary Planning Guidance (SPG) documents embody a range of different approaches to regulating the live/work building. The London Borough of Hackney (LBH) produced the first in 1996, approving the construction of 1,336 live/work units between 1995 and 2004.[8] While achieving its primary aim as 'an innovative, pragmatic planning policy to encourage private investment into run-down buildings in run-down parts of a run-down borough',[9] this was revoked just seven years later. Something had, apparently, gone horribly wrong.

This can be explained as follows: live/work captured the imaginations of the creative middle classes. As we have seen in Chapter Two, the term was coined to sell apartments that were intended to embody the bohemian, creative qualities of the original SoHo artists' lofts. While the primary regenerative aim was achieved with unexpected efficacy, the London Borough of Hackney planning department became increasingly agitated by some unexpected outcomes of their radical new policy. First, developers were making disproportionate profits from the almost residential prices they achieved on the sale of live/work units built on disused, often neglected and therefore cheap light-industrial sites.[10] And consequent research seemed to show that few people were actually working in the live/work buildings, so that precious light-industrial land was unintentionally being lost to residential use.[11] In addition, developers were 'side-stepping employment promotion and affordable housing policy requirements that they would otherwise have had to meet'.[12] London Borough of Hackney planners came to the conclusion that the whole movement was a scam to enable developers to profit from the conversion of light-industrial land to residential use. And so they revoked their SPG, saying:

We do not support live/work as a policy position; it hasn't worked. A lot of employment areas have been degraded because most live/

work units developed in the Borough are not operating as live/work, but are being used purely as residential accommodation.[13]

Scratch the surface of this controversy, however, and a more complex picture emerges. Most live/work buildings were not, indeed, designed to meet the needs of the home-based workforce, but were part of the immensely successful marketing campaign for loft-style apartments that had started in New York.[14] But the movement touched a nerve. Many people found the promise of buildings specifically intended for home-based work immensely attractive. And, despite the buildings often being inappropriately designed, many home-based workers moved in and, indeed, still live and work there. A photographer, working part-time while she has young children, inhabits one of 114 live/work units in a 2001 development. Her so-called live/work unit is, in fact, a maisonette (so much less alluring a name …). It has a ground-floor open-plan living/kitchen/dining room with a tiny desk-space corner by the entrance, and three bedrooms and a bathroom upstairs [**Fig. 5.3**].

My living room doubles as studio-space: I use it once or twice a week and move all the furniture. The sofa is light and goes on top of the dining table; I roll the rug up and move the chairs out. I have a big white paper background that goes across the space and fold-up flash lighting. I do two-hour shoots. My child goes to a friend or out with my husband, who works a four-day week. I would definitely prefer to have a separate studio, but hire studios cost £150 a day; it would double my costs and make my work unaffordable. It works fine; I book two families on one day, and so minimize the number of times I have to shift the furniture.

This inconvenience is tolerated because the natural light and spatial qualities are good and the property is part of a successfully branded live/work scheme inhabited by like-minded creative people. Seven years after the initial 2005 interview, now with two children, this photographer continues to shift furniture several times a week to accommodate her work.

13. *Interview with Mark Powney, policy planner, London Borough of Hackney, 13 October 2006.*

14. *Zukin, op. cit.*

15. *London Residential Research, op. cit.*

FIG. 5.3 *Photographer has to move the furniture in her live/work unit whenever she works*

But this part-time transformation of living space to workspace is not what London Borough of Hackney planners had in mind when they authorized large numbers of live/work units. This type of inhabitation, involving ancillary work, is permitted in any dwelling. They conceptualized work-dominated or equal-status workhomes housing light-industrial and service industries with numbers of employees. However, without the planners understanding the distinction, many live/work buildings were designed and marketed as home-dominated workhomes. And so, despite a rapidly growing home-based workforce, obvious demand, and a wide range of benefits to both the individual and society as a whole, London Borough of Hackney planners rejected the whole concept. This, in turn, led to the collapse of the live/work property market in the UK. Developers and property owners scrambled to get their properties reclassified as residential, despite, in many cases, their ongoing use as workhomes. Recognizing the inherent good sense of designing for home-based work, waves of subsequent SPGs have tried to address this anomaly. But the difficulty of determining what is and is not live/work has meant they have generally been unsuccessful. The UK live/work guru Tim Dwelly even went so far as to stipulate at his 2008 live/work conference that for it to be true live/work, the workspace had to be on the ground floor.

Of course, this is nonsense. As we have already seen, the diversity of the UK home-based workforce makes such a prescriptive approach meaningless. And so a deep-seated confusion about live/work remains. What does live/work mean? Is it compulsory to carry out paid employment in a live/work unit, and, if so, how can this be enforced? And does this paid employment count, in the planners' eyes, if it is, say, IT-based and could just as easily be carried out in an ordinary bedroom? How much work are people allowed to do in their home, before they need planning permission? Are people allowed to live in commercial premises? And if not, why not? How is work distinct from other aspects of life, and how are those distinctions maintained or blurred by home-based workers? Local planning authorities have puzzled over, and tried to answer, these questions when writing increasingly directive live/work SPGs. In an attempt to close loopholes and resolve some of these issues, the London Borough of Hackney commissioned a piece of research on the field. It concluded that 'conditions and planning agreements to secure live-work are in effect unenforceable'.[15]

A logical but narrow response to the live/work confusion, this overlooked the much larger issue of design for home-based work at both the building and the urban scale. And, in doing so, a key opportunity to clarify the issue was missed. In reality, the workhome is a building type as varied as the dwelling, and so single-shot spatial or environmental prescriptions are bound to fail. To be effective, the governance of this largely forgotten building type needs to encompass and support the development of all three of its forms: home-dominated, work-dominated and equal-status.

Despite all the controversy and confusion, the LBH's pioneering work around live/work generated some fine buildings inhabited by communities of home-based workers. But their automatic classification as composite hereditaments[16] has led to many individuals requesting the reclassification of their units as dwellings, because occupants of such buildings often have to pay a double property tax. An artist cleared out his studio and converted it temporarily into a living room. Once his work/live unit had been reassessed as residential, he reinstated it and often works there for 12 or 15 hours a day. This is common. Its downside is that local authorities think that nobody works in their live/work units, and that there is therefore no call for buildings that combine dwelling and workplace. Neither assumption is true. A national planning guideline, created in 2005 and classifying live/work as *sui generis* (i.e. a class of its own), has shelved rather than resolved the issue.[17]

There has been some movement in planning policy, however. As the rationale for functional zoning has largely been removed by the deindustrialization of major cities and pollution control, and Jacobs' ideas have filtered through, 'mixed-use' has become a new orthodoxy in post-industrial urban planning. In London, on average, 40 per cent of all development across the 33 boroughs were classified as mixed-use in 2006–2007.[18] Intended to break down isolated residential, commercial or light-industrial districts and their dependency on the car, this policy is, however, having limited success. In the USA, it usually involves a combination of residential and commercial; mixing two or more commercial uses alone, such as shops and offices, does not comply.[19] In the UK, mixed-use developments often take the form of self-contained blocks with shops and restaurants on the ground floor and offices and/or apartments above. Housing-led mixed-use schemes often include a community facility such as a gym or a crèche.[20] Theoretically this is mutually beneficial, giving shopkeepers, restaurateurs and the like captive customers while residents have shops and other facilities a few moments from their homes. In practice, however, it is more problematic. In London, a quarter of the ground-floor commercial premises of apartment-based developments remain empty for years after they are built.[21] And many so-called successful schemes consist of flats built over a supermarket. While this is an improvement on the suburb that has no amenities, such mixed-use developments have not brought the hoped-for new life and diversity to town and city.

This may be because mixed-use as it is currently conceived does not offer structural change. In the UK, for example, the mono-functional Use Class Order remains intact, and so while widespread mixed-use developments combine residential and non-residential elements, they do not accommodate the 'intricate minglings' of home-based work.

While working practices are changing radically and rapidly, planning regulations lag behind. And so the British population increasingly hides what it thinks will not be allowed. The few valiant organizations

16. In UK law, 'hereditament' is used to refer to any kind of building that can be inherited.

17. Office of the Deputy Prime Minister, 30/2005. The UK ODPM was replaced in May 2006 by the Department of Communities and Local Government.

18. R. Cooper, G. Evans and C. Boyko (eds), Designing Sustainable Cities (2009), p. 194.

19. Ibid., p. 193.

20. Ibid., p. 195.

21. Ibid., p. 196.

22. See Tim Dwelly's Live/work Network, available at: www.liveworknet.com

Valuation bands

Council Tax valuation bands	Ranges of values in England	Ranges of values in Wales
A	up to £40,000	up to £44,000
B	over £40,000 and up to £52,000	over £44,000 and up to £65,000
C	over £52,000 and up to £68,000	over £65,000 and up to £91,000
D	over £68,000 and up to £88,000	over £91,000 and up to £123,000
E	over £88,000 and up to £120,000	over £123,000 and up to £162,000
F	over £120,000 and up to £160,000	over £162,000 and up to £223,000
G	over £160,000 and up to £320,000	over £223,000 and up to £324,000
H	over £320,000	over £324,000 and up to £424,000
I		over £424,000

Please note that the valuation bands differ in Scotland.

FIG. 5.4 *UK Council Tax Bands, October 2012*

that stand up for live/work have an uphill struggle.[22] In general, the growing home-based workforce opts to live at their workplace or work in their home covertly, shaping the space to accommodate the combined functions as best they can. That this is far from ideal has already been touched on in Chapter Three; it will be discussed further in Chapter Six.

But even if these planning policies were reviewed, and reconfigured to support and encourage rather than obstruct the design of buildings and cities around home-based work, this would currently have little effect on bringing the home-based workforce and the workhome into view. This is because it is a toxic combination of outdated planning policies and a punitive tax system that drives the UK home-based workforce underground.

Income tax is not the issue. Most home-based workers in the UK pay this tax. The problem lies with property taxation. The current UK system is organized around a binary vision of business as distinct from home that works poorly for the home-based workforce. Council Tax is levied on all houses and flats in bands according to property value [**Fig. 5.4**]. It is set and collected by every local authority to fund neighbourhood services such as police, street lighting and refuse collection. Business rates, calculated on a rateable value per square metre of non-domestic property, are set and distributed by central government. They also pay for local services. Buildings assessed as part domestic and part non-domestic are accommodated, but clumsily. Any workhome that has a dedicated workspace is classified by the antiquated term 'composite hereditament', with Council Tax liable on the dwelling part and business rates on the workplace part. This would be a straightforward and workable system if the two taxes were equivalent to each other and calculated in the same way, as they are in Japan, where a similar system, which will be discussed in more detail later in this chapter, works well.

But this is not the case. The two taxes were conceived independently, and have no regard for each other. One is paid to central, while the other goes to local, government. And, as a result, they are often punitive to those who inhabit buildings that combine dwelling and workplace, because a clash in the way the two taxes are calculated means such people often have to pay twice for their local services. Council Tax is commonly levied on the value of the whole building and then business rates are charged on top of it. This affects a great many home-based workers across the UK, particularly in London, where residential property values are high.[23]

Impatient with a system that tries to charge them twice for their local services, many home-based workers respond by keeping their head down below the radar. And, as a result, large numbers of otherwise law-abiding citizens live and work under a cloud of anxiety about being caught. The hairdresser, whose salon in a rear extension to her house is unusable for any other purpose, is liable for business rates under current regulations. Since she already pays Council Tax and income tax, her turnover could not support the payment of the additional business rates. And she finds it difficult to see how the double taxation can be justified, as she runs a modest business and makes her contribution to local services through Council Tax. So she keeps her head down and her business operates on a word-of-mouth basis only.

23. In 2012, house prices averaged £364,000 and so most properties sit comfortably in the top Council Tax band. The workplace element of an ordinary London terraced house, which is worth £650,000 even in the most deprived boroughs, would have to be valued at more than £330,000 for the property to drop into a lower band and for the home-based worker to pay the correct property tax. This is an improbable scenario.

A substantial proportion of the UK home-based workforce is liable to pay twice for their local services in this way, and this is not popular. Many consider business rates to be a stealth tax for which they receive nothing. They argue that, because High Street lock-up shopkeepers operate from two locations, it is fair that they pay the two taxes as, in effect, they use two sets of streetlights, pavements and roads. By contrast, the home-based worker uses only one set of services. One shopkeeper, living above his shop, says: 'I think it is a rip-off paying both business rates and Council Tax as the services are duplicated … police, fire, ambulance, road sweeping, street lighting …'

Another concurs:
It is ridiculous. It amounts to double payment for local services … basically Council Tax and business rates are supposed to be providing the same services, it just doesn't make sense, the council is just making extra money out of us … The council are aware … they still charge double.

Home-based work is therefore hidden wherever possible, and only those unable to avoid it pay the double tax. Inevitably these are the visible home-based workers, the shopkeepers, publicans, hoteliers, restaurateurs and funeral directors living on the premises, who are unable to escape the attentions of the agency that assesses properties for tax. Live/work units, by their nature and name, also fall into this trap. Many are reclassified as residential properties, despite on-going home-based work, to avoid this double taxation.

If that was not bad enough, capital gains tax (CGT) is also levied at a percentage of the value of the work element on the sale of a composite hereditament, despite the fact that primary residences are meant to be exempt. This is a further incentive for home-based workers to avoid having their workhome classified in this way. Common strategies include operating covertly or ensuring the building does not have a dedicated workspace. The children of a home-based company director do their homework in his office, which is also used for drying laundry and to store items from the rest of the house precisely for this reason. This is not ideal either in terms of his efficiency or his occupational identity, an issue that will be discussed further in Chapter Six.

The UK: other problematic areas

There are many other ways in which governance affects home-based work adversely. For the past 100 years residents of UK social housing have had to sign tenancy agreements that at best discourage and at worst prohibit home-based work. One, for a flat inhabited by a young home-based entrepreneur, includes the following clause:

'Use of Premises: To use the premises for residential purposes only and not to operate a business at the premises, and not to use the premises for any illegal or immoral purpose.'

It is revealing that running a business is paralleled with using the premises for an illegal or immoral purpose. Presumably the two practices were considered to be on a par when the document was written. The illustrator hides his business, only advertising on the Internet [**see Fig. 3.68**]. A child-minder lives and works on a large estate run by a major UK housing association. Approaching retirement age, she decided she would prefer to spend the rest of her working years looking after children in her home rather than continuing to work in a care-home for the elderly. Once qualified and registered, she asked her social landlord for permission to work as a child-minder in her flat, because her tenancy agreement included the following clause:

You must get our written permission before you can run a business from your home. We will not withhold permission unless we have a good reason. We will refuse permission if the business would cause a nuisance to or annoy neighbours, or damage the property. We may withdraw our permission at any time if we have good reason. We will let you know why.

Permission was refused, but ('because I went to school') the child-minder protested, insisting she should be given permission unless they had good reason to refuse. The housing association finally conceded, on condition she did not cause any problem to the neighbours. Her response was that she had lived there for eighteen years and had never caused her neighbours any trouble. As the only registered child-minder on an estate of more than 1,200 homes, she is aware of dozens of other women on the estate who are child-minding informally, largely as a result of the justifiable fear that they may be refused consent to work at home if they formalize their work. This raises a range of issues, including the children's health and safety and the child-minder's occupational identity. The UK government, in fact, made a pledge to lift the ban on social tenants starting businesses in their own homes in their 2010 Coalition agreement.[24] But the idea that such people should not work in their homes is so deeply ingrained that housing associations and local authorities are not implementing this shift in policy. It is no coincidence that unemployment runs at twice the rate among UK residents of social housing as in the overall population.[25]

As well as the huge issues it raises, the conceptual separation between dwelling and workplace generates a myriad of smaller irritations for UK home-based workers. Utility companies have different pricing structures for workplaces and private dwellings; people in dual-use buildings often have to pay the higher commercial rate throughout. One shopkeeper, charged commercially for water in his flat, was told: '… even if you don't have a WC downstairs in your shop, you still have to use the upstairs one during the day, don't you?'

24. HM Government, The Coalition: Our Programme for Government (2010), p. 10.

25. Social Exclusion Team, Greater London Authority Intelligence Update, 2006–2011 (2011).

Electricity is often wired on a single circuit and similarly charged at the commercial rate throughout in older composite hereditaments. Many home-based workers are exasperated at the waste of resources involved in having two small separate weekly refuse collections to the same address, one commercial, for which they have to pay, and one domestic, funded from Council Tax. At the other extreme, a live-in school caretaker's refuse collections and mail deliveries are suspended during the school holidays, leading to maggots in his bins and Christmas cards received in January. Shopkeepers speak of the problems of receiving deliveries in areas where residential parking schemes do not meet their needs: one reports that his milkman regularly receives parking tickets. An illustrator, inhabiting a live/work unit with dwelling and workplace entrances on parallel streets and therefore with two addresses, had to battle not to be charged twice for utilities and her TV licence. A furniture-maker living above his workshop had difficulty getting his children into his local school because a Council Tax receipt to prove residency is a necessary part of the application, and he pays only business rates.

These large and small ways in which current UK governance systems do not work for the home-based worker help to explain the low profile of this workforce. It is better to keep quiet than face the confusion, difficulty and additional cost that come from trying to operate openly. But that two-thirds of the 76 UK participants in the research work covertly or illicitly in some way is deeply counterproductive, for the individual, for the economy and for society as a whole.

The USA

And in the USA it is little different. In the view of US architect and academic, Howard Davis, the number of home-based workers and businesses is probably higher than is routinely reported. This is because of the ability for the 'new economy' to accommodate home-based businesses and because the current high US unemployment rate causes people to move away from corporate employment to form new, small home-located businesses.

The first comprehensive zoning ordinance, regulating land use as well as building form, was instituted in New York City in 1916 and the US Supreme Court affirmed the constitutionality of zoning in 1926, but Davis points out that there is no national legislation of home-based businesses. Each US municipality has its own land-use and zoning regulations and, as a result, cities differ greatly from each other in how home businesses are regulated. While small professional offices may be permitted, manufacturing, retail, or service occupations like hairdressing or auto repair, particularly attractive to people with low incomes, are generally not. Such businesses therefore need to exist 'under the radar', supported by informal business networks. Some cities are taking steps toward the relaxation of codes that prevent home-based businesses, but Davis concludes that the thousands of individual ordinances that exist along with mono-functional land-use patterns, partly the result of almost a hundred years of zoning, are likely to ensure that home-based work continues to be largely hidden from view in the USA.[26]

A number of interviews with home-based workers in California, carried out as a foil to the 76 English interviews, reinforce this view.[27] Two highly successful home-based businesses, one run from a residential and the other from a light-industrial zone, considered the risk of being interviewed for this book too great. The first of these was a chef who caters for exclusive events, for small or large numbers of people at around $150/head, in a large timber shed in the back yard of his house. The impact on his garden is not dissimilar to that of the UK surveyor's Portakabin office. Despite often employing five people, his operation is covert and illicit, because it happens in a residential zone. But how hidden can this much cooking be? His neighbours clearly do not mind, as no one has complained in five years. But he still feels the need to keep out of view of the authorities. The second non-interview involved a metalworker in a parallel but diametrically opposed situation. He runs a sophisticated prototyping, contract manufacturing and product development business, employing ten people in a large 1920s industrial workshop, and lives there, both covertly and illicitly. Using the most advanced CNC machinery, his work ranges from developing cutting-edge medical equipment to restoring historic monuments. Few people know that his workspace also conceals his home.

Both people find it stressful that, despite being mainstream members of society, they are in some important way outside the law and have

FIG. 5.5 *An illicit US picture-framing workshop*

28. *No external photographs were permitted because the building contravenes the zoning ordinance.*

to operate covertly. Their dual use of mono-functional zones does no harm. Indeed, it can be argued that their 24-hour inhabitation contributes to the creation of the busy, vibrant, socially engaged neighbourhoods that planners and politicians love to talk about but find so difficult to achieve in practice.

Two participants adversely affected by zoning were, however, happy to be interviewed. A picture-framer started out in his garage. After 15 years in a live/work unit, he has returned to having an illicit garage workshop [**Fig. 5.5**].[28] Although he is careful to conceal his work, it seems unlikely his neighbours are unaware of it: woodworking machinery is noisy. A mechanic's home-based work, though also illicit, is highly visible [**see Fig. 3.59**]. Someone complained to the authorities as soon as he first moved in and started mending cars on the empty site next to his house. However, since he sorted out an oil run-off problem and became known locally, there have been no further complaints despite the fact that, at any one time, he has between fifteen and twenty vehicles in his yard. Indeed, he is now an integral part of the neighbourhood, a friendly, watchful presence on the street, who keeps everyone's cars running.

FIG. 5.6 *The US Batle Studio on the 'crack' between residential and light-industrial zones*

FIG. 5.7 US kinetic sculptor and landscape architect's workhome in a nineteenth-century dairy

Other participants, finding ways around various restrictive ordinances, combine home and work legitimately. Agelio Batle's workhome, discussed in Chapter Two, is positioned bang on the junction between a residential zone and a light-industrial zone. With workshop/studio/office downstairs and apartment upstairs, family life, work and home flow between the two spaces. The neighbours are pleased at the dual-use building on the crack (as it were) between the two zones [**Fig. 5.6**]. They consider the 24-hour occupation of the building keeps the district safer and even increases the value of their properties. More on these benefits in Chapter Six.

A kinetic sculptor and a landscape architect combine a large workshop/studio space with design office and family home in a nineteenth-century dairy building [**Fig. 5.7**]. Despite being in a residential zone, the building has, for historic reasons, permission for combined light-industrial and residential use. The light-industrial use has to be constant, however. If it lapses, the building will be reclassified as residential to fit in with its neighbourhood.

FIG. 5.8, 5.9 US artist's studio built to footprint of a previous garage, front and interior views

A fine artist has built a detached top-lit studio behind her house, precisely to the footprint of the garage that was there before, so that aerial surveys of her district will not detect it [**Fig. 5.8, 5.9**]. The director of a Buddhist organization lives in her high-end three-storey house way up in the hills. Few people know she and her husband both work there. A building contractor and agent for converting cars

FIG. 5.10 *Separate doors for home and workplace with different coloured doorbells*

to run on chip fat, however, has built a two-storey workhome; the ground-floor office has its own entrance, adjacent to the front door of the house, with a differently coloured doorbell [**Fig. 5.10**]. Because it is in a rare 'mixed-use residential' zone, this workhome is legitimate; signage advertising his business is even permitted.

And, finally, the vast disused smelting works in which the US contact juggler lives and works with 350 other young creative people has live/work permission. It was converted in the 1980s, as a part of the early live/work movement, into 62 units of 100–500 square metres. Part of an industrial wasteland by railway tracks, the complex has its own café, recording studio and thrift shop/art gallery/bike repair shop. In effect, a gated community, and therefore secure, it invites collaboration and connections through its open-door policy. The juggler and I wander through narrow, winding corridors, numerous small courtyards and a series of increasingly theatrical rehearsal spaces. In one, a clown plays the 'Moonlight Sonata', ignoring our intrusion; in another, two acrobats construct a frame. This series of buildings houses a very real community, in many senses of the word: a great many young people living and working collectively in close proximity to each other; a shared passion for their art; a shared contempt for more conventional ways of life. It opens a conversation about ways in which we could build differently for a future revolving about home-based work, thus encouraging collaboration and the social and temporal freedoms that come with it, all of which, as a side effect, help to prevent social isolation.

In his 2012 book, *Live-Work Planning and Design*, Thomas Dolan includes a meticulous analysis of the complex regulatory and planning policy implications of design for home-based work in the USA. He discusses the challenge live/work poses to US governance frameworks, particularly the underlying strictly zoned segregation for residential, commercial and industrial use. And he unpicks the various ways that planners and code-writers have attempted to accommodate live/work within existing frameworks. That this takes more than 100 pages is an indication of the scale and complexity of the problem. His approach is practical; he is an architect with decades of experience building live/work developments in the USA and his book is aimed at helping others to navigate the complexities of the field.

This book, by contrast, aims to highlight a more widespread, even global, need for change, without prescribing how this might be implemented in any particular place. UK and US regulatory and policy frameworks, developed in the wake of slum clearances and Ebenezer Howard's radical ideas about Town-country Garden Cities, are predicated on the separation of dwelling from workplace. Piecemeal change aimed at accommodating the current rapid rise in home-based work is complicated and often ineffectual. One can only continue patching an old system to fit a new situation for so long. Sooner or later the whole system has to be re-conceptualized. We are now at that point with home-based work, as this workforce is growing rapidly and will continue to grow. In the UK, the number of people working mainly from home doubled in size between 1991 and 2001,[29] and has increased a further 21 per cent since then.[30] It is now estimated that 25 per cent of the working population lives at their workplace or works at or from home for at least eight hours per week, the point at which it is considered to be spatially significant.[31]

This rapid growth is echoed across the world. It is possible that going out to work will in years to come be viewed as a disruptive twentieth-century aberration. The social, economic and environmental pressures discussed in the next chapter and a reduced need for most occupations to be carried out in collective workplaces are likely to result in home-based work becoming the dominant working practice, supported by rapidly developing teleconferencing technologies, neighbourhood hubs, etc. It is also likely that technological developments will result in many other functions, like medical procedures, that are currently carried out in specialized workplaces, being transferred to the home.

This represents a radical change in our society. It has huge implications for how we inhabit, think about and regulate our homes, workplaces and cities. Adverse governance frameworks contribute to this change happening surreptitiously in many parts of the world, with negative consequences for both the individual and for society as a whole. In other places, however, only slightly different policies and governance systems have the effect of supporting and encouraging home-based work and the development of workhomes. These deserve scrutiny as they are potentially replicable models.

Japan

As we saw at the beginning of this book, Japan's social, political and economic history sets it apart in this field. The tradition of home-based work has been continuous there since feudal times. And, maybe as a consequence, important areas of Japanese policy and governance, blind to the ingrained separation of dwelling

29. The UK Census (2001).

30. Analysis of UK Labour Force Survey statistics by Andy Lake at Flexibility. co.uk, available at: www. flexibility.co.uk/flexwork/ location/homeworking-statistics-2009.htm

31. Holliss, op. cit (2007).

and workplace in the West, accommodate this working practice and facilitate the development of workhomes. Planning policy, for example, permits 49 per cent employment use (or 50 square metres; whichever is smaller) in any dwelling, in even the strictest residential districts in Tokyo. It is common, as a result, for people to live at their workplace or work in their home.[32] In addition, property taxation for both commercial and residential property is charged by area. The rate is the same, just paid to a different body. So there is no fiscal deterrent to openly working at home, living at the workplace or building workhomes. These buildings are, as a result, commonplace. Half the buildings designed by Koh Kitayama are workhomes of one sort or another; the same applies to many other architects. Buildings like Atelier Knot's house for the vegetable seller or Tadao Ando's Yoshida House, modern interpretations of an old tradition, are easily incorporated into the city. Atelier Bow-Wow's own combined house and studio, where fourteen interns and employees graft from early in the morning until late at night, effortlessly rubs shoulders with its residential neighbours. Principal Tsukamoto's 'we can see and hear, but we don't' helps to explain an attitude that facilitates this. Four of the six workhomes in Kitayama's Klarheit building were, at the last report, in use solely as workplaces. No problem. And if someone wanted just to live there, that would not be a problem either.

Aware of the social, environmental and economic benefit of home-based work, particularly in the context of an ageing population and a falling birthrate, in 2003 the Japanese government included the following in a series of radical, far-sighted 'e-policies':

By the year 2010, the government aims to increase teleworkers to 20% of the working population, so that an environment can be established in which each individual can maximize their capabilities in a job regardless of their location.[33]

Furthermore, it pledged that 'conventional labor regulations will be reviewed, applying them to the telework model'.[34] And it set up an Action Plan for Doubling the Teleworking Population in May 2007. The Ministry of Internal Affairs and Communications (MIC) stated that it was committed to implementing this

steadily and speedily by means such as performing demonstration experiments and nationwide dissemination/educational seminars to spread telework. The MIC has also introduced a telework program for MIC employees, thereby taking the leadership in adopting telework for government officials.[35]

A policy review that aims for this level of impact is needed in both the UK and the USA, and in other countries such as India, where governance systems initially modelled on those of the UK during colonial times have resulted in similar difficulties.[36] The environmental consequences alone of such an intervention would make it a major achievement. This will be discussed in the next chapter. Also, inherently flexible governance systems and policies allow Japanese buildings to change function over time. This has a liberating effect on

32. Interview with Koh Kitayama and Hiroko Hasama, Koh Kitayama + architecture WORKSHOP, 8 July 2008.

33. E-Japan Strategy II 2003, 'Teleworker' is defined here as a person who works outside the conventional workplace for more than eight hours per week (regardless of time or place) using IT-related tools.

34. Ibid.

35. Available at: www.soumu. go.jp/english/icpb/index. html (accessed 3 Oct. 2012).

36. 'Modern town planning [in India] emerged from the British intervention in Indian cities. These were modelled heavily on the prevailing ideologies and movements in Town Planning in England... The Bombay Town Planning Act, 1915, was the first to be introduced in India and was applied to the present states of Maharashtra and Gujarat. Such laws empowered the local authorities to control the use of land and development through the instruments of zoning and building regulations...' See S. Ballaney, The Town Planning Mechanism in Gujarat, India (2008), p. 13-14. The Indian legal system is based on English Common and Statutory Law; and commercial and residential property tax rates differ, as in the UK.

what is designed and built. The workhome is a building type taken for granted in Japan, both traditionally and in the new generation of buildings designed to meet the needs of creative practitioners and e-generated employment practices.

Increasingly, inappropriate and outdated conceptual frameworks for governance, based on the spatiality of industrial rather than informational capitalism, are a central cause of the invisibility, in the UK, the USA and elsewhere in the Global North, of home-based workforces and their associated buildings.[37] In the Global South, where home-based enterprises are often essential in the struggle against poverty, construction of informal workplace extensions to the home that contravene official zoning mandates is widespread [**Fig. 5.11**]. Maybe as a consequence the conversation about how to accommodate home-based work in planning frameworks is more advanced.[38] Nigerian planner Nkeiru Ezeadichie asks whether planners in the Global South

should ignore the urban informal economy, condemn it, or strategize to accommodate it, recognizing that it is no longer a temporary trend as earlier speculated but another kind of economy that is here to stay in contemporary developing countries?[39]

Similar questions may be asked about the relationship of planning frameworks to home-based work in more developed countries.

This chapter shows how regulations rooted in the industrial past discourage this working practice and as a consequence severely restrict the possibility of developing buildings and city districts appropriate to contemporary home-based employment practices, in part, generated by informational capitalism. Changes to planning frameworks and, in the UK, property taxation systems and tenancy agreements in social housing are urgently needed. They would help bring this practice and these buildings out from the shadows.

37. See Manuel Castells, (2000), for a discussion of informational capitalism.

38. See, for example, M. Nohn, Mixed Use Zoning and Home-Based production in India (2012); N. Ezeadichie, 'Home-based Enterprises in Urban Space: Obligation for Strategic Planning?' (2012).

39. Ezeadichie, op. cit.

FIG. 5.11 *Pottery, Dharavi, Mumbai*

Sustainability

Sustainability

1. The IPCC reviews and assesses the most recent scientific, technical and socio-economic information produced worldwide relevant to the understanding of climate change. Its primary goal is to provide rigorous and balanced scientific information to decision-makers.

2. In 2007, the IPCC's best estimate of future change was that globally-averaged surface temperatures would be 2.5°C–4.7°C higher by 2100 compared to pre-industrial levels. The full range of projected temperature increases by 2100 was found to be 1.8°C–7.1°C, based on the various scenarios and uncertainties in climate sensitivity. See the Royal Society, Climate Change: A Summary of the Science (2010).

3. See UK Government, The Carbon Plan (2011).

4. Some 21% of dwellings were built before 1919; 16% between 1919 and 1945, while only 12% have been constructed since 1990. See Department for Communities and Local Government, English Housing Survey: Housing Stock Report (2008), p. 9.

The way we live our lives and use our homes and workplaces, our villages, towns and cities is changing. In the past the *idea* of home-based work was thought to undermine 'home' as a domestic refuge from the male world of work, while the *practice* was thought to be bad for people's health and well-being. And so, as we have seen, society was organized to restrict and even prohibit this working practice. These attitudes persist and still have some lingering currency. But in the context of the digital revolution and more women in employment than ever before, home-based work can be viewed through a very different lens: as a cutting-edge practice with the potential to ease a range of contemporary social problems. And this is not true only for middle-class professionals; blue-collar home-based work has equal potential. This chapter will explore how the idea of home-based work can contribute to the debate about how to achieve a more sustainable future.

An environmentally sustainable working practice

There is overwhelming evidence that human activity is causing dangerous levels of climate change. Since 1988, the Intergovernmental Panel on Climate Change (IPCC)[1] has reported the urgent need for reductions in greenhouse gas emissions, mainly carbon dioxide. Policies are being developed globally to address this.[2] In the UK, the Climate Change Act of 2008 established a legally binding target to reduce these emissions by at least 80 per cent below the 1990 base year levels, by 2050. The main strategy proposed to achieve this is the development and application of new technologies to produce low-carbon buildings, transport, industry and electricity.[3]

But the technical difficulty and cost of achieving this are immense. If we look at just one area, low-carbon buildings, the scale of the problem becomes apparent. England has one of the oldest building stocks in Europe: 88 per cent of its 22.5 million dwellings were built before 1990 and 37 per cent before 1945.[4] Limits on heat loss in buildings were first introduced in 1965 and have since periodically

5. Department of Trade and Industry, *Energy White Paper: Our Energy Future – Creating a Low Carbon Economy* (2003) p. 34.

6. G. Killip, *Built Fabric and Building Regulations*, 40% House Project, (2005), p. 4.

7. J. Anable, B. Lane, and T. Kelay, *An Evidence Based Review of Public Attitudes to Climate Change and Transport Behaviour* (2006), p. 28.

8. When setting out the government's modernizing agenda, Tony Blair declared that what counts is what works (H.T.O. Davies et al. *What Works? Evidence-based Policy and Practice in Public Service* (2000), cited in Anable et al. op. cit., p. 5.) The implication of this is that policy-making would be driven by evidence of what is proven to be effective in addressing social problems and achieving desired outcomes.

9. Anable et al., op. cit., p. 6.

been tightened. The government claimed the stricter 2002 regulations would cut heating requirement of a new home by 50 per cent compared to 1990 levels.[5] But many would argue that current controls remain insufficiently stringent, and it is unlikely the national building stock can be brought up to the necessary standard by 2050,[6] unless, as environmental engineer Max Fordham once suggested, the country is put on a war footing to tackle the crisis. And there are equivalent problems with upgrading transport and the production of electricity to low-carbon solutions. It is therefore likely that we will also need to change our behaviour. This proposition is not yet a major part of political debate, but consciousness is changing and people increasingly recognize that their own behaviour is part of the problem.[7]

Home-based work can reduce carbon emissions by helping us to travel less, heat less and make less, while simultaneously improving people's quality of life. This seems to offer a win/win solution.

Travel less

A 2006 study for the UK Department for Transport acknowledged that:

If the requisite reductions in CO_2 are to be achieved, the transport sector must play a significant role … With more or less coercive policies such as national road pricing being at best a long way off, there is an urgent need to understand and deliver what works[8] in policy terms to encourage behaviour shifts to contribute to transport energy reduction in the shorter as well as the longer term.[9]

One of the defining characteristics of home-based work is that it reduces how often and how far people travel to work. Individual home-based workers' stories underline this. A BT manager, leading an intercontinental team from his modern detached suburban home [**Fig. 6.1**] says: 'Environmentally, working at home is a great improvement. I was working 45 miles away, and driving 30,000 miles a year. I still have a company car, but now I only drive 10,000 miles per year.'

FIG. 6.1 *BT manager's workhome*

A pair of graphic designers used to drive two cars for an hour across London to their studio each morning so that one could make an early return to collect children from school. They sold their second car when they moved their studio into the converted attic of their terraced house, a stone's throw from their children's school, and reduced their mileage by a factor of ten. Such individual actions are not significant on their own but, when multiplied by the 4.2 million UK workers who usually work at home and the millions more who are home-based for at least part of the week,[10] let alone the 100 million estimated home-based workers worldwide,[11] they could combine to effect a substantial and globally significant reduction in carbon emissions. While most UK workers drive a car to work, 50 per cent of London commuters travel by train, underground or bus.[12] Although considerably cleaner than cars, the CO_2 emissions of public transport are therefore also an important part of the picture. If large numbers of people stay at home, then fewer trains will have to run: London's Victoria Line underground trains run almost every minute in the rush hour.

The findings of the 2004 research project SUSTEL (Sustainable Teleworking) carried out across five European countries to investigate the environmental sustainability of telecommuting (i.e. home-based employees working remotely, using telecommunications) support this idea.[13] They indicate that teleworking significantly reduces non-business travel even when 'rebound' effects (i.e. increases in travel that result from not commuting) are taken into account. In a review four years later of the environmental impact of homeworking by its employees, one of the original participants, British Telecom (BT), found a saving of around 7,000 tonnes of carbon emissions a year on a net basis, with rebound effects accounting for less than 10 per cent of the saving.[14] The most recent UK census attributes a drop of 5.5 per cent in people commuting to work by car between 2001 and 2011 to an increase in home-based work.[15]

Make less

The current dominant practice of going out to work leaves homes empty during the working day and workplaces deserted at night and at the weekend. This is an inefficient use of space. Workhomes, in contrast, tend to be occupied around the clock. A more intensely inhabited building stock could then potentially be smaller; indeed, BT reports that teleworking has 'substantially contributed to halving the size of its property portfolio'.[16] BAA has released an entire building as a result of its home-based work policy. And the UK company, Word Association, has given up having a central office at all. Everyone now works at home.[17]

In the UK, home-based work is often carried out in under-used domestic space, or in spaces that transform between domestic and workplace functions according to the time of day.[18] A BT manager converted his dining room into an office; a curtain-maker works in

10. Labour Force Survey, ONS, Characteristics of Home Workers, 2014, available at: www.ons.gov.uk/ons/rel/lmac/characteristics-of-home-workers/2014/rpt-home-workers.html (accessed 20 June 2014); Holliss, op. cit. (2007).

11. S. Sinha, Rights of Home-based Workers (2006).

12. UK Office for National Statistics, Commuting to Work (2011), available at: www.ons.gov.uk/ons/dcp171776_227904.pdf (accessed 17 Dec. 2013).

13. P. James, Is Teleworking Sustainable? An Analysis of its Economic, Environmental and Social Impacts (2004), p. 23.

14. P. James, Homeworking at BT: The Economic, Environmental and Social Impacts, (2008), p. 36; BT Group PLC, Sustainability Review (2011), available at: www.bt.com/betterfuture, p. 9 (accessed 19 Nov. 2012).

15. UK Office for National Statistics, Table KS15, in Travel to Work (UK Census 2001); Table CT0015 in Method of Travel to Work (UK Census 2011).

16. Hopkinson and James, op. cit., p. 18.

FIG. 6.2 *Musician's workspace addition to his terraced house*
FIG. 6.3 *Graphic designer's garden home-office*

17. N.J. Millard, Clouds, Crowds and Customers: Doing Business as 'Unusual' (2010); Hopkinson and James, ibid., p. 17.

18. Holliss, op. cit. (2007).

19. Hopkinson and James, op. cit., p. 21.

her garage; a social policy researcher and a curator both work on their dining-room tables when their families are out of the house. Even when new space is constructed to turn home or workplace into workhome, for example, when a musician adds a workroom to his terraced house [**Fig. 6.2**] or a graphic designer builds an office in her garden [**Fig. 6.3**], ancillary spaces such as the kitchen and the WC remain in dual use. Home-based work therefore intensifies the use of property and contributes, without the need for new buildings, to more densely populated villages, towns and cities. So long as the new spaces are well insulated, this is good for the environment. It also generates a wide range of social benefits that will be discussed later.

Heat less

People who go out to work generally warm their home in the morning, leave it to go cold during the day and then re-warm it in the evening, while workplaces are heated during the day and then left to go cold overnight. This is inherently wasteful. The SUSTEL study assumes that the amount of energy consumed in the home rises in direct proportion to the increased amount of time spent at home as a result of home-based work.[19] But interviews with UK home-based workers do not support this hypothesis. While environmental sustainability is not yet a common priority, most home-based workers are frugal with heat because they have to pay the bills themselves. This energy cost-consciousness leads people to adapt their behaviour, to minimize the amount they heat their homes during the working day. A winter email exchange about this with a SUSTEL researcher revealed him to be typing in his home office (aka his garage) wearing two pullovers, thick socks and slippers and still verging on cold to keep his heating costs down. A journalist wears a woolly hat while she works and takes brief 'fire-breaks' in front of an electric heater. An artist living and working collectively with six other artists says:

We tried heating the studios – we all had electric heaters – and then we had an electricity bill of £4000. So we had to stop that. We don't heat the studios at all now and it gets cold in there, really cold. We put on two jumpers, two trousers and two pairs of socks to go to work.

Most of the home-based workers interviewed for this book heat their homes minimally during the working day. This, together with a demonstrably shrinking building stock and the fact that people are less careful with heat when their employer is paying the bill, suggests that home-based work can contribute to an overall reduction in energy use for heating. The SUSTEL project reached the same conclusion.[20]

The rebound phenomenon

More research is, however, needed to develop and disseminate an understanding of the rebound phenomenon. While most studies of teleworkers' travel habits show a reduction in overall travel, a few report the opposite.[21] This is because some people spend the money they save by not commuting on activities that involve high carbon emissions, such as holidays in the sun, while others replace regular short work-orientated journeys with longer, less frequent trips. A Cornish home-based worker, for example, flies to monthly meetings in London. Geographically isolated home-based workers can find that trips that would previously have been part of their journey to work, such as driving to the shop, taking kids to school or visiting the doctor, still have to be made. In such cases home-based work can increase, not reduce, travel and therefore carbon emissions. If corporations do not reorganize and downsize their property portfolios, home-working policies can lead to under-used and unnecessarily heated corporate buildings. And a shift from working in a well-insulated workplace to a heated but poorly insulated workhome can increase, not reduce, carbon emissions. These rebound effects will reduce as awareness of the imperative to reduce carbon emissions grows. Public transport routes will grow to cover less densely populated areas more effectively. Teleconferencing technologies will improve and be more widely used. Fewer people will fly to holiday destinations, even if they can afford to. Under-used space will become less common, and priority will be given to insulating buildings that are used day and night.

People currently work at home or live at their workplace primarily for social and/or economic reasons. If carbon emissions are reduced as a result, this is a side effect. Unless a technological leap provides us with unlimited non-polluting energy, home-based work is likely to be a necessary though not sufficient condition of combating dangerous climate change. Environmental sustainability is the overriding contemporary challenge. Thousands of organizations are striving globally for a low carbon future. These include worldwide intergovernmental organizations, government departments in almost every country in the world, international non-government organizations, as well as continental and national organizations. And millions of individuals are also working to lower their carbon footprint.

20. Ibid., p. 21.

21. For example, B.E. Koenig, D.K. Henderson, and P.L. Mokhtarian, 'The Travel and Emissions Impacts of Telecommuting for the State of California Telecommuting Pilot Project', (1996), pp.13–32; R. Hamer, E. Kroes, and H. Van Ooststroom, 'Teleworking in the Netherlands: An Evaluation of Changes in Travel Behavior', (1991), pp. 365–82, cited in S. Cairns et al., Smarter Choices: Changing the Way We Travel (2004); C. Penfold, S. Webster, H. Neil, H. Ranns and J. Graham, Understanding the Needs, Attitudes and Behaviours of Teleworkers (2009).

The idea that home-based work offers an additional strategy for reducing carbon emissions can contribute to this intensifying debate.

An economically sustainable working practice

Hard economics, not the potential to contribute to global carbon reductions, is driving the current rapid increase in home-based work. In highly developed and developing economies alike, this working practice creates economic growth in three ways: (1) by increasing the efficiency of large organizations; (2) by encouraging new businesses; and (3) by supporting economic activity amongst marginal members of society.

There remains a fairly widespread view that working at home encourages skiving and causes management problems. But there is plenty of evidence that the opposite is true. Employing home-based workers increases the profitability of major corporations by reducing overheads. BT reports annual savings of £6,000 in overheads on each of its 15,000 home-based employees, a total of £90 million a year.[22] And being home-based makes their employees happier and more productive, which increases profits further. BT's home-based call-centre workers handle a fifth more calls than their office-based counterparts. They take a third less time off sick and have a 99 per cent return-to-work rate after maternity leave.[23] This is in the context of almost half the 440,000 women pregnant annually in Great Britain experiencing some form of disadvantage at work, simply for being pregnant or taking maternity leave, and 30,000 being forced out of their jobs each year.[24]

BT is not alone in pursuing home-based work as an economic strategy. The SUSTEL study tells us that:

Telecom Italia's Info412 call-centre operation has almost a quarter of its workforce teleworking. They spend 15% less time on calls than non-teleworkers. For this and other reasons they take 3.3% more calls per hour. Similar results came from a carefully monitored pilot scheme amongst Bradford Council benefits staff who process all claims electronically. The teleworkers achieved an 11–38% productivity improvement (measured as claims processed per hour), with an overall average gain of 25%, compared to non-teleworkers. Accuracy levels have remained similar. The teleworkers also had an 80% reduction in absenteeism rates.[25]

Home-based work makes sound business sense in large organizations, facilitating growth by reducing overheads, raising the productivity of existing workers and increasing the size of the workforce without capital outlay on premises.

This working practice also creates growth at the other end of the scale. Most businesses start from home to minimize overheads and ease the long hours that are often required to get an enterprise off the ground. Walt Disney started up in his uncle's garage in Los

22. BT, Flexible Working: Can Your Company Compete Without It? (2007).

23. Ibid.

24. Equal Opportunities Commission, Greater Expectations; Final Report of the EOC's Investigation into Discrimination against New and Expectant Mothers in the Workplace, (2005).

25. James, op. cit. (2004).

Angeles in 1923; the company achieved a gross income of over $42 billion in 2012. The Body Shop, bought by L'Oréal for $1.14 billion in 2006, began with Anita Roddick mixing ingredients at home with her daughters. Apple Computers [**Fig. 6.4**], Hershey's chocolate empire and the Ford Motor Company also started from home. This working practice is a hidden economic driver in advanced economies globally. Nearly one million Australians run a business from home, from an overall population of 21.4 million.[26] And the US Small Business Association reports that more than half the businesses registered in the United States are home-based, contributing more than $530 billion annually to the US economy.[27] In the UK, a third of all enterprises remain home-based.[28] Of these, one in ten has a turnover of more than £250,000 per annum.[29] The collective value of home-based business to the UK economy is difficult to verify because there are no studies that provide a detailed economic profile of this sector.[30] However, small and medium sized enterprises (SMEs) overall accounted for more than half of employment (59.1 per cent) and almost half of turnover (48.8 per cent) in the UK private sector at the start of 2012.[31] Although they are generally smaller than their premises-based counterparts,[32] in 2009, the commentator Emma Jones of Enterprise Nation estimated the annual contribution of home-based businesses to the UK economy at £284 billion.[33]

And there is yet another layer of the economy that depends on home-based work. Marx labelled the people working in it 'petty commodity producers'. They are the diverse, marginal, informal workers.[34] Although it is historically dismissed as an anomaly, sociologists and economists increasingly accept this sector as a 'necessary outgrowth' and driver of both developing economies and advanced capitalism.[35] The World Bank estimates that this 'shadow economy' contributes substantially globally.[36] An investigation of 151 countries in 2010 found that its contribution ranged from 8.5 per cent of Swiss GDP to 66.1 per cent of Bolivian GDP and thus raised this aspect of the economy into view by recognizing its impact and value.[37] This sector is diverse. In less developed countries it tends to include street food traders and refuse workers, as well as the menders and makers of a wide variety of goods. In the UK, two aspects of it exist side by side: people knit, sew, iron and provide informal childcare. They sell cheap clothing from bin-liners in their living rooms, bake cakes and make fried delicacies for sale in neighbourhood corner shops. But they also make music and art, design furniture, clothing and software, run pop-up cafés and courses on street art. The inherent marginality of all aspects of this shadow economy, however, in every part of the world, generally means these people either work in their homes or live at their workplaces. Such home-based micro-businesses form a substantial and stable segment of the economies of both less and more developed countries.[38] The Kathmandu Declaration on Women Workers in the Informal Sector (2000) noted the existence of more than 50 million informal home-based workers in South Asia.[39] The World Bank study considers it 'obvious' that

26. According to Australian Government initiative, See www.business.gov.au/BusinessTopics/Homebasedbusiness/Pages/default.aspx (accessed 15 Jan. 2013).

27. See www.startupnation.com/business-articles/8990/1/2007-home-based-100.htm (accessed 15 Jan. 2013).

28. In 2006/7, 51% of businesses were home-based at start-up. See Annual Small Business Survey 2006/7, Department for Business, Enterprise and Regulatory Reform, (2007), cited in C. Mason, S. Carter, and S. Tagg, (2008), p. 5.

29. Mason et al., op. cit., p. 2.

30. Ibid., p. 6.

31. Parliamentary Select Committee on Small and Medium Sized Enterprises, Roads to Success: SME Exports (2013).

32. Mason et al., op. cit., p. 16.

33. E. Jones, Home Business Report (2009), p. 2. Estimate calculated from the regional datasets given for Small and Medium Enterprise Statistics for the UK and Regions (2008) by the Department for Business Innovation and Skills.

34. C.O.N. Moser, 'Informal Sector or Petty Commodity Production: Dualism or Dependence in Urban Development?', (1978), pp. 1041–64.

FIG. 6.4 *Apple Computers started in Steve Jobs' parents' garage in Los Altos, CA*

35. S. Sassen, 'The Informal Economy: Between New Developments and Old Regulations', (1994), pp. 2289–304. See also M. Castells and A. Portes, 'World Undernеath: The Origins, Dynamics and Effects of the Informal Economy', (1989), p. 11.

36. Defined as including all market-based legal production of goods and services that are deliberately concealed from public authorities for any of the following reasons:
(1) to avoid payment of income, value added or other taxes,
(2) to avoid payment of social security contributions,
(3) to avoid having to meet certain legal labor market standards, such as minimum wages, maximum working hours, safety standards, etc., and
(4) to avoid complying with certain administrative procedures, such as completing statistical questionnaires or other administrative forms', but excluding 'crimes like burglary, robbery, drug dealing, etc.

37. F. Schneider, A. Buehn, and C.E. Montenegro, 'Shadow Economies All over the World: New Estimates for 162 Countries from 1999 to 2007', (2010).

38. R.M. Sudarshan and S. Sinha, Making Home-based Work Visible: A Review of Evidence from South Asia (2011).

one of the big challenges for every government is to undertake efficient incentive-orientated policy measures in order to make work less attractive in the shadow economy and, thus, to make work in the official economy more attractive.[40]

But many would disagree, as they view this informal economy as an essential and valuable component of developed capitalism, providing a flexible workforce able to respond rapidly to fluctuating economic conditions and driving creativity.[41] Owning the means of production, albeit on a tiny scale and as a result of rejecting regulation, releases this workforce from more centralized relations of capitalist production and exchange. This can help vulnerable people who might otherwise be excluded, such as the poorly educated, the sick and the elderly, to work. It can also provide the creative sector with unhampered opportunities to experiment and innovate.

Home-based work contributes to growth in the global economy in these three ways. It is curious, therefore, that it is rarely included in social and economic policy or in the wider debate about sustainable economics. WIEGO,[42] campaigning to support home-based women workers in the informal sector, reports:

Few governments try to find out how many home-based workers there are, in what sectors they are working, and what their economic contribution really is. So, there are hardly any official statistics on home-based workers. They are usually ignored in economic development programmes, employment legislation and social security systems. When they are noticed, governments tend to classify them all as 'entrepreneurs' rather than the 'workers' that many are – let alone as workers with rights under law.[43]

Both the International Labour Organization (ILO) and the Organization for Economic Co-operation and Development (OECD) have developed policies on home-based work. But, piecemeal and fragmented, these focus on individual areas of concern. And there is a problem with terminology. 'Home-based work', 'home-work', 'homework' (some of which refer to children's after-school work), 'telework' and 'telecommute' are sometimes used interchangeably. But they are also used to differentiate between different sorts of home-based work, particularly between informal sweated labour in developing countries and flexible working practices in developed countries. The resultant policies tend to focus on issues concerning one particular group and therefore have limited application. This may explain why the ILO C177 Home Work Convention (1996), for example, has been ratified by only seven of the ILO's 185 member countries. An analysis of research in the field found 30 different terms used for home-based workers, each defined slightly differently to refer to a distinct subset of the whole.[44]

It is this whole, however, that is of real interest here. And what is currently lacking and urgently needed is an analysis that locates *all* contemporary home-based work in advanced capitalism, from the poorest slum-dweller working on their own account in India to the UK Prime Minister in Downing Street. This book aims to address this. Using the term 'workforce' to describe all home-based workers may be sociologically contentious, as it appears to ignore basic Marxist principles by incorporating the owners of the means of production, workers and petty commodity producers into a single group. But considering all people who live at their workplaces or work in their homes as a workforce can help us to understand and support through appropriate policies the part this working practice could play in creating a more economically sustainable future.

It could also help to prevent the repetition of past mistakes. There is a strong similarity, for example, between contemporary movements to clean up and regulate informal home-based work in India, and the nineteenth-century UK slum clearances. A reported 60 per cent of Mumbai's 20 million people are slum-dwellers. Most live and work in tiny single-room 'hutments' or in a room over a workshop. Metalworkers and potters, chilli-crushers and shoemakers, cooks and tailors live and work cheek by jowl **[Fig. 6.5]**. The BBC recently estimated the annual turnover of Dharavi, one of Mumbai's largest slums, at $650 million, with goods being exported all around the world.[45] A great deal could be learned about sustainable urban

39. M. A. Chen, R. Jhabvala and F. Lund, 'Supporting Workers in the Informal Economy: A Policy Framework', (2002).

40. Schneider et al., op. cit. (2010) p. 36.

41. For example, ILO, Women and Men in the Informal Economy: A Statistical Picture (2002); A. Weston, 'Creativity in the Informal Economy of Zimbabwe', PhD, Kingston University (2012).

42. WIEGO (Women in Informal Employment: Globalising and Organising) is a global research-policy-action network that seeks to improve the status of the working poor, especially women, in the informal economy.

43. C. Mather, 'We Are Workers Too! Organising Home-based Workers in the Global Economy' (2010).

44. Holliss, op. cit. (2007), p. 51.

FIG. 6.5 *Metalworkers and potters, chilli-crushers and shoe-makers, cooks and tailors live and work cheek by jowl, Dharavi, Mumbai*

45. See http://news.bbc.co.uk/1/shared/spl/hi/world/06/dharavi_slum/html/dharavi_slum_intro.stm (accessed 22 Jan. 2013).

46. V. Mukhija, *Squatters as Developers? Slum Redevelopment in Mumbai* (2003), p. 7.

47. A. Sen, 'Poor, Relatively Speaking', the Fifteenth Geary Lecture, *The Economic and Social Research Institute* (1982).

48. A. Sen, *Development as Freedom* (1999), p. 29.

development from these settlements. But instead, as with the nineteenth-century East End London slums, widespread clearances are being carried out. Apparently motivated by improving poor sanitation and overcrowding, organizations like the Mumbai Slum Rehabilitation Authority permit developers to profit from demolishing informal settlements and building 'free-sale' buildings, on the condition that eligible slum structures are replaced. On the face of it, this is a progressive policy. But the bleak replacement housing is reminiscent of early twentieth-century UK social housing [**Fig. 6.6**]. Designed to Western standards to be hygienic and also, specifically, to discourage home-based work, it lacks the intricate multi-layered urban qualities of the slum [**Fig. 6.7**]. Such regeneration policies benefit developers while leaving slum-dwellers in a worse situation than before, transformed into property-owners but robbed of their ability to earn a living.[46] The economist and Nobel Laureate, Amartya Sen, makes the powerful argument that the assessment of a standard of living should focus on

neither commodities, nor characteristics, nor utility, but something that may be called a person's capability.[47]

Being deprived of the capability to work, as part of a micro-enterprise or of the informal home-based workforce that hovers around the periphery of all modern economies, is a basic 'unfreedom'.[48] This approach to deprivation turns conventional thinking about poverty on its head. The Mumbai slum-dweller, with the capability to 'truck, barter and trade' but with only a communal toilet and tap, emerges as less deprived than the UK social tenant whose home, despite having a private bathroom, is designed to discourage and managed to prohibit home-based economic activity. Sen argues that: 'Top down interventions, by state or international organizations, not sensitive to local livelihoods will destroy the existing capabilities

FIG. 6.6 *Replacement housing, Dharavi, Mumbai, 2009*

49. A.A. Frediani, 'The World Bank, Turner and Freedom in the Urban Arena', (2009), p. 10.

50. M. Nussbaum and A. Sen (eds), The Quality of Life (1993), p. 36.

51. W.A. Lewis, The Theory of Economic Growth (1955), pp. 98–9, cited in H.W. Arndt, Economic Development (1987), p. 177.

52. A. Colantonio, 'Social Sustainability: An Exploratory Analysis of its Definition, Assessment Methods, Metrics and Tools', in Measuring Social Sustainability: Best Practice from Urban Renewal in the EU (2007), pp. 6–7.

acquired by dwellers and will generate further difficulties for the poor to emerge from poverty.'[49]

This seems to be exactly what is happening. Demolishing the Indian slums and replacing them with slabs of medium-rise housing built to a pattern specifically developed in the UK to discourage home-based work deprives the poor of the basic capability to work. And this brings with it a loss of complex functionings, such as being happy, achieving self-respect, taking part in the life of the community, appearing in public without shame, a loss which is suffered by many residents of UK social housing.[50] It also has a negative impact on the economy. The opposite approach is needed. UK social housing reconceived to embody the urban and economic qualities of the Mumbai slum would transform both the city and the lives and prospects of its occupants.

But this working practice, with its potential to promote economic sustainability, remains stubbornly invisible. Even the New Economics Foundation (NEF), the most likely of UK think-tanks, makes no reference to home-based work, though its strapline is 'Economics as if people and the planet mattered', and its mission statement is 'We aim to improve quality of life by promoting innovative solutions that challenge mainstream thinking on economic, environment and social issues. We work in partnership and put people and the planet first.' And this is despite the fact that NEF has a major interest in local money and how it can stay local, rather than be swallowed up by the big corporations.

The development economist and Nobel Laureate Arthur Lewis wrote:

The advantage of economic growth is not that wealth increases happiness, but that it increases the range of human choice … The case for economic growth is that it gives man greater control over his environment, and thereby increases his freedom.[51]

FIG. 6.7 *Intricate multi-layered urban qualities of the slum, Dharavi, Mumbai, 2009*

This incontrovertible benefit of home-based work will be discussed in the next section.

A socially sustainable working practice

Social sustainability can be defined as the ability of a community to develop processes and structures that meet the needs both of current members and of future generations. It blends traditional social objectives and policy areas, such as equity and health, with issues concerning the economy, the environment and, more recently, notions of participation, social capital, happiness, well-being and quality of life.[52] This section explores the impact home-based work has on our lives and communities, and its potential in terms of social sustainability.

This is an emerging concept. The least studied dimension of sustainable development, it is often overlooked. Reviewing the field, urban geographer and economist Andrea Colantonio refers to it as 'an end state in which all human activities can be maintained within the existing capacity of the planet'. He identifies a number of key

53. Ibid., p. 6.

54. M. Marmot, The Status Syndrome: How Your Social Status Directly Affects Your Health and Life Expectancy (2004), p. 2.

55. Ibid., p. 39.

56. As elsewhere in this book, the term 'work' is used here to refer to paid productive, rather than unpaid reproductive, work. But, especially in the case of artists, the work in question is not necessarily monetized.

57. R. Layard, 'Happiness: Has Social Science a Clue?' (2003), pp. 5–9.

FIG. 6.8 *Andrea Colantonio's thematic dimensions to social sustainability*

Dimension	Key theme area
Social	1. Acess to resources 2. Community needs (e.g. are communities able to articulate their needs?) 3. Conflicts mitigation 4. Cultural promotion 5. Education 6. Elderly and aging 7. Enabling knowledge management (including access to E-knowledge) 8. Freedom 9. Gender equity 10. Happiness 11. Health 12. Identity of the community / civic pride 13. Image transformation and neighbourhood perceptions 14. Integration of newcomers (especially foreign in-migrants) and residents 15. Leadership 16. Justice and equality 17. Leisure and sport facilities 18. Less able people 19. Population change 20. Poverty eradication 21. Quality of Life 22. Security and Crime 23. Skills developmemt 24. Social diversity and multiculturalism 25. Well being
Socio-Institutional	26. Capacity Building 27. Participation and empowerment 28. Trust, voluntary organisations and local networks (also known as Social Capital)
Socio-economic	29. Economic security 30. Employment 31. Informal activities / economy 32. Partnership and collaboration
Socio-environmental	33. Inclusive design 34. Infrastructures 35. Environmental Health 36. Housing (quality and tenure mix) 37. Transport 38. Spatial / environmental inequalities

thematic areas [**Fig. 6.8**].[53] The practice of home-based work has a bearing on many of these.

The people interviewed for this book spoke articulately and at great length about the problematic aspects of working at home or living at their workplace. Their comments stretch to 28 pages of data, densely spaced and in a small font. And yet, despite these outpourings of frustration and discontent, only five of the 86 say they would prefer to go out to work. Why is this?

A fundamental benefit, mentioned by most of the people interviewed, is that home-based work increases the control they have over their lives. Epidemiologist Michael Marmot found that: 'Autonomy – how much control you have over your life – and the opportunities you have for full social engagement and participation are crucial for health, wellbeing, and longevity.'[54] His studies of the 'exquisitely stratified' British civil service found 'the men at the bottom of the office hierarchy have, at ages forty to sixty-four, four times the risk of death of the administrators at the top of the hierarchy'.[55]

This increase in control is independent of occupation or status. The Mumbai slum-dwelling handbag-maker can take as much pleasure in having a break from her work to go upstairs and read her child a story in bed as the British Prime Minister in 10 Downing Street. The inherent flexibility of this working practice allows people to combine the different aspects of their lives, creative, economic, domestic and caring, in the way that best suits them, no matter how menial (or important) the work. This improves the quality of their lives.

There has been a revolution in gender roles since the 1950s and most women, globally, now expect to work.[56] Many expect to have a career, control their own finances and make an equal contribution to the domestic economy. Similarly, a growing number of men expect to play an equal role in parenting and in the domestic realm. But caring responsibilities make erratic demands. One of the shocks of becoming a parent to a school-age child in the UK is that school finishes at 3.30 p.m., halfway through the working day for many of us. And children get ill, need to be taken to the dentist and have half-term holidays. What are we meant to do? Many people manage this by employing a web of child-minders and nannies. But an increasing number shift to home-based work, organized around their children's routines.

For some, like the father who set up in business at home so he could support his wife in the care of their severely disabled first-born child or the hairdresser who started a home-based salon when she became a single parent, this social dimension is primary. For others it is one of a number of factors. A BT manager leading a trans-continental team worked intolerably long days when office-based. Taking conference calls across time zones both early in the morning and late at night, he rarely saw his young son. Now that he works at home his irregular working hours fit neatly around his child's life. And he is able to work shorter hours and take time out in the middle of the day with his son, which was impossible when he worked in an office 45 miles from home.

Home-based work allows almost half the people interviewed for this book to interweave their productive work and caring roles, including people with responsibility for a sick family member or their elders. An alternative health practitioner lives in the same block of flats as her mother:

So part of my day is popping in on my 91 year-old mother downstairs; I usually visit her twice, one reasonable visit (about an hour, usually around lunchtime, I sometimes make her lunch) and one short one. The second visit is usually between clients in the afternoon, just to check that she's all right, or to see if she wants me to go and buy her some cigarettes up the road ...

Such close but light-touch contact extends older people's independence. Both generations are able to get on with their lives, knowing that problems can be identified and resolved speedily, saving both the cost and the indignity of residential care.

Home-based work has other social benefits. It reduces time spent commuting, which most people hate. Layard, a sociologist with an interest in happiness, cites a study in which 1,000 working Texan

FIG. 6.9 *Academic and mother of three's study is a doorless extension to her kitchen*

58. G. Topham, 'Vogue's Alexandra Shulman Joins Backlash Against Working from Home', The Guardian, 2 March 2013.

59. See BT, 'Flexible Working Drives Down More Than Costs', available at: www. globalservices.bt.com/uk/en/ insights/more_productivity_ from_your_force (accessed 31 Oct. 2013); Global Workplace Analytics, Costs and Benefits: Advantages of Telecommuting for Companies, available at: www. globalworkplaceanalytics. com/resources/costs-benefits (accessed 3 Oct. 2013).

women were asked to analyse their different daily activities and attribute how they felt to each one.[57] On average they felt least happy on their morning commute, closely followed by working and the evening commute. These three most miserable activities were pursued for a total of 7.9 hours on average per day. In contrast, 94 per cent of the albeit much smaller sample in this research report positively enjoying their home-based work.

Home-based work also helps people to manage the domestic aspects of their lives. Running a home used to be considered a full time job, but is now usually carried out in parallel with paid work. Many home-based workers ease their domestic workload by tucking housework and cooking into the working day. An academic and mother-of-three's study is a door-less extension to her kitchen [**Fig. 6.9**]. It is designed specifically so she can move between computer and stove when stuck or just thinking, making the evening meal while she works. Similarly a social policy researcher says: 'I often think about the structure of a report or something while I am unloading the dishwasher, you don't stop thinking about it because you are doing something else.'

This does not just apply to women. An internationally renowned (male) photographer, working at a self-designed stand-up workstation in a dedicated workspace in his end-of-terrace house [**Fig. 6.10**], commented:

Yesterday I really enjoyed doing a day's work and the laundry at the same time as it meant I could come out [of the studio] and get a breath of fresh air, throw the washing over the line and get a bit of sun … almost the only bit of physical activity yesterday was running up and downstairs with baskets of laundry.

This does not imply, as was recently suggested by the editor of British *Vogue*,[58] that home-based workers are less focused or hard-working. Offices are notoriously inefficient places and people need to take breaks from their work. When at home these breaks can contribute to the efficient management of a busy household; in the office they are often taken up with gossip or social media. Research studies repeatedly show home-based workers to be more productive than their office-based colleagues, despite widespread stereotyping to the contrary.[59]

People also use home-based work to bypass workplace discrimination. A 70-year-old translator gets her work via the Internet and telephone. Since she has a 'young' voice, her clients, whom she never meets, have no idea of her age. It is not relevant and she has no plan to retire. A home-based illustrator, similarly, works entirely via the Internet:

FIG. 6.10 *Photographer's self-designed stand-up workstation*

I like the fact that I am anonymous. There's no judgement being made on me about what I look like, people just take me for my work. I get work from my website. It's very rare I meet customers. I'm not very confident in that department.

Her relief, as a young, mixed-race woman, at being judged on the quality of her work alone is one of the factors that keeps her working in a home-based studio. A heavily pregnant graphic designer and an obese writer, also sourcing and delivering work only via their websites, express similar relief. Home-based work is also good for those who cannot work in the conventional workplace for cultural reasons or for reasons of illness, disability or poor education. A pioneering scheme in the UK supports people with low levels of literacy to foster children in their homes.[60]

60. Community Foster Care, Gloucestershire.

61. Cited in R. Putnam, Bowling Alone: The Collapse and Revival of American Community (2000), p. 19.

62. A fireman from 1950, Ian McMurtrie was Assistant Fire Master at Lauriston Fire Station for decades. His great-grandfather, grandfather and two great-uncles were all firemen; his two sons are in the Fire Service today. Mr Mac, as he is affectionately known in the fire-station, although now retired from the fire service, is Honorary Curator of the Museum of Fire at Lauriston.

63. Interview with former Lauriston fireman, Martin Kerr (June 2013).

As well as affecting individual lives, home-based work has a positive impact on the social capital of the neighbourhood. The progressive reformer L.J. Hanifan first defined this in 1916 as

the tangible substances [that] count for most in the daily lives of people: namely good will, fellowship, sympathy, and social intercourse among the individuals and families who make up a social unit … The individual is helpless socially, if left to himself. If he comes into contact with his neighbor, and they with other neighbors, there will be an accumulation of social capital, which may immediately satisfy his social needs and which may bear a social potentiality sufficient to the substantial improvement of living conditions in the whole community. The community as a whole will benefit by the cooperation of all its parts, while the individual will find in his associations the advantages of the help, the sympathy, and the fellowship of his neighbors.[61]

Historically this was often an inevitable consequence of home-based work, and was taken for granted. At the Scottish fire station discussed in Chapter Two, as well as working together the firefighters lived together as neighbours. Their 20 or so children played on the deck-access balconies to their homes that overlooked the rear fire-yard, and watched their fathers and their friends' fathers training. Maybe as a direct consequence of this close contact, working in the fire service runs in families.[62] Once the working day was over at 5.30 p.m., they were allowed to play down there. When it was cold they went up to the top-floor communal laundry where the wives did their washing. There they could play in the drying-yard, a large open-plan space that was always kept warm so clothes would dry swiftly. Even firefighters' wives who did not live at the station dried their clothes there.[63] Firefighting was considered a vocation, not just a job, and the fire-station had a collective social life that involved monthly dances, birthday and Christmas parties. At New Year families would go from flat to flat, first-footing each other. And the social impact and sense of community extended beyond the fire station itself. The pub opposite was the 'firefighters' pub', where the men and their families socialized. The fire station supported two local shops and the children all went to the same school. And, as in any closely knit community, there were also arguments and fights.

Loss of social capital is an unexpected consequence of the shift to going out to work. Built through ordinary daily contacts between family members, neighbours, local shopkeepers, tradespeople, etc., it inevitably diminishes when people spend long days working away from home. And in primarily commercial or industrial areas there is little chance of it developing. The 24-hour inhabitation of workhome and neighbourhood, inherent in home-based work, contributes to creating more socially engaged districts. It stimulates the local economy and promotes local social networks and cohesion, as home-based workers tend to shop locally and use local services. In 2006, 78 per cent of BT's registered homeworkers made more use of local services such as shops and sports facilities than they had when office-based.[64] A home-based London architect (and mother of four), with eight employees working in a mews office at the bottom of her garden, comments:

Another point about home-based work is that it creates and supports a mixed economy. I can think of at least five other people who live and work around our square as well as ourselves – all of whom go to the local shops, go out to eat at lunch time, have clients coming to the area, use the public spaces and public transport throughout the day. It is an ideal urban model in that there is integration between different activities bringing life throughout the day which impacts economically and socially. It means also that I can stay involved in various local community and school things that would be difficult to get to if I worked in a separate place. It seems to me that more people are working from home now in this local area than ten or even five years ago, and this definitely has a positive impact on the quality of life and urban spaces.

The fine-grained mix of uses that home-based work brings to the village, town and city makes areas busier, livelier and safer, as Jane Jacobs observed: 'This is something everyone knows: a well-used city street is apt to be a safe street. A deserted city street is apt to be unsafe.'[65]

This positive social impact can be seen in radically different communities of home-based workers. Twenty-five of the interviews for this book were carried out in a small UK village where most people live in their workplace or work in their home in one way or another. The newsagent, open from 5 a.m. to 7 p.m., says: 'Because it is a village we are friendly with our customers – we go into their homes and they come into ours' [**Fig. 6.11, see Fig. 3.63**]. The garage proprietor says she 'knows everyone in the village'. She does her paperwork at the kitchen table because 'there's too much going on out there to sit and do accounts and things' [**see Fig. 3.13**]. Although she sells petrol at a higher price than the supermarket in the nearest town, she says, 'a lot of people come here because they wouldn't go anywhere else because they're from the village'. She and her family

64. James, op. cit. (2008), p. 25.

65. Jacobs, op. cit. p.44

FIG. 6.11 *Village newsagent*

66. Puttnam, op. cit., p. 403.

also look after people if they are ill or have a problem: 'Very often people knock on your door when they are in trouble.' An engineer and an art gallery/framing workshop proprietor, whose combined home and workplaces open onto the village square [**Fig. 6.12, 6.13, 6.14**], also consider they have a duty of care to the village. They have developed a relaxed and flexible lifestyle around their work and family, and their long working hours mean they take time out when they want to:

If someone comes into the workshop I haven't seen for a while, I'll stop work for half an hour. You can't equate that to losing money, you can't even think about that. And [his wife] can spend a whole day listening in the shop ... It is a very social role. People come in for a coffee, or to use the WC. We see it as a social service; the fabric of life has broken down, people have no support. It's a privilege for us to be able to do it. It is a very valuable aspect of a village.

This social capital is equally palpable in communities of artists where work and home lives are indistinguishable and supported by a shared commitment to art and performance [**Fig. 6.15**]. Open-door policies mean that people wander in and out of each other's space, which leads to impromptu interactions. Friendships and collaborations develop as carpenters, product designers, drummers, filmmakers, musicians, record producers, painters and sculptors gather around a fire in the yard behind the east London buildings in which they live and work [**see Fig. 3.65**]. And in Oakland, CA, in the USA, individuals build trust, community and a sense of neighbourhood by collaborating, preparing food for each other and tending collective areas [**Fig. 6.16**].

Home-based work builds social capital, however, only when it is carried out openly, when people are aware of, and get to know, others working in their field or offering services in their neighbourhood and community. Most of the home-based workers in the rural village inhabit traditional visible, generally live-nearby or

live-adjacent, workhomes built over the past 300 years. Those in the artists' communities have collectively appropriated disused, run-down and therefore cheap industrial buildings that are known locally as centres of creativity. As US sociologist Robert Putnam says, 'Actions by individuals are not sufficient to restore community, but they *are* necessary.'[66]

When hidden, however, this working practice has the opposite effect of introducing fear and mistrust. UK suburbs teem with people working in their semi-detached homes. The relatively low density leads to many purpose-built workhome extensions. However, rather than contributing openly to the life of the neighbourhood, a great many suburban home-based workers operate in a state of constant anxiety about getting 'caught', or being 'shopped' by

FIG. 6.15 *UK, artists' collective workhome*

their neighbours. This is also the case for homeworking residents of UK social housing, who hide their work for fear of eviction. In both cases this working practice is pushed underground for fear of adverse governance frameworks: in suburbia relating to planning permission and payment of property tax, and in social housing relating to tenancy agreements that prohibit home-based work. The consequences, of neighbours living in fear of each other and people operating outside important frameworks such as the Fire Regulations or Child-minder Registration, are corrosive. In these circumstances, home-based workers become isolated and disempowered members of disconnected communities. Any sense of community identity or civic pride is eroded, and newcomers are seen as a threat. When atomized and hidden, this workforce can struggle to thrive.

Social isolation is a problem for many contemporary home-based workers. A journalist says:

It's not very good for you, mentally, to spend so much time alone … I have a pal, and I email her a lot, but it isn't real … she's in her little hole and I'm in my little hole … I need to keep an eye on myself in terms of isolation and mental health.

An architect also struggles with isolation:

It can get really depressive working at home on my own, I enjoy it to a certain extent; I enjoy having my own space … it gives me a break from my partner, or from colleagues. But sometimes I feel as if am not socializing a lot. It can be a very isolating experience.

The need to avoid such social isolation, paradoxically, often drives development of the social capital discussed earlier. The managing director of a manufacturing company, for example, is part of a lunch club with six other home-based workers in his village who, although working in different occupations, interact as colleagues. He also has a circle of twelve close village friends who regularly meet up for a drink,

FIG. 6.16 Community-building through tending collective areas

and go on holiday together. The two networks help to prevent the isolation he could feel as both a home-based worker and the parent of a severely disabled child. Home-based workers often interpret loosely what a 'colleague' is. A poet's colleagues take the form of a writing group and a writing buddy. She meets up with them regularly in a local community bookshop. A chronically ill website designer walks 20 minutes down the road to see a costume designer every day. Although they work in different fields, both are home-based and they relate as colleagues as well as friends.

She is my 'co-worker at the water cooler', I know all the stuff she's working on, and vice versa, so it does become an environment where you can go in and talk about little bits of progress you have made and so on, frustration with a client.

The brief daily excursion gets him out of his flat, helps his condition, and gives him the chance to share the ups and downs of his work. Despite working in different occupations, their issues overlap and both find the fresh perspective helpful.

Many home-based workers use digital media to combat isolation. A BT manager texts and chats with friends when they are online. An architect has developed 'essential relationships' with other home-based workers via a number of on-line support groups. An academic writes a popular daily blog, which gets lots of responses.

But for many, isolation simply is not a problem. They include those with employees; those whose work involves interactions with members of the public; those with large families or busy social lives outside their work; those (like musicians or artists) who have developed a discipline about solitary work, and those where there is more than one member of the household in home-based work. Only a fifth of the people interviewed for this book find it a problem. And most of these have developed a creative solution that, in turn, contributes to increasing local social capital. The 2005 US Office

of Personnel Management (OPM) survey of Federal Government agencies found 87 per cent of Federal employees were interested in teleworking. Of the 13 per cent who would not telework if given the option, only just over half (in other words, just 7 per cent of the overall total) said isolation was the primary deterrent.[67] The SUSTEL survey found 46 per cent of BT's registered homeworkers felt more isolated from their colleagues in the two years from 2006 to 2008. But it also found that 61 per cent of BT's field workers and 32 per cent of their office-based workers did so too, suggesting that being home-based was not the primary factor.[68]

The social isolation of home-based workers is made worse by cities designed to protect the privacy and gender-defined roles of the nuclear family. As Danish urban designer Jan Gehl says: 'First we shape the cities, then they shape us.'[69] Community and collectivity, including shared space, can reduce isolation. A furniture-maker speaks of the industrial estate where he lives and works with his family:

It's a lovely community, buying the freehold means we are all committed to each other and the community. It's very friendly and neighbourly. There are no other kids, and only three units where people are living [as well as working]. No one would grass us up [their residential use is illicit]. Everyone likes it that we live here as well as work here; it provides an extra pair of eyes, makes it more secure. We've recently put in new collective bike racks, and we do collective gardening.

A photographer in a gated live/work development comments:

I really enjoy being part of the community – there are creative people around all day … I have no sense of isolation. I have the big doors open in summer, and meet people because they walk past … we just talk to each other.

But the opportunity to incorporate collective space in workhome developments is often missed; an architect inhabiting a live/work unit said:

It's quite handy having a whole bunch of other people doing similar things around. Occasionally I borrow things, or they borrow things, or we do things together … I'm in the corner here, so if I leave the door open, people don't tend to walk in, but I've got a friend next to the lift and the staircase and he gets to see a lot of what is going on. I know a lot of people here … We need a shared space, but it hasn't happened, apart from the formal Indian restaurant [on the ground floor]. We really needed a bar, or a café where people could have breakfast. It's a missed opportunity.

A start-up businessman in an affordable live/work unit concurs:

There is no collective space for the eight units in the scheme, that includes a photographer, an IT specialist, an on-line fashion designer,

67. CDW Government Inc., 2005 Federal Telework Report. See http://newsroom.cdwg.com/news-releases/news-release-01-31-05.html (accessed 1 Nov. 13).

68. James, op. cit. (2008), p. 25.

69. V. Law and J. Gehl, The Progressive (Dec. 2012/Jan. 2013), p. 37 (this echoes Sir Winston Churchill: 'We shape our buildings and afterwards they shape us', (meeting in the House of Lords), 28 October 1943).

some ceramics designers, a craft import business and myself in corporate finance. We bump into each other in the corridor ... but rarely go into each other's units. If there was some collective space it would be excellent.

Shared space is, as a result, often appropriated space. A graffiti artist, part of a community of 200 young creative people living and working in a series of industrial buildings, also speaks of the importance of community: 'It's almost like an art-house film I'm living. The yard is a collective external space where the community gathers. Sometimes there are fifteen people chilling out there, sitting on sofas around a big fire of pallets.'

Similarly, a yard behind a photographer's workhome, intended for car parking, is a social space in the summer, where the people living and working in the block can share a beer after a day's work.

Gehl identifies the importance of creating opportunities for social interaction in cities:

I'd say the most important thing is the daily encounters – we need shared spaces where we meet our fellow citizens. That's an important part of a good democracy – that you can actually meet your fellow citizens of all walks of life on a daily basis.[70]

This can be provided by intermediary places such as cafés, hubs, libraries and community centres, as well as playgrounds, parks, squares and leisure centres.

Home-based work has the potential to promote such social sustainability only if it is visible.[71] As we have seen, many buildings that seem to be houses are also workplaces. This invisibility results in problems with occupational identity for some home-based workers.

French philosopher Henri Lefebvre's work provides a framework for interpreting home-based workers' attitudes to their work and buildings.[72] Rejecting the idea of space as a fact of nature, an empty vessel in which activities take place, Lefebvre thinks of space as a product of the ideas, and in particular the power relationships, of the society that produces it.[73] He proposes the social production of space, describing the city as 'a space that is fashioned, shaped and invested by social activities during a finite historical period'.[74] His concept of 'lived' space, which centres on the ideas that people have about spaces in their heads, is useful when thinking about design for home-based work.

As lived space, different workspaces (the corporate office, the designer's or artist's studio, the factory, the hairdressing salon) conjure up particular images in our minds. Some are formal, even opulent, some casually chic, while others are clinical and hygienic or chaotic, untidy and even dirty. They do not, however, usually incorporate

70. Jan Gehl, *The Progressive* (Dec. 2012/Jan. 2013), p. 38.

71. Parts of this section were first published in *Sociological Research Online* (May 2012).

72. 'Henri Lefebvre, the most prolific of French Marxist intellectuals, died during the night of 28–29 June 1991, less than a fortnight after his ninetieth birthday. During his long career, his work has gone in and out of fashion several times, and has influenced the development not only of philosophy but also of sociology, geography, political science and literary criticism.' M. Kelly, 'Henri Lefebvre, 1901–1991' (1992).

73. H. Lefebvre, *The Production of Space* (1991), pp. 1–67.

74. *Ibid.*, p. 73.

FIG. 6.17 Artist in double-height studio

either children or domesticity. Since occupational identity is closely associated with such spaces, what happens to it when we engage in home-based work?

The design and inhabitation of the workhome affect home-based workers' occupational identities in different ways. **Figure 6.17** shows an artist standing in his double-height studio filled with a painter's paraphernalia, a number of works in progress on the walls. Upstairs a completed painting hangs on the wall, but his compact living space is chaotic [**Fig. 6.18**]. Laundry is draped over the stair; papers and meal remnants cover the table; there are piles of clutter throughout. While earning his living mainly as an academic, this home-based worker's occupational identity is embedded in his creative work and this dominates his workhome. To him, his untidiness contributes to his identity as an artist:

FIG. 6.18 Artist's mezzanine living space

FIG. 6.19 *Architect's
kitchen/technical library
devoid of personal
artifacts*

*Clients come to my studio, it doesn't matter to me that it's my home
as well. Mostly they don't come upstairs, but it doesn't bother me
anyway, people expect artists' studios to be untidy. I don't need to
keep my world private. It's very personal work, so I'm opening up
my personal world anyway; I don't have to keep up some kind of an
image.*

The converse is true of many other home-based workers. While
the design and inhabitation of the artist's double-height studio and
untidy mezzanine living quarters reinforce his sense of who he is, the
architect who inhabits the self-designed live/work unit in **Figure 3.6**
is concerned that his work may not be taken seriously, primarily
because the building is at a domestic scale: 'An architect's office
should be a barn-like structure with a 6-metre high ceiling, open
trusses and big industrial windows, just like in Shoreditch. That is
what I would like.' His kitchen also, doubling as a technical library, is
kept spotlessly clean, tidy and, like the rest of the building, devoid
of personal artifacts or evidence of domestic inhabitation [**Fig. 6.19**].
The domestic and personal are erased in an attempt to imprint a
professional identity on the building and its spaces. For both the artist
and the architect, therefore, ideas of what their working environment
should be like seem to drive the way they inhabit their space and
make it conform to and reinforce their occupational identities.

Only five interviewees would prefer to go out to work if they had
the option, just 6 per cent of the total. Of these, four are architects
and one works in financial services, and the central problem they
all have is with their occupational identity as a home-based worker.
Their workhomes do not match up to their aspirations and each is
concerned that their work is not taken seriously because they work in
a domestic context.

Many home-based occupations involve interaction with the public.
Those undertaken by people interviewed for this book include baker,

FIG. 6.20 *Curator's invisible work disappears when family life appears*

car mechanic, publican, funeral director, child-minder, manager of a historic house, rector and school caretaker. Most of these people live at their workplaces rather than working in their homes. These workhomes are often publicly identifiable, and as a result these people receive recognition and respect for their home-based work and for the role that they play in their communities. The imprint of the buildings they inhabit on the built fabric of the neighbourhood reinforces their occupational identities [**see Fig. 1.26**, **3.5**, **3.13**, **3.24**, **3.27**, **3.36**].

In contrast, many home-based workers inhabiting home-dominated workhomes face serious difficulties, both with carving out appropriate space in which to work and with asserting and maintaining their occupational identities. The images of a social policy researcher at work [**see Fig. 3.21**, **3.25**] provide clues to work-related struggles between herself, her domestic partner, her children, and even visiting friends and relations. Papers strewn across her kitchen table have to be moved when her children return home from school. And when people come to stay, she loses her workroom. Neither kitchen nor guest-room provides her with a formal space in which she can work in a 'business-like way'. Her role as wife and mother takes precedence. The exterior of her workhome [**see Fig. 3.51**] gives no clues to passers-by, or to the neighbourhood at large, about the work that is carried out inside, since both work and worker are invisible. Similarly, a home-based curator, who works at the table in her dining room, says: 'I would never call it my workroom. It is invisible work that disappears; when the rest of family life appears, I put it all away' [**Fig. 6.20**]. Both these home-based workers organize meetings in spaces outside their workhome, at colleagues' or clients' premises or in cafés, restaurants or bars, as a way of maintaining their professional identity.

Men and women work equally in the generally invisible IT-based occupations, such as writing, illustration or translation, that do not involve face-to-face interaction with members of the public. A similar balance is found among home-based workers, such as hairdressers or car mechanics, child-minders or shopkeepers, who work closely with the public. There is, however, a substantial gender imbalance in terms of the type of buildings these people inhabit. Nearly two-thirds of the home-based workers interviewed for this book who live at their workplace are male, while the same proportion of those working in their homes are female. This tendency is emphasized if we look at the visible and socially valued home-based worker inhabiting recognizable, generally work-dominated, buildings specifically designed for dual functions, like the pub, the funeral parlour, the school caretaker's house or the rectory. More than eight out of ten of these people are men.

In these cases, the dominant function of the workhome has a major impact on the occupational identity of the home-based worker. As well as being designed, or at least organized, to facilitate particular occupational processes, these buildings also fulfil a semiotic function. They communicate the social and economic value of the associated work to the home-based workers themselves, to their family and to the neighbourhood. This reinforces their occupational identity. The converse is often true about the workers, mainly women, who inhabit home-dominated workhomes. Here work is squeezed into house or flat, often to the detriment of both functions and the occupational identity of the home-based worker. That more men inhabit work-dominated workhomes and more women inhabit home-dominated workhomes suggests that problems with occupational identity are more common for home-based working women than for men.

The invisibility of home-based work is at the core of this problem. But workhomes, even home-dominated ones, can be designed so that the work function is explicit and visible from the street, thus reinforcing home-based workers' occupational identities. Alison Brooks Architects' 2009 housing scheme at Newhall in Harlow achieves this. The room closest to the street could be a living room or a bedroom. But, with a separate entrance and a large window overlooking the street, it also provides an ideal workspace for a variety of occupations from acupuncture to journalism, curtain-making to computer repair, and offers scope for both social interaction with passers-by and discreet signage advertising a service [**Fig. 6.21**]. Tony Fretton Architects' radical 2011 social housing scheme on Constantijn Huygenstraat in Amsterdam also achieves this by providing flexible space, with generous floor-to-ceiling heights and no load-bearing walls, equally suitable for residential and non-residential use. The governance of the scheme sets out that a fixed percentage of the space is to be in residential and non-residential use. Although not explicitly encouraging home-based work, this type of development offers a model for how the workhomes of the future might be built and managed.

FIG. 6.21 *Newhall, Harlow. Alison Brooks Architects, 2009*

Signage can increase home-based workers' visibility and reinforce their occupational identity. Booth noted people working in their homes who used signs to advertise their work. Some, selling food from their houses, had 'notices badly written on boards in front of some [houses] inviting the wayfarer to winkles, watercress, eggs and cake'.[75] Professionals had brass plates engraved with their name and occupation. This practice is still common in France and the Netherlands. But, in the UK and the USA at least, governance issues tend to stand in the way of home-based work being celebrated and openly promoted in this way.

So home-based work can contribute to social sustainability in a number of ways. By increasing the control people have over their lives, it increases their happiness, well-being and sense of freedom. By facilitating the care of dependants, it contributes to gender equality. By helping people who are older, disabled, or sick to remain or become economically active, it improves their quality of life. By rooting people more firmly in their neighbourhoods, it encourages collaboration and partnerships in the development of local social networks and local economies. By promoting these, it provides an effective tool for developing local social capital and cohesion. The idea of home-based work should be part of any discourse about social sustainability. For it to be effective, however, both a supportive corporate culture and a supportive legislative framework will be necessary.

Conclusion

Conclusion

1. Available at: www.
bbc.co.uk/blogs/
louisestewart/2011/02/
prime_minister_says_living_
abo.html> (accessed 2 Jan.
2013).

How and where we work has a major impact on our lives, on the economy and, currently, on global warming. A century in which going out to work has been the dominant working practice has resulted in home-based work being overlooked at every level of society. Both Margaret Thatcher and David Cameron have identified being Prime Minister as living above the shop, with Cameron reporting that, 'far from seeing less of [his family]' as Prime Minister, 'it was actually easier' because of this.[1] But people tend to have a stereotype in mind when they think of home-based work: maybe exploited piece-working manufacturers, penniless artists in their lofts or start-up entrepreneurs. And as a result they do not generally identify their political leaders, their neighbours, or even themselves as being members of this workforce. On a recent research trip to visit Singaporean shop-houses, I heard from a public sector worker that there is no contemporary home-based work in Singapore. When I probed his own lifestyle, however, it emerged that he works at home regularly, often until 3 a.m. Having his desk in the bedroom makes it difficult for his wife to sleep and so he is in the process of building an extra, dedicated, workroom.

Such blindness to home-based work and its social and spatial consequences is common. Layers of ideology and policy, compacted over a century, have pushed this working practice into the shadows. As a result, this workforce generally operates invisibly and often covertly in the Global North, while the slums of the Global South are being swept away and replaced with medium-rise housing in the mistaken belief that the home-based work they teem with is a problematic symptom of a backward society. This makes change difficult; home-based work is notably absent from contemporary discourses about how a more sustainable world might work. However, this working practice, properly planned and built for, could contribute to rejuvenating economies, reducing global warming, changing the shape of our buildings and cities, and improving the quality of life of millions of people globally.

People in all walks of life increasingly live at their workplaces or work in their homes. Each member of the home-based workforce, from the least to the most powerful, contributes in a small way to a more socially, environmentally and economically sustainable future. Home-based work is not a panacea that can single-handedly solve current global problems. But it is an idea that could promote a more sustainable world.

Formally easing the distinction between work and home is a substantial task. Current silos of government and ways of thinking are deeply embedded; such obstacles are different for every country and sector. But, though this presents a significant challenge, this shift offers potentially disproportionate benefit. Layard, clear that happiness must be the business of government, quotes Thomas Jefferson:

2. R. Layard, Happiness: Lessons from a New Science (2011), p. 256.

'The care of human life and happiness, and not their destruction, is the only legitimate object of good government.'[2]

In discussing happiness at work, Layard agrees with the sociologist Marmot that, though our earnings are important, increased control over our work and therefore over our lives may be an even more powerful motivating force. Home-based work can actively encourage this, no matter who we are or what our occupation or social status is. The environmental and economic arguments that support the expansion of this working practice are equally convincing.

We cannot, however, ignore the fact that working at home or living at our workplace can also be problematic. This may be because of noisy neighbours behind thin walls or floors; or because of suburban isolation and loneliness; or a result of combining family and work in already-too-small accommodation or of inhabiting cheap, but cold and damp space. Evidence gathered from hundreds of home-based workers between 2001 and 2013 indicates that the design of the buildings we live and work in and their relationship to the city are the key to making this working practice either heaven or hell.

This brings us back, full circle, to the architecture and urbanism of home-based work. There is a long tradition to draw on, when designing for this working practice, at both the building and the urban scale. Part of the essence of the historic city is a fine-grained morphology that results from it having grown up organically around home-based work. Short blocks, mews, courtyards, squares and alleyways housed myriad home-based occupations, and in many places continue to do so. Artists, when they find disued (and often apparently unusable) buildings and spaces to live and work in, create a modern version of an ancient lifestyle, which is frequently played out in spaces that resemble the medieval city. Their lives and occupations can be so closely interwoven that there is, ultimately, no difference between them. As we saw in Chapter Two, the live/work movement drew on this to stimulate the production of loft-style apartments in developed cities across the world.

However, despite some developers and architects being committed to design for home-based work, this resulted primarily in a form of commodification, creating a product that was, briefly, highly profitable for them. It did not address the real spatial, environmental and social requirements of the home-based workforce. And as a result it was a largely ephemeral movement, merely touching on what is possible. If we truly build to meet the needs of this rapidly growing population, then the buildings we inhabit and our cities will change beyond recognition.

In twenty-first-century advanced capitalism, architecture is mainly approached as a commodity: as buildings, design expertise, architectural education and also as a mechanism for attracting capital and tourists.[3] This generally results in innovation being restricted to the buildings of the wealthy, the philanthropic or the alternative fringe. As elsewhere in the market, many producers maximize profit by creating the cheapest product they can and selling it for as much as they can get away with.

This short-sighted approach reduces standards.[4] Examples of developers using scaled-down furniture to make diminutive rooms in their show-homes look bigger are common, for example.[5] It also sets up problems for the future. Buildings have a long lifespan and the damage caused by building inappropriately can impact on many generations. Taking a longer view on return on investment allows social, economic and environmental sustainability to be factored in. As has been repeatedly stated in this book, the way we live our lives is changing; the current rapid increase in home-based work looks likely to continue. A result of the information revolution among other things, this is the biggest social change since the Industrial Revolution. In the nineteenth century new building types sprang up to accommodate innovatory industrial processes: factories and mills, railway and power stations. The same is happening today, but the primary new building type that is being thrown up, the workhome, is centuries old and generally invisible. This is largely because it is, in many parts of the world, extremely difficult to build. A leading American design practitioner and theorist bought a light-industrial building when she settled in London. Her apartment sits on the top floor above the two levels of her design practice – illegally. 'It's nuts,' she says.

It is more serious than that. The rigid web of rules and regulations that determine what can and cannot be built is currently having a profoundly destructive effect; driven by prime cost economics, most contemporary buildings do not meet the needs of a rapidly changing society. A few slip through the net: Alison Brooks Architects' Newhall workhome development was shortlisted for the prestigious 2013 Stirling Prize. And Carl Turner's Slip House, a modern interpretation of living above the shop, was commended in the *Architectural Review's* 2013 International House of the Year competition [**Fig. C.1, C.2**].

3. This was evident at the 2013 Economic Value Workshop for the UK Farrell Review of Architecture. While asking the core question "In what ways does architecture and built environment design contribute to the UK economy?" the discussion was framed in terms of commodification.

4. UK new-build space standards are the lowest in Western Europe; this limits the scope for workhome/ flexible usage; see R. Roberts-Hughes, The Case for Space: The Size of England's New Homes (2011), p. 10.

5. For example, L. Bachelor, 'Does Buying a New-Build Home Leave You on Shaky Foundations?', The Observer, Sunday, 31 March 2013.

FIG. C.1, C.2 *Slip House, Hackney, London. Carl Turner Architects, 2013. View of front elevation and Plans.*

But Brooks says that, in every scheme she has designed since, the workspace has been deleted to maximize profit. And, beautiful as it is, Turner's workhome, built for himself, does not provide a widely applicable economic model.

This affects the poor disproportionately. In the private sector, home-based work is often accommodated through under-occupation: people use a spare room, a large landing or a disused garage as a workspace, or they build a shed at the bottom of their garden. But in the public sector these options are not generally available. In the Global South, land that the poor have trucked and traded on for generations is being taken from under their feet, while in the Global

North subsidized housing is still being built and regulated to a pattern specifically designed to prevent home-based work.

Few contemporary home-based workers live and work in conditions that suit them. But they could. Home and workplace could be combined in an infinite number of ways to make workhomes. Streets of houses could alternate with streets of workplaces, linked by private gardens or courtyards inside each urban block to create mews or *machiya*-style workhomes. Or dwellings and workplaces – shops, offices, bakeries, restaurants, workshops, consulting rooms, studios – could alternate along the street. Apartment buildings could include intermediate levels of workspace, managed collectively by inhabitants or by a hub organization. These could be designed around the requirements of a range of occupations, including catering or sewing, sculpture or furniture-making, hairdressing or child-minding, not just desk-based work. And, conversely, office buildings could interleave residential floors or wings. Huge dwellings could incorporate tiny workspaces or, vice versa, compact living space could be fitted into vast industrial units. Courtyard workhomes could be designed with workspaces facing the street and homes facing inwards, or the other way around, with homes onto the street and workplaces in the courtyard. Clusters of workhomes could be designed around noisy, dirty occupations such as sculpture or mechanics, and others around families with dependent children or elders. High street cafés and bars with free wifi already provide an extension to home-based workspace that helps combat social isolation. This could be expanded to provide hubs in the supermarket or chemist, the launderette or sports centre. The possibilities are endless. And once legitimized, this workforce could advertise discreetly, as their Victorian predecessors did. Making home-based services visible and accessible in this way would contribute to increasing neighbourhood connectivity, and thus stimulate the local economy. Unexpected problems would be bound to arise (how do young home-based workers meet and fall in love?) and be solved (flirting benches with wifi?[6]). And so, incrementally, a markedly different world could emerge.

6. This idea comes from a student project by Kevin Haley of Aberrant Architecture.

This is unlikely to happen, however, until home-based work is introduced into the discourse about a sustainable future. One of the aims of this book, therefore, is to stimulate this conversation. The idea of home-based work could provide a simple but powerful unifying strategy for those working globally towards social, economic and environmental sustainability. Although a major shift for some people and institutions in how they think about the world and what they consider to be beneficial or desirable, for others this will simply be a matter of common sense. Pioneering corporations such as BT at one end of the spectrum, and the shoe-mender living above his shop at the end of the street at the other, demonstrate the economic argument. An understanding of the damage and stress caused by our crowded urban rush hour and by clogged motorways returning commuters to their suburbs underpins the environmental argument.

And an awareness of the increasing diversity of the global workforce reinforces the social argument. But our cities, homes and workplaces still largely continue to be designed and organized around the outdated model of the husband going out to work, while the wife stays at home tending house and children. Rethinking this presents an important and pressing challenge.

Appendix

Appendix

Charles Booth's home-based occupations

A selection of home-based occupations referred to in the Booth notebooks for south-east London, Bethnal Green and Hackney, 1886–1903.

Manufacture: artificial flower-making, baker, bead-work, bed-frame maker, bicycle-maker, bookbinder, boot-finisher, boot-maker, boot-repairer, brush-drawer, brush-maker, cabinet-maker, cardboard box-maker, carver, chair and couchwood carver, clock-maker, clothier, cordwainer, corset-maker, dairy, dressmaker, doll-maker, fancy leather goods maker, fish-curer, furrier, fur-puller, fur-sewer, fur-worker, glass-blower, gold-leaf beaters, hoop-makers, horse-collar makers, ice-cream maker, mantle-making, market bag-maker, matchbox makers, mathematical instrument-maker, milliner, musical instrument-maker, needlework, oar-maker, packing case makers, paper-sorting, pocket-book maker, sack-making, sewing-machine workers, ship's mattress maker, shirt-makers, shoe-makers, slipper-makers, splint-cutter, tailor, tanner, tie-maker, toy horse and towel horse maker, toy makers, toy whip maker, venetian blind maker, watchmaker, weaver, wire workers

Service industry: beer-house on-licence, beer-house off-licence, brothel, common lodging house, domestic service, eating house, fire fighters, fully licensed public house, haircutter, hotel, housekeeper, insurance agent, landlord and landlady, laundry, mangling, mechanic, music teaching, pawn shop, police, prostitution, stabling, umbrella repairer, wood-chopper

Trade: baked-potato hawker, coal and coke merchant, draper, florist, flower-seller, food-vendor, grocer, ice-cream hawker, milk vendor, pawnbroker, rag-dealer, salt-seller, soap-boiler merchant

Agriculture: market gardening, orchard foreman

Religion, education and caretaking: clergy and lady helpers, cathedral with resident priests, parsonage, vicarage, head master's house and porter's lodge, school-keeper, caretaker to Presbyterian church, curate or caretaker to Mission Clubroom, superintendent to baths and washhouse, foreman to brewery, foreman to Pickfords depot, foreman to builder's yard, caretaker to Star Omnibus Co, attendant to public baths

Professions: architect, artist, dentist, doctor, insurance agent, ladies school, photographer, solicitor, veterinary surgeon

Building industry: builder, carpenter, marble mason, plumber

Illustration credits

The author and publishers would like to thank the following individuals and institutions for giving permission to reproduce material in this book. We have made every effort to contact copyright holders, but if any errors have been made we would be happy to correct them at a later printing.

Epigraph, 'In Front of Your Nose' by George Orwell (Copyright © George Orwell, 1946). Reprinted by permission of Bill Hamilton as the Literary Executor of the Estate of the Late Sonia Brownell Orwell.

Figure 1.0: © Tower Hamlets Local History Library & Archive
Figure 1.1: © English Heritage
Figure 1.2: © The Clothworkers' Company
Figure 1.3: © English Heritage
Figure 1.4: © Frances Holliss
Figure 1.5: © London Metropolitan Archives, City of London: SC/PHL/01/387 (55/0817)
Figure 1.6: © Tower Hamlets Local History Library & Archive
Figure 1.7: © Tower Hamlets Local History Library & Archive
Figure 1.8: © Margaret Tomlinson, from a collection deposited by Victoria County History
Figure 1.9: Reproduced by permission of English Heritage
Figure 1.10: © John Prest (*The Industrial Revolution in Coventry* by John Prest (1960), Figure 7 from p. 84 (adapted), by permission of Oxford University Press)
Figure 1.11: Reproduced by permission of English Heritage
Figure 1.12: © John Prest (*The Industrial Revolution in Coventry* by John Prest (1960), Figure 8 from p. 86 (adapted), by permission of Oxford University Press)
Figure 1.13: © Coventry History Centre
Figure 1.14: © John Prest (*The Industrial Revolution in Coventry* by John Prest (1960), Plate 5a by permission of Oxford University Press)
Figure 1.15: Reproduced by permission of English Heritage
Figure 1.16 © Neville Parker
Figure 1.17: © Tower Hamlets Local History Library & Archive

Figure 1.18: © Library of the London School of Economics and Political Science (LSE/Booth/A/19)
Figure 1.19: © British Library
Figure 1.20: © Scottish Fire and Rescue Service Museum of Fire
Figure 1.21: © City of Edinburgh Council, Archives, www.capitalcollections.org.uk
Figure 1.22: © Frances Holliss
Figure 1.23: © Forgotten Books
Figure 1.24: © Forgotten Books
Figure 1.25: © Historic Resources Branch, Manitoba Culture, Heritage and Tourism, 2006
Figure 1.26: © Frances Holliss
Figure 1.27: © Frances Holliss
Figure 1.28: © Frances Holliss
Figure 1.29: © Frances Holliss
Figure 1.30: © Frances Holliss
Figure 1.31: © Frances Holliss
Figure 1.32: © Frances Holliss
Figure 1.33: © Frances Holliss
Figure 1.34: © Frances Holliss
Figure 2.0: © Kazunori Fujimoto (Flickr Creative Commons)
Figure 2.1: © Giles Walkley (*The Artists' Studio-House in London, 1764–1914* by Giles Walkley (1994) Scolar Press, Figure 178 from p. 219, by permission of Giles Walkley)
Figure 2.2: © Giles Walkley (*The Artists' Studio-House in London, 1764–1914* by Giles Walkley (1994) Scolar Press, Figure 35 from p. 51, by permission of Giles Walkley)
Figure 2.3: © Frances Holliss
Figure 2.4: © Giles Walkley (*The Artists' Studio-House in London, 1764–1914* by Giles Walkley (1994) Scolar Press, Figure 126 from p.156 (adapted), by permission of Giles Walkley)
Figure 2.5: © Frances Holliss
Figure 2.6: © Viktor Jak
Figure 2.7: © Paul Louis/DACS 2014
Figure 2.8: © TEEMU008 (Flickr Creative Commons)
Figure 2.9: © Bernt Rostad (Flickr Creative Commons)
Figure 2.10: © Shelly Pietrzak (Flickr Creative Commons)
Figure 2.11: © DACS 2014
Figure 2.12: © Ben Garrett (Flickr Creative Commons)
Figure 2.13: © John Lord (Flickr Creative Commons)
Figure 2.14: © Iqbal Aalam. www.flickr.com/photos/iqbalaalam/1920556138/in/set-72157602373912133
Figure 2.15: © FLC/ ADAGP, Paris and DACS, London, 2014
Figure 2.16: © FLC/ ADAGP, Paris and DACS, London, 2014
Figure 2.17: © FLC/ ADAGP, Paris and DACS, London, 2014
Figure 2.18: © Frances Holliss
Figure 2.19: © Mark Lyon
Figure 2.20: © Frances Holliss
Figure 2.21: © Mark Lyon
Figure 2.22: © Colin Davies
Figure 2.23: © Eames Office LLC

Figure 2.24: © Peter Shep
Figure 2.25: © Joe Low / RIBA Library Photographs Collection
Figure 2.26: © 1972 Henry Smith-Miller
Figure 2.27: © Charles Nesbit, Photographer, 1972
Figure 2.28: © Thomas Heinser
Figure 2.29: © Thomas Heinser
Figure 2.30: © Tanner Leddy Maytum Stacy
Figure 2.31: © Nick Hufton
Figure 2.32: © Frances Holliss
Figure 2.33: © Frances Holliss
Figure 2.34: © Frances Holliss
Figure 2.35: © Frances Holliss
Figure 2.36: © Frances Holliss
Figure 2.37: © Frances Holliss
Figure 2.38: © Frances Holliss
Figure 2.39: © Kazunori Fujimoto (Flickr Creative Commons)
Figure 2.40: © Tadao Ando
Figure 2.41: © Tadao Ando
Figure 2.42: © Tadao Ando
Figure 2.43: © Frances Holliss
Figure 2.44: © Atelier Knot
Figure 2.45: © Atelier Bow-Wow
Figure 2.46: © Frances Holliss
Figure 2.47: © Frances Holliss
Figure 2.48: © Frances Holliss
Figure 2.49: © Atelier Bow-Wow
Figure 2.50: © Daici Ano
Figure 2.51: © Daici Ano
Figure 2.52: © Daici Ano
Figure 2.53: © Daici Ano
Figure 2.54: © Daici Ano
Figure 2.55: © Koh Kitayama + ARCHITECTURE WORKSHOP
Figure 2.56: © Daici Ano
Figure 3.0: © Frances Holliss
Figure 3.1: © Frances Holliss
Figure 3.2: © Frances Holliss
Figure 3.3: © Thomas Heinser
Figure 3.4: © Frances Holliss
Figure 3.5: © Frances Holliss
Figure 3.6: © Frances Holliss
Figure 3.7: © Frances Holliss
Figure 3.8: © Frances Holliss
Figure 3.9: © Frances Holliss
Figure 3.10: © Frances Holliss
Figure 3.11: © Frances Holliss
Figure 3.12: © Frances Holliss
Figure 3.13: © Frances Holliss
Figure 3.14: © Frances Holliss
Figure 3.15: © Frances Holliss
Figure 3.16: © Frances Holliss
Figure 3.17: © Frances Holliss

Figure 3.18: © Frances Holliss
Figure 3.19: © Frances Holliss
Figure 3.20: © Frances Holliss
Figure 3.21: © Frances Holliss
Figure 3.22: © Frances Holliss
Figure 3.23: © Frances Holliss
Figure 3.24: © Frances Holliss
Figure 3.25: © Frances Holliss
Figure 3.26: © Frances Holliss
Figure 3.27: © Frances Holliss
Figure 3.28: © Frances Holliss
Figure 3.29: © Frances Holliss
Figure 3.30: © Frances Holliss
Figure 3.31: © David Anderson
Figure 3.32: © Arthur Adler
Figure 3.33: © Frances Holliss
Figure 3.34: © Frances Holliss
Figure 3.35: © The Roald Dahl Museum and Story Centre
Figure 3.36: © Frances Holliss
Figure 3.37: © Frances Holliss
Figure 3.38: © Frances Holliss
Figure 3.39: © Frances Holliss
Figure 3.40: © Frances Holliss
Figure 3.41: © Caroline Ede
Figure 3.42: © Frances Holliss
Figure 3.43: © Frances Holliss
Figure 3.44: © Frances Holliss
Figure 3.45: © Frances Holliss
Figure 3.46: © Frances Holliss
Figure 3.47: © Frances Holliss
Figure 3.48: © Frances Holliss
Figure 3.49: © Frances Holliss
Figure 3.50: © Frances Holliss
Figure 3.51: © Frances Holliss
Figure 3.52: © Frances Holliss
Figure 3.53: © Frances Holliss
Figure 3.54: © Frances Holliss
Figure 3.55: © Frances Holliss
Figure 3.56: © Frances Holliss
Figure 3.57: © Frances Holliss
Figure 3.58: © Frances Holliss
Figure 3.59: © Frances Holliss
Figure 3.60: © Frances Holliss
Figure 3.61: © Thomas Heinser
Figure 3.62: © Frances Holliss
Figure 3.63: © Frances Holliss
Figure 3.64: © Frances Holliss
Figure 3.65: © Frances Holliss
Figure 3.66: © Frances Holliss
Figure 3.67: © Frances Holliss
Figure 3.68: © Frances Holliss

Figure 3.69: © Frances Holliss
Figure 3.70: © Frances Holliss
Figure 3.71: © Daici Ano
Figure 4.0: © Museum of London
Figure 4.1: Reproduced by permission of English Heritage
Figure 4.2: © Hertfordshire Archives and Local Studies (HALS)
Figure 4.3: In public realm
Figure 4.4: © Hertfordshire Archives and Local Studies (HALS)
Figure 4.5: © Hertfordshire Archives and Local Studies (HALS)
Figure 4.6: © Frances Holliss
Figure 4.7: © Tony Ray-Jones/RIBA Library Photographs Collection
Figure 4.8: © Museum of London
Figure 4.9: © Tower Hamlets Local History Library & Archive
Figure 4.10: © In the public realm
Figure 4.11: © English Heritage
Figure 4.12: © English Heritage
Figure 4.13: © H.J. Malby/Victoria and Albert Museum, London
Figure 4.14: © Museum of London
Figure 4.15: © Museum of London
Figure 4.16: © Museum of London
Figure 4.17: From the Woburn Abbey Collection
Figure 4.18: © Frances Holliss
Figure 4.19: © Frances Holliss
Figure 4.20: © Frances Holliss
Figure 4.21: © David Shankbone (Flickr Creative Commons)
Figure 4.22: © Frances Holliss
Figure 4.23: © Frances Holliss
Figure 4.24: © Frances Holliss
Figure 4.25: © Frances Holliss
Figure 4.26: © Mirrorpix
Figure 4.27: © Frances Holliss
Figure 4.28: © Frances Holliss
Figure 4.29: © Frances Holliss
Figure 4.30: © Frances Holliss
Figure 4.31: © Frances Holliss
Figure 4.32: © Frances Holliss
Figure 4.33: © Frances Holliss
Figure 4.34: © Heirs Ben Merk, collection City Archives Amsterdam (B00000000604)
Figure 4.35: © Daici Ano
Figure 5.0: © Thomas Galvez (Flickr Creative Commons)
Figure 5.1: © Frances Holliss
Figure 5.2: © Frances Holliss
Figure 5.3: © Frances Holliss
Figure 5.4: In the public realm
Figure 5.5: © Frances Holliss
Figure 5.6: © Frances Holliss
Figure 5.7: © Thomas Heinser
Figure 5.8: © Frances Holliss
Figure 5.9: © Frances Holliss
Figure 5.10: © Frances Holliss

Select bibliography

ACA Architecture, available at: http://acaarchitecture.com/Mag58.htm

Anable, J., Lane, B., and Kelay, T., *An Evidence Based Review of Public Attitudes to Climate Change and Transport Behaviour*, London: Transport for London (2006).

Ando, T. and Dal Co, F., *Tadao Ando: Complete Works*, London: Phaidon (1995).

Arndt, H.W., *Economic Development*, Chicago: University of Chicago Press (1987).

Bachelor, L., 'Does Buying a New-Build Home Leave You on Shaky Foundations?', *The Observer*, Sunday, 31 March 2013.

Badger, E., 'Mixed-Use Neighborhoods May Be Safer, Too', *The Atlantic Cities*, March 13 2013.

Ballaney, S., *The Town Planning Mechanism in Gujarat, India*, Washington, DC: The World Bank (2008).

Banham, R., 'Ateliers d'Artistes: Paris Studio Houses and the Modern Movement', *Architectural Review*, August 1956.

Barnwell, P., Palmer, M. and Airs, M. (eds), *The Vernacular Workshop: From Craft to Industry 1400–1900*, York: Council for British Archaeology (2004).

Batchelor, R., 'The Pullens Story'. Available at: http://iliffeyard.co.uk/gallery-view/guest-gallery---the-pullen-s-story).

Bell, D.F. and Jayne, M., *City of Quarters: Urban Villages in the Contemporary City*, Aldershot: Ashgate (2004).

Benton, T., *The Villas of Le Corbusier, 1920–1930*, New Haven, CT: Yale University Press (1987).

Booth, C., *Life and Labour of the People in London*, London: Macmillan and Co (1902).

Booth, C., *LSE Booth Archive (1886–1903)*, available at: www.booth.lse.ac.uk

Booth, C. and Steele, J., *The Streets of London: The Booth Notebooks*, London: Deptford Forum (1997).

Braverman. H., *Labour and Monopoly Capital: The Degradation of Work in the Twentieth Century*, New York: Monthly Review Press (1974, reprint 1998).

BT, 'Flexible Working Drives Down More Than Costs', available at: www.globalservices.bt.com/uk/en/insights/more_productivity_from_your_force.

BT, *Flexible Working: Can Your Company Compete Without It?* London; BT (2007).

BT Group PLC, *Sustainability Review*, London: BT (2011).

Buckingham, J.S., *National Evils and Practical Remedies, with the Plan of a Model Town ... Accompanied by an Examination of Some Important Moral and Political Problems*, London: Peter Jackson (1849).

Bythell, D., *The Sweated Trades; Outwork in Nineteenth-century Britain*, London: Batsford (1978).

Cairns, S., Sloman, L., Newson, C., Anable, J., Kirkbride, A. and Goodwin, P., *Smarter Choices: Changing the Way We Travel*, London: UK Department for Transport (2004).

Castells, M., *The Rise of the Network Society The Information Age: Economy, Society and Culture*, Vol. 1, Oxford: Blackwell (2000).

Castells, M. and Portes, A., 'World Underneath: The Origins, Dynamics and Effects of the Informal Economy', in A. Portes, M. Castells, and L.A. Benton (eds.) *The Informal Economy: Studies in Advanced and Less Developed Countries*, Baltimore, MD: Johns Hopkins University Press (1989).

CDW Government Inc., *Federal Telework Report*, Vernon Hills, IL: CDW Government Inc. (2005).

Chen, M.A., Jhabvala, R. and Lund, F., 'Supporting Workers in the Informal Economy: A Policy Framework', Working Paper on the Informal Economy, Geneva, International Labour Organization (2002).

Chesterton Planning and Developments, *Live/Work Developments: An Analysis of Their Role in Economic Regeneration*, Shoreditch: Our Way (2003).

Colantonio, A., 'Social Sustainability: An Exploratory Analysis of Its Definition, Assessment Methods, Metrics and Tools', *Measuring Social Sustainability: Best Practice from Urban Renewal in the EU*, Oxford: Oxford Institute for Sustainable Development (OISD), International Land Markets Group (2007).

Cooper, R., Evans, G. and Boyko, C. (eds), *Designing Sustainable Cities*, Oxford: Blackwell (2009).

Cross, A.W.S., *Public Baths and Wash Houses*, London: B.T. Batsford (1906).

Curtis, W.J.R., 'Ronchamp Undermined by Renzo Piano's Convent, France', *Architectural Review*, 24 July 2012.

Davies, C., *The Prefabricated Home*, London: Reaktion Books (2005).

Davies, H.T.O., Nutley, S.M. and Smith, P.C., *What Works? Evidence-based Policy and Practice in Public Service*, Bristol: Policy Press (2000).

Davis, H., *Living over the Store: Architecture and Local Urban Life*, London: Routledge (2012).

Davis, H., 'Making the Marginal Visible: Micro-Enterprise and Urban Space in London', paper presented at the ARCC Conference (2013).

Davis, M., 'Historical Introduction to the Campaign for Equal Pay', Centre for Trade Union Studies, London Metropolitan University (2007), available at: www.unionhistory.info/equalpay,

Defoe, D., *A Tour through the Whole Island of Great Britain*, London: Dent Printing ([1727] 1974).

Dernie, D. and Carew-Cox, A., *Victor Horta*, London: Academy Press (1995).

Dickens, C., *Hard Times* (1854).

Dictionary of Scottish Architecture, available at: www.scottisharchitects. org.uk/building_full.php?id=212368

Dolan, T., *Live-Work Planning and Design: Zero-Commute Housing*, Hoboken, NJ: John Wiley and Sons (2012).

Dunbar, R.I.M., 'Neocortex Size as a Constraint on Group Size in Primates', *Journal of Human Evolution*, Vol. 22 (Issue 6) (June 1992).

Ehrenhalt, A., 'Inspired Amateurs', *Planning*, Vol. 67, Part 6, ISSN 0001-2610 (June 2001).

E-Japan Strategy II (2003) Available at: www.kantei.go.jp/foreign/policy/it/0702senryaku_e.pdf

Eliot, G., *Silas Marner* (1861).

Equal Opportunities Commission, *Greater Expectations; Final Report of the EOC's Investigation into Discrimination against New and Expectant Mothers in the Workplace*, London: Equal Opportunities Commission (2005).

Evans, G., Foord, J. and Shaw, P., *Creative Spaces: Strategies for Creative Cities*, London Development Agency (2006).

Ezeadichie, N., 'Home-based Enterprises in Urban Space: Obligation for Strategic Planning?' *Urban Fringe, Berkeley Planning Journal*, September 20, 2012.

Felstead, A., Jewson, N. and Walters, S., *Changing Places of Work*, Basingstoke: Palgrave Macmillan (2005).

Frediani, A.A., The World Bank, Turner and Sen: Freedom in the Urban Arena, Working Paper No. 136, Development Planning Unit, University College London (2009).

Freedman, A., 'Jane Jacobs', *Globe and Mail*, June 9, 1984.

Friedman, A.T., 'Girl Talk: Marion Mahony Griffin, Frank Lloyd Wright and the Oak Park Studio', in D. Van Zanten (ed.), *Marion Mahony Reconsidered*, Chicago: University of Chicago Press (2011).

Gage, A., *Archaeologia* Vol. XXV (1834).

Gaskell, S.M., *Slums*, Leicester: Leicester University Press (1990).

Gehl, J., *Cities for People*, Washington, DC: Island Press (2010).

Geirtz. L.M. and Hughes, N.J., *Abridged Building Classification (ABC)*, Dublin: An Foras Forbartha (1981).

Gies, F. and Gies, J., *Life in a Medieval Village*, New York: Harper and Row (1990).

Global Workplace Analytics, *Costs and Benefits: Advantages of Telecommuting for Companies*, available at: www. globalworkplaceanalytics.com/resources/costs-benefits

Goldsmith, S. and Elizabeth, L. (eds), *What We See: Advancing the Observations of Jane Jacobs*, Oakland, CA: New Village Press (2010).

Guillery, P. (ed.) *Built from Below: British Architecture and the Vernacular*, London: Routledge (2011).

Gurstein, P., *Working at Home in the Live-in Office: Computers, Space and the Social Life of Households*, PhD, University of California, Berkeley, CA (1990).

Gurstein P., 'Planning for Telework and Home-based Employment: Reconsidering the Home/Work Separation', *Journal of Planning Education and Research*, Vol. 15, Issue 3 (April 1996). pp. 212–24

Gurstein, P., *Wired to the World, Chained to the Home: Telework in Daily Life*, Vancouver: UBC Press (2001).

Gurstein, P. and Marlor, D., *Planning for Telework and Homebased Employment: A Canadian Survey on Integrating Work into Residential Environments*, Centre for Human Settlements, Vancouver: UBC Press (1995).

Hakim, C., *Social Change and Innovation in the Labour Market: Evidence from the Census SARS on Occupational Segregation and Labour Mobility, Part-Time Work and Student Jobs, Homework and Self-Employment*, Oxford: Oxford University Press (1998).

Hall, P., *Cities of Tomorrow and Intellectual History of Urban Planning and Design in the Twentieth Century*, Oxford: Blackwell (1998, reprint 2002).

Hamer, R., Kroes, E. and Van Ooststroom, H., 'Teleworking in the Netherlands: An Evaluation of Changes in Travel Behavior', *Transportation*, Vol. 18 (1991).

Harrison, B., *Not Only the 'Dangerous Trades': Women's Work and Health in Britain, 1880–1914*, London: Taylor & Francis (1996).

Holliss, F., 'The Workhome... A New Building Type?', PhD, London Metropolitan University (2007).

Holliss, F., 'Beyond Live/work', *Planning in London*, Issue 67 (Oct–Dec 2008).

Holliss, F., 'From Longhouse to Live/work Unit: Parallel Histories and Absent Narratives', in P. Guillery (ed.) *Built from Below; British Architecture and the Vernacular*, London: Routledge (2010).

Holliss, F., 'House with Associated Office?' in S. Wigglesworth (ed.) *Around and About Stock Orchard Street*, London: Routledge (2011).

Holliss, F., 'Space, Buildings and the Life-Worlds of Home-Based Workers', *Sociological Research Online*, 31 May 2012, available at: http://www.socresonline.org.uk/17/2/24.html

Holliss, F., 'Home Is Where the Work Is: The Case for an Urban Revolution', *The Conversation*, 24 July 2012.

Holliss, F., 'Home-based Work: A Quiet Casualty of the Bedroom Tax', *The Conversation*, 21 May 2013.

Home, R.K., *A Township Complete in Itself: A Planning History of the Becontree/Dagenham Estate*, London: Libraries Department, London Borough of Barking & Dagenham and School of Surveying, University of East London (1997).

Hopkinson, P. and James, P., *UK Report on National SUSTEL Fieldwork*, Bradford: Sustainable Telework (2003).

Hosking, T., *Family Life in Medieval Britain*, Hove: Wayland (1994).

Howard, E., *To-Morrow: A Peaceful Path to Real Reform*, London: Swann Sonnenschein (2003).

Howard, E., *Garden Cities of Tomorrow: Being the Second Edition of 'To-Morrow: A Peaceful Path to Real Reform'*, London: Swan Sonnenschein (1902).

Howard, E., *To-Morrow: Aa Peaceful Path to Real Reform*, original edition with new commentary by P. Hall, D. Hardy, and C. Ward, London: Routledge (2004).

Hutton, T.A., *The New Economy of the City: Restructuring, Regeneration and Dislocation in the Twenty-First Century Metropolis*, London: Routledge (2008).

International Labour Organization, *Women and Men in the Informal Economy: A Statistical Picture*, Geneva: ILO (2002).

Jacobs, J., *The Death and Life of Great American Cities*, New York: The Modern Library (1961. reprint 1993).

James, P., *Is Teleworking Sustainable? An Analysis of its Economic, Environmental and Social Impacts*, Brussels: USTEL, European Communities (2004).

James, P., *Homeworking at BT: The Economic, Environmental and Social Impacts*, Bradford: SustainIT and University of Bradford (2008).

Jinnai, H., *Tokyo: A Spatial Anthropology*, Berkeley, CA: University of California Press (1995).

Jones, E., *Home Business Report*, London: Enterprise Nation (2009).

Kelly, M. 'Henri Lefebvre, 1901–1991', *Radical Philosophy*, Vol. 060 (Spring 1992).

Killip, G., *Built Fabric and Building Regulations*, 40% House Project, Oxford: Environmental Change Institute: University of Oxford (2005).

Koenig, B.E., Henderson, D.K. and Mokhtarian, P.L., 'The Travel and Emissions Impacts of Telecommuting for the State of California Telecommuting Pilot Project', *Transportation Research Part C*, Vol. 4, Issue 1 (Feb. 1996).

Labour Force Survey, *Characteristics of Home Workers, 2014*, available at: http://www.ons.gov.uk/ons/rel/lmac/characteristics-of-home-workers/2014/rpt-home-workers.html. London: ONS.

Layard, R., 'Happiness: Has Social Science a Clue?' Lionel Robbins Memorial Lecture (March 2003).

Layard, R., *Happiness: Lessons from a New Science*, Harmondsworth: Penguin Books (2011).

Lefebvre, H., *The Production of Space*, Oxford: Basil Blackwell (1991).

Lewis, W.A., *The Theory of Economic Growth*, London: George Allen and Unwin (1955).

Linné, C.V. and Freer, S., *Linnaeus' Philosophia Botanica*, Oxford: Oxford University Press (2002).

Live/work Institute Available at: www.live-work.com

Live/work Network Available at: www.liveworknet.com/

London Borough of Hackney, *Live/Work Supplementary Planning Guidance* (1996) London: LBH.

London Borough of Hillingdon, *Supplementary Planning Guidance for Live/work Accommodation* (2006) Available at: www.hillingdon.gov.uk/media.jsp?mediaid=8415&filetype=pdf

London Residential Research, *Review of Live-Work Policy in Hackney*, London: London Borough of Hackney (2005).

Marcel Breuer Digital Archive. Available at: www.breuer.syr.edu

Marchant, H., 'Feature Family: The Braggs', *Ford Family*, Vol. 1 (April 1952).

Marmot, M., *The Status Syndrome: How Your Social Status Directly Affects Your Health and Life Expectancy*, London: Bloomsbury (2004).

Marsh, J., 'Gender Ideology and Separate Spheres in the 19th Century', Victoria and Albert Museum article. Available at: www.vam.ac.uk/content/articles/g/gender-ideology-and-separate-spheres-19th-century/ (2013).

Mason, C., Carter, S. and Tagg, S., *Invisible Businesses: The Characteristics of Home-based Businesses in the United Kingdom*, Glasgow: Hunter Centre for Entrepreneurship (2008).

Mather, C., *We Are Workers Too! Organising Home-based Workers in the Global Economy*, WIEGO, available at: www.wiego.org (2010).

Maxcy, S.J., 'The Teacherage in American Rural Education', *The Journal of General Education*, Vol. 30 (1979).

Mearns, A., *The Bitter Cry of Outcast England: An Inquiry into the Condition of the Abject Poor*, London: James Clarke (1883).

Meirion Jones, G., 'The Long House', *Medieval Archaeology 17* (1973).

Melhuish, C., *Modern House 2*, London, Phaidon (2000).

Millard, N.J., *Clouds, Crowds and Customers: Doing Business as 'Unusual'*, London: BT (2010).

Moran, J., 'Defining Moment: Streets in the Air Arrive on Britain's Housing Estates, 1961', *Financial Times Magazine*, 5 June 2010.

Moser, C.O.N., 'Informal Sector or Petty Commodity Production: Dualism or Dependence in Urban Development?', *World Development*, Vol. 6 (1978).

Mukhija, V., *Squatters as Developers? Slum Redevelopment in Mumbai*, Aldershot :Ashgate (2003).

Nohn, M., *Mixed Use Zoning and Home-based Production in India* WIEGO Technical Brief, (rban Policies, No. 3 (2011). Available at: www.wiego.org

Nussbaum, M. and Sen, A. (eds), *The Quality of Life*, Oxford: Clarendon Press (1993).

Office of the Deputy Prime Minister, Circular 30/2005, London: TSO.

Park, P.B., *My Ancestors Were Manorial Tenants*, London: Society of Genealogists (2002).

Penfold, C., Webster, S., Neil, H., Ranns, H. and Graham, J., *Understanding the Needs, Attitudes and Behaviours of Teleworkers*, London: UK Department for Transport (2009).

Pennington, S. and Westover, B., *A Hidden Workforce; Homeworkers in England, 1850–1985*, Basingstoke: Macmillan Education (1989).

Power, A., *Hovels to High Rise: State Housing in Europe Since 1850*, London: Routledge (1993).

Prest, J.M., *The Industrial Revolution in Coventry*, Oxford: Oxford University Press (1960).

Pullens Estate, available at: http://iliffeyard.co.uk/gallery-view/guest-gallery---the-pullen-s-story

Pullens Estate, available at: www.pullensyards.co.uk/category/open-studios/

Putnam, R., *Bowling Alone: The Collapse and Revival of American Community*, New York: Simon & Schuster (2000).

Roberts-Hughes, R. (2011) *The Case for Space: The Size of England's New Homes*, London: RIBA.

Robson, E.R., *School Architecture: Being Practical Remarks on the Planning, Designing, Building, and Furnishing of School-Houses*, London: John Murray (1874).

Rosen, B. and Zuckermann, W. *The Mews of London: A Guide to the Hidden Byways of London's Past*, Exeter: Webb and Bower (1982).

Royal Commission, *Royal Commission Enquiring into the Condition of Framework-Knitters*, London: the Royal Commission (1845).

Rubenstein, A. *Just Like the Country*, London: Age Exchange (1991).

Sassen, S., 'The Informal Economy: Between New Developments and Old Regulations', *The Yale Law Journal*, vol. 103 (1994), pp. 2289–304.

Schneider, F., Buehn, A., and Montenegro, C.E., 'Shadow Economies All over the World: New Estimates for 162 Countries from 1999 to 2007', Policy Research Working Paper 5356, Washington, DC, The World Bank Development Research Group (2010).

Schneider, T. and Till, J., *Flexible Housing*, London: Architectural Press (2007).

Seccome, W., 'Patriarchy Stabilised: The Construction of the Male Breadwinner Norm in Nineteenth-Century Britain', *Social History*, vol. 11, issue 1 (1986).

Sen, A., 'Poor, Relatively Speaking', Fifteenth Geary Lecture, The Economic and Social Research Institute (1982).

Sen, A., *Development as Freedom*, Oxford: Oxford University Press (1999).

Shelton, B., *Learning from the Japanese City*, London: E. & F.N. Spon (1999)

Sheppard, F., 'Spitalfields and Mile End New Town', *Survey of London*, Vol. XXVII, London: Athlone Press (1957).

Shrimpton, D.M., *The Parkers of Rantergate : Framework Knitters*, Ruddington: Ruddington Framework Knitters Museum Trust (1989).

Sidwell, S., 'The Weavers and Watchmakers of Hillfields', unpublished report, courtesy of Coventry City Records (1972).

Simpson, D., *CFA Voysey: An Architect of Individuality*, London: Lund Humphries (1979).

Sinha, S., *Rights of Home-based Workers*, New Delhi: National Human Rights Commission (2006).

Social Exclusion Team, *Greater London Authority Intelligence Update, 2006–2011*, London: Greater London Authority.

Stedman Jones, G., *Outcast London: A Study in the Relationship between Classes in Victorian Society*, London: Penguin (1971, reprint 1984).

Steer, F.W. (ed.), *Farm and Cottage Inventories of Mid-Essex, 1635–1749*, Chelmsford: Essex Record Office (1950).

Stewart, L., www.bbc.co.uk/blogs/louisestewart/2011/02/prime_minister_says_living_abo.html

Sudarshan, R.M. and Sinha, S., 'Making Home-based Work Visible: A Review of Evidence from South Asia', in Urban Policies Research Report No.10, Women in Informal Employment: Globalising and Organising

(2011), available at: www.wiego.org

Swenarton, M., *Homes Fit for Heroes: The Politics and Architecture of Early State Housing in Britain*, London: Heinemann Educational (1981).

Tarn, J.N., *Working-class Housing in 19th-Century Britain*, London: Architectural Association Papers (1971).

Taut, B., *Houses and People of Japan*, Tokyo: The Sanseido Co. Ltd, (1937).

The Royal Society, *Climate Change: A Summary of the Science*, London: The Royal Society (2010).

Tomalin, C., *Samuel Pepys: The Unequalled Self*, London: Viking (2002).

Topham, G. 'Vogue's Alexandra Shulman Joins Backlash Against Working from Home', *The Guardian*, 2 March 2013.

Tyng, A., *Beginnings: Louis I. Kahn's Philosophy of Architecture*, Chichester: Wiley (1984).

UK Department for Communities and Local Government, *English Housing Survey: Housing Stock Report*, London: TSO (2008).

UK Government, *The Carbon Plan*, London: TSO (2011).

UK Government, *The Coalition: Our Programme for Government*, London: TSO (2010).

UK Office for National Statistics, Table KS15, in *Travel to Work* (Census 2001), London: ONS (2001).

UK Office for National Statistics, Table CT0015, in *Method of Travel to Work* (Census 2011), London: ONS (2011).

UK Office for National Statistics, *Commuting to Work, 2011*, available at: www.ons.gov.uk/ons/dcp171776_227904.pdf

UK Parliamentary Select Committee on Small and Medium Sized Enterprises, *Roads to Success: SME Exports*, London: TSO (2013).

Unwin, R., *Cottage Plans and Common Sense*, Fabian Tract No. 109, London: The Fabian Society (1902).

Vellay, D., *La Maison de Verre: Pierre Chareau's Modernist Masterwork*, London: Thames and Hudson (2007).

Walkley, G., *Artists' Houses in London*, 1764–1914, Aldershot: Scolar Press (1994).

Webb, B., *My Apprenticeship*, Vol. II, London: Penguin Books Ltd (1938).

Weston, A., 'Creativity in the Informal Economy of Zimbabwe', PhD, Kingston University (2012).

Woolgar, C.M., *The Great Household in Late Medieval England*, New Haven, CT: Yale University Press (1999).

Wright, G., 'Architectural Practice and Social Vision in Wright's Early Designs', in C.R. Bolon, R.S. Nelson and L. Seidel (eds), *The Nature of Frank Lloyd Wright*, Chicago: University of Chicago Press (1988).

Wright, L., *Clean and Decent: The Fascinating History of the Bathroom and Water Closet*, London: Routledge and Kegan Paul (1960).

Young, T. and Baldwin, S.B.E., *Becontree and Dagenham*, Becontree: Becontree Social Survey Committee (1934).

Zukin, S., *Loft Living: Culture and Capital in Urban Change*, London: Radius (1988).

Zurich News, 'Fire Damage to Schools', 27 March 2003.

Acknowledgements

I am very grateful to London Metropolitan University, the Arts and Humanities Research Council, the Economic and Social Research Council and the Daiwa Anglo-Japanese Foundation for their financial and institutional support, and to the Society of Architectural Historians of Great Britain for their publication grant.

I am also grateful to Daphne Turner for her editing, Rex Henry for his design, and to Colin Davies, Graeme Evans, Adam Hart, Suzy Nelson, Kim Randall, Barry Shaw and Ken Worpole for their thoughtful comments on earlier drafts or draft chapters. Any mistakes are, of course, my own.

I am indebted to all the interviewees and research participants, in the UK, the USA and Japan, for their generosity in sharing their lives and workhomes with me.

Special thanks are due to Colin Davies and Jo Foord for supervising the doctoral research that lies behind this book.

Special thanks are also due to Sue Bagwell, Russell Brown, Peter Conradi, Ayona Datta, Howard Davis, Eames Demetrios, Julia Dwyer, Caroline Ede, Mike Falk, Fran Ford, Louise Goodison, Kevin Haley, Peter Hall, Craig Harrison-Smith, Hiroko Hasama, Thomas Heinser, Martin Holliss, Patty Hopkins, Colin Hughes, Yoko Inoue, Viktor Jak, Peter James, Ryo Kinoshita, Koh Kitayama, Takeshi Kohari, David Kohn, Miko Kurosawa, Andy Lake, Angela Lee, M.J. Long, Helen Mallinson, Ian McMurtrie, Robert Mull, Lucy Musgrave, Viv Nicholls, Jim O'Neill, Andrew Parry, Joseph Kohlmaier and Stefan Kraus of Polimekanos, Naomi Pollock, David Powell, Lynne Prather, John Prest, Oliver Rehm, Sue Ridge, Chi Roberts, Bob Rubin, Keith Shearer, Pat Thomas, Yoshiharu Tsukamoto, Marc Vellay, Seth Wachtel, Giles Walkley, Graham Watts, Ned White, Peter White, Sarah Wigglesworth, Antje Witting, Carol Wolkowitz and John Worthington.

And finally I thank my family, Adam Hart, Ruben Holliss and Maya Holliss, for their support and love.

Index

Page numbers in *italics* refer to illustrations